CW00322057

WORLD ATLAS
& ALMANAC

Table of Contents

Europe

Asia

Oceania

Africa

North and Central America

South America

Map locator

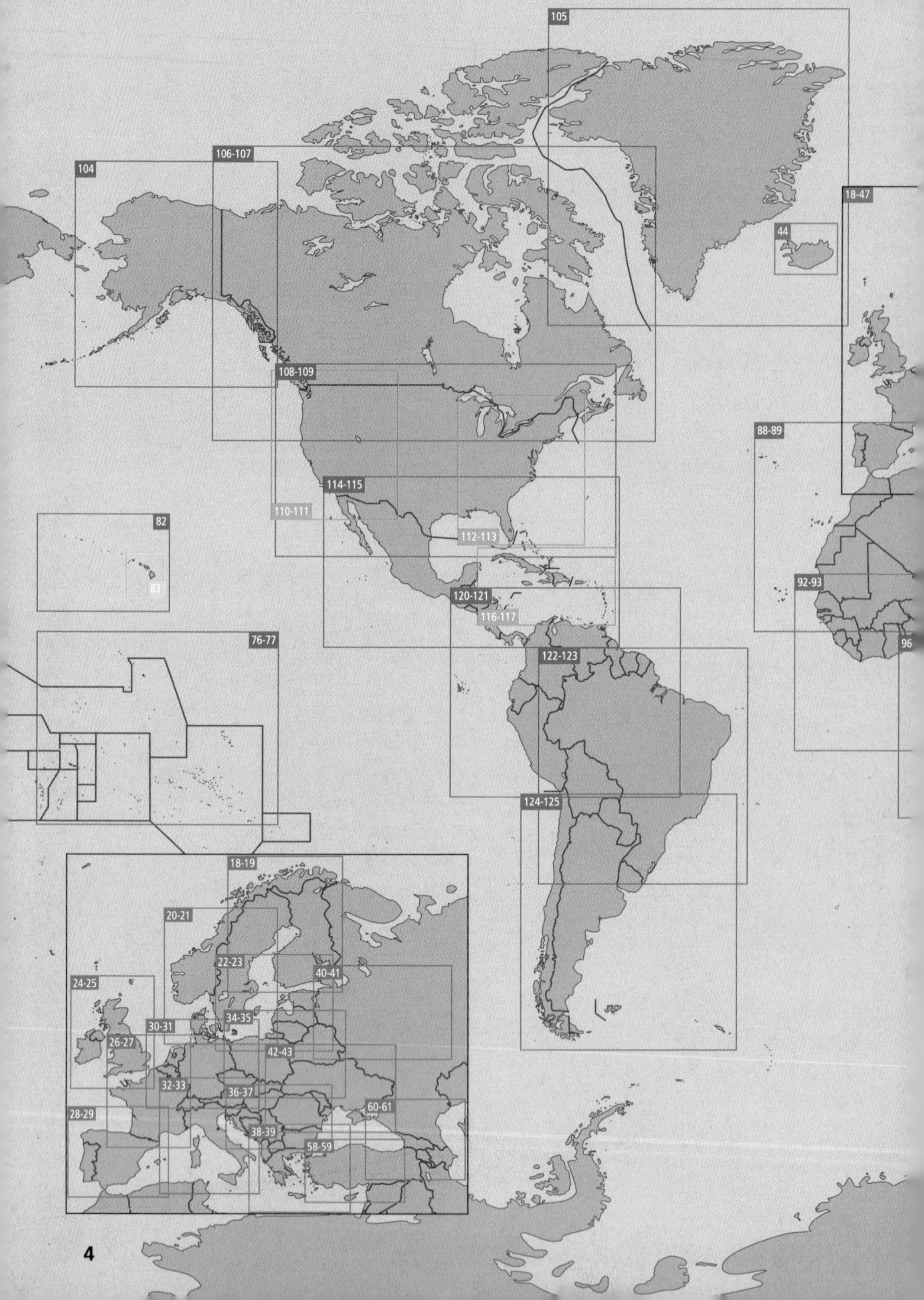
105
104
106-107
18-47
44
108-109
88-89
114-115
110-111
82
112-113
83
92-93
120-121
116-117
76-77
96
122-123
124-125
18-19
20-21
22-23
40-41
24-25
30-31
34-35
26-27
42-43
32-33
36-37
60-61
28-29
38-39
58-59

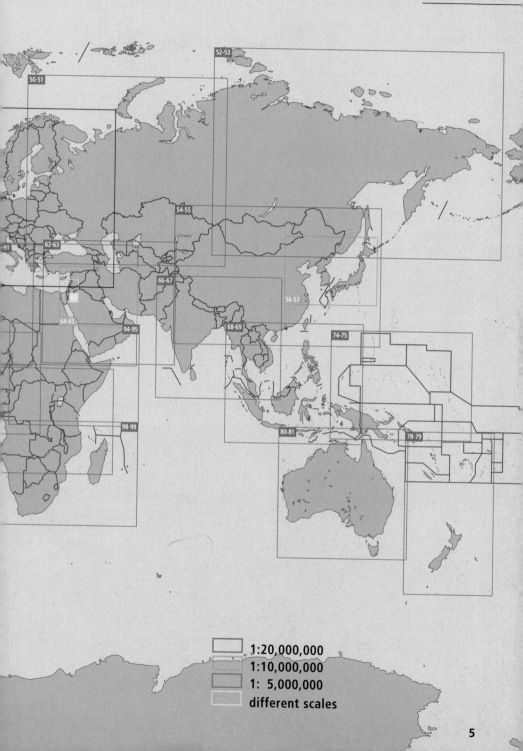

50-51
52-53
54-55
62-63
-91
62
66-67
56-57
64-65
94-95
68-69
74-75
98-99
80-81
78-79

1:20,000,000
1:10,000,000
1: 5,000,000
different scales

Legend

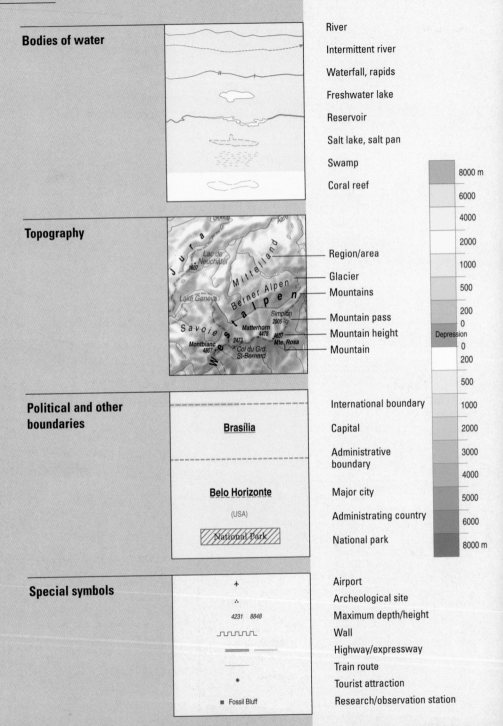

Bodies of water

River
Intermittent river
Waterfall, rapids
Freshwater lake
Reservoir
Salt lake, salt pan
Swamp
Coral reef

Topography

Region/area
Glacier
Mountains
Mountain pass
Mountain height
Mountain

Political and other boundaries

Brasília

Belo Horizonte

(USA)

National Park

International boundary
Capital
Administrative boundary
Major city
Administrating country
National park

Special symbols

Fossil Bluff

Airport
Archeological site
Maximum depth/height
Wall
Highway/expressway
Train route
Tourist attraction
Research/observation station

8000 m
6000
4000
2000
1000
500
200
0
Depression
0
200
500
1000
2000
3000
4000
5000
6000
8000 m

Type faces

PACIFIC OCEAN	Ocean
Caribbean Sea	Sea, gulf, bay
Atacama Trench	Underwater topography
Lake Superior, *Mississippi*	Lake, river
Great Plains	Region/area
ANDES, **Coast Ranges**	Mountain chain/system
Aconcagua	Mountain
Punta Pariñas	Cape
Greater Antilles, *Martinique*	Islands, Island
BRAZIL	Nation
Mato Grosso	Administrative area
São Paulo	
Belo Horizonte	The size of the type faces reflects not
Belém	only the population of a city or town
Pôrto Velho	but also its overall signifigance in the
Macapá	region.
Fonte Boa	

**Classification of
cities and towns**

▣	more than 5,000,000 inhabitants
☐	more than 1,000,000
◉	more than 500,000
◎	more than 100,000
◦	more than 50,000
○	less than 50,000

Place locator

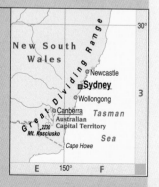

Search for the name of the sought after area/city in the alphabetically arranged map index. The place names are followed by the page numbers of relevant maps as well a number-letter combination indicating the area's location the map. Letters indicate the east-west position and numbers the north-south position of an area.

Examples: **Sydney 81 F3**
Page **81**
Map section **F3**

The Earth, the so-called blue planet, is the third planet from the sun and the fifth largest planet in the solar system. Formed from a cloud of dust and gas around 4.5 billion years ago, the Earth travels in an elliptical orbit at distances between 147 to 152 million kilometers away from the sun.

The Earth is not a perfect sphere; the area around the poles being relatively flat. The polar diameter of the Earth measures 12,714 kilometers, about 42 kilometers less than the equatorial diameter of the planet. The maximum circumference of the Earth measures 40,075 kilometers. Our planet has a total area of 510 million square kilometers; 71% of the Earth's surface is covered by bodies of water and 29% by land.

The World

Physical and
political maps

1 : 145 000 000   0 1450 2900 4350 km

The World: Political

140° 120° 100° 80° 60° 40° 20° 0°

80°

A R C T I C C

Ellesmere Island

Grønland
(Greenland)
(Denmark)

Spitsbergen (Norway)

Victoria Island

Baffin Island

Jan Mayen (Norway)

Reykjavík **ICELAND** *Faroe Islands (Den.)* **NORWAY** **SWE**

Alaska (U.S.)

Arctic Circle

Yellowknife

Oslo Stoc

60° Anchorage

UNITED KINGDOM **DENMARK** Copenhagen

Aleutian Islands

C A N A D A

Vancouver

Winnipeg

Ottawa

Montreal

Dublin Berlin
IRELAND London 2 **GERMANY**
3
Paris 8 7
12 13 15 **Roma**
FRANCE 14 (Rome)

PORTUGAL Madrid **ITALY**
Lisboa **SPAIN**
(Lisbon)

40°

Chicago

Washington

Azores (Port.) *Canary Islands (Sp.)* Algiers Tunis
TUNIS
Rabat Trip
MOROCCO

P A C I F I C

San Francisco
Los Angeles

UNITED STATES

Houston

Bermuda (U.K.) A T L A N T I C

ALGERIA L

Guadalupe (Mexico)

Tropic of Cancer

BAHAMAS Nassau

Port-au-Prince **HAITI**

Western
Sahara

MAURITANIA
Nouakchott

Hawaii (U.S.) Honolulu

20°

La Habana
(Havana)
MEXICO **CUBA**
Ciudad de México
(Mexico City)
Guadalajara

Santo Domingo **DOMINICAN REPUBLIC**
Puerto Rico (U.S.)
Basseterre **SAINT KITTS AND NEVIS**
St. John's **ANTIGUA AND BARBUDA**
Roseau **DOMINICA**
Castries **SAINT LUCIA**
Belmopan Bridgetown **BARBADOS**
BELIZE Kingston Port of Spain **TRINIDAD AND TOBAGO**
Georgetown **GUYANA**
Paramaribo **SURINAME**
French Guiana (Fr.)

CAPE VERDE
Praia

MALI **NIGER**
Bamako Niamey N'djame

Palmyra (U.S.)

GUATEMALA Guatemala
EL SALVADOR San Salvador
HONDURAS Tegucigalpa
NICARAGUA Managua
COSTA RICA San José
PANAMA Panamá

JAMAICA

Caracas

VENEZUELA

Bogotá

SENEGAL Dakar
GAMBIA Banjul
GUINEA-BISSAU Bissau
GUINEA Conakry
SIERRA LEONE Freetown
LIBERIA Monrovia

NIGERIA
2 3 4 Abuja
Malabo
8

0° Equator

Galápagos Islands (Ecuador) Quito
ECUADOR
COLOMBIA

Manaus

Belém

GABON Libreville Kinst
Brazzaville

KIRIBATI

PERU
Lima

B R A Z I L

Brasília

Luanda
ANGO

20°

Cook Islands (N.Z.)

French Polynesia (Fr.)
Papeete

Pitcairn Island (U.K.)

Tropic of Capricorn

Sala y Gómez (Chile)
Easter Island

San Félix (Chile)
San Ambrosio

La Paz
BOLIVIA

PARAGUAY
Asunción

Rio de Janeiro
São Paulo

Trindade

Martim Vaz (Brazil)

St.-Helena (U.K.)

NAMIBIA
Windhoe

O C E A N

CHILE
Santiago

Islas Juan-Fernández (Chile)

URUGUAY
Buenos Montevideo
Aires

O C E A N

Tristan da Cunha (U.K.) Cape To

40°

ARGENTINA

Gough

60°

Punta Arenas

Falkland Islands (U.K.)

South Georgia (U.K.)

South Orkney Islands (U.K.)

South Sandwich Islands (U.K.)

Bouvet Island (Norway)

South Shetland Islands (U.K.)

Antarctic Circle

MIDDLE AMERICA
1 **SAINT VINCENT AND THE GRENADINES** Kingstown
2 **GRENADA** St. George's

EUROPE
1 **NETHERLANDS** Amsterdam
2 **BELGIUM** Brussels
3 **LUXEMBOURG** Luxembourg
4 **CZECH REPUBLIC** Praha (Prague)
5 **SLOVAKIA** Bratislava
6 **SWITZERLAND** Berne
7 **LIECHTENSTEIN** Vaduz
8 **AUSTRIA** Wien (Vienna)
9 **HUNGARY** Budapest
10 **SLOVENIA** Ljubljana

11 **CROATIA** Zagreb
12 **ANDORRA**
13 **MONACO**
14 **SAN MARINO**
15 **VATICAN CITY**
16 **BOSNIA AND HERZEGOVINA** Sarajevo
17 **SERBIA AND MONTENEGRO** Beograd (Belgrade)
18 **ALBANIA** Tiranë
19 **MACEDONIA** Skopje
20 **MALTA** Valletta

140° 120° 100° 80° 60° 40° 20° West 0° East

1 : 145 000 000   0   1450   2900   4350 km

40°   60°   80°   100°   120°   140°   160°   180°

O   C   E   A   N

80°

Franz Josef Land
North Land

Novaya
Zemlya
New Siberian Islands

Wrangel Island

Arctic Circle

.AND

.kki

St. Petersburg
ESTONIA
:finn
ATVIA   Moskva
LITHUANIA   (Moscow)
BELARUS
·sk
·wa   Kyïv (Kiev)
·vi   UKRAINE
·ANIA   MOLDOVA
·Bucureşti (Bucharest)
·tia   BULGARIA
·liya)   Ankara
CE
TURKEY
·Athens)   SYRIA   Baghdad
Nicosia   Dama-
·YPRUS 2   scus
Cairo   IRAQ
EGYPT   SAUDI
·   Riyadh
ARABIA

R   U   S   S   I   A

Alaska
(U.S.)

60°

Yekaterinburg
Novosibirsk

Samara

Astana
KAZAKHSTAN
Irkutsk
Ulaan Baatar

A l e u t i a n   I s l a n d s

MONGOLIA

GEORGIA   UZBEKISTAN   Almaty   Ürümqi
Tbilisi   Bıshkek
Baki (Baku)   Tashkent
KYRGYZSTAN
ARMENIA   TURKMENISTAN   Dushanbe
Ashgabad   TAJIKISTAN
I R A N   AFGHANISTAN
Teheran   Kabul
Islamabad
Kuwait
KUWAIT   New   NEPAL   BHUTAN
Abu   Delhi   Kathmandu   Thimpu
U.A.E.   Dhabi   PAKISTAN
Muscat   BANGLADESH
OMAN   I N D I A   Dhaka
Mumbai

Peking

K u r i l   I s l a n d s

40°

NORTH KOREA
Pyongyang
SOUTH (Seoul)
KOREA   Seoul
JAPAN   Tokyo
Nanjing
Shanghai

C H I N A

P A C I F I C

O C E A N

Vientiane

Taipei

Macao

TAIWAN
Tropic of Cancer   Hawaii
(U.S.)   20°
Honolulu

·hartoum   ERITREA   Sanaa
·UDAN   Asmara   YEMEN
AL   Addis Ababa   Djibouti
·an   ETHIOPIA
·JC
·ANDA   Kampala   SOMALIA
·RATIC   Kigali   Nairobi   Mogadishu
·INDA
·LIC   Dodoma
·iO   TANZANIA

MYANMAR
Rangoon   VIET-
Laccadive   THAILAND   NAM
Islands   Chennai   Krüng Thep
(India)   (Bangkok)   Phnom
Colombo   Penh   CAMBODIA
SRI LANKA   Kuala Lumpur
Male   MALAYSIA
MALDIVES   SINGAPORE
Sumatra

Hanoi

Manila
Northern
Mariana Islands
Guam   (U.S.)
(U.S.)
Koror
Palikir
PALAU

Victoria
SEYCHELLES   Chagos Archipelago
(U.K.)

PHILIPPINES

MARSHALL
ISLANDS

M i c r o n e s
a
M e l a
n
e
s
I N D O N E S I A

Java
Jakarta

MICRONESIA

Dili
EAST TIMOR

PAPUA
NEW GUINEA

Palmyra
(U.S.)

Darrit
Dalap-Uliga-

Bairiki

Equator   0°

K I R I B A T I

·MBIA   MALAWI   COMOROS
·ke   Lilongwe   Moroni
·BABWE
·arare   Antananarivo
·WANA   MADAGASCAR
·one   Maputo

Cocos Islands
(Australia)

Port Moresby

Honiara
SOLOMON
ISLANDS

Vaiaku
TUVALU

Tokelau
(N.Z.)

American
SAMOA   Samoa
(U.S.)

Port Louis   I N D I A N
Réunion
MAURITIUS   (Fr.)

VANUATU   Port
New   Vila
Caledonia
(Fr.)

FIJI
Apia
Suva
TONGA

Niue
(N.Z.)

Cook Islands
(N.Z.)

20°

·ia   Mbabane   SWAZILAND
·H   Maseru   LESOTHO
·A

Nukualofa
Tropic of Capricorn

AUSTRALIA

Norfolk
(Australia)

O C E A N

Amsterdam
(Fr.)
St.-Paul

Perth

Lord Howe
(Australia)

Canberra   Sydney
Melbourne

NEW
ZEALAND   Wellington

40°

Crozet Islands
(Fr.)

Kerguelen Islands
(Fr.)

Tasmania

Prince Edward Islands
(South Africa)

Heard
(Australia)

Macquarie Islands
(Australia)

60°

Antarctic Circle

AFRICA
1 BURKINA FASO Ouagadougou
2 IVORY COAST Yamoussoukro
3 GHANA Accra
4 TOGO Lomé
5 BENIN Porto-Novo
6 CAMEROON Yaoundé
7 EQUATORIAL GUINEA Malabo
8 SÃO TOMÉ AND PRÍNCIPE São Tomé
9 BURUNDI Bujumbura

ASIA
1 LEBANON Beirut
2 ISRAEL Jerusalem
3 JORDAN Amman
4 AZERBAIJAN Baki (Baku)
5 BAHRAIN Al Manama
6 QATAR Doha
7 BRUNEI Bandar Seri Begawan

A N T A R C T I C A

● Capital

40°   60°   80°   100°   120°   140°   160°   180°

Europe: Physical

14   1 : 20 000 000

F Cape
30°
G
40°
H Barents Sea
Kolgujev
50°
J
60°
1
Varangerfjord
m. Kanin Nos
poluostrov
Kanin
Narodnaja
1894
K
Inari
järvi
Murmansk
Pečora
Kola Peninsula
lapland
Lake Imandra
Arhangel'sk
White
Timan Ridge
U
R
A
L
Oulu
Oulujärvi
Severnaja Dvina
Onega Bay
Onega
Kamskoe
vdhr.
Soumenselkä
Karelia
Northern Uvals
Perm
2
Salpausselka
Lake
Onega
50°
Helsinki
Gulf of Finland
St. Petersburg
Lake
Ladoga
Belaja
M
O
U
Tallinn
Lake
Peipus
Rybinsk
Reservoir
Volga
Kama
Kujbyševskoe
vdhr.
Obsjtsji Syrt
N
T
Riga
Valdai
Hills
343
Daugava
Moskva
(Moscow)
Volga
Volgogradskoe
vdhr.
Mugodzhar Hills
A
I
50°
munas
Vilnius
Minsk
Dnepr
Central Russian Upland
Don
Volga Upland
Žaýk
Caspian Depression
3
Aral Sea
N
S
Warszawa
(Warsaw)
Polesye
Pripet
Marshes
Kyjiv
(Kiev)
3745
Cimljanskoe
vdhr.
Volga
-22
Astrakhan
Podil's'ka vysočyna
Doneck
Dnieper
Donets'kyy
Kryazh
Don
Ustjurt Plateau
-132
Galicia
CARPATHIAN
MOUNTAINS
Bessarabia
Chişinău
Sea
of Azov
Caspian
Karabogaz
Gol
2305
Pietrosu
Odessa
Crimea
Kerčens'ka protoka
-28
Türkmenbašy
40°
Mureş
rad
ade
Moldoveanu
2543
Transylvanian Alps
Walachia
Bucureşti
(Bucharest)
Prut
Constanţa
C A U C A S U S
5642
Elbrus
Sea
Baki
(Baku)
Kura
ld
Sofija
(Sofiya)
opje
Balkan Mts
2376
Botev
Danube
Black
Sea
2155
Tbilisi
3937
Kačkar
Pontic Mountains
Yerevan
5165
Ararat
Araks
Elburz Mountains
4
Musala
2925 Rhodope Mts
Istanbul
Köroglu
Dağları
2499
Bosporus
Sea of
Marmara
Ankara
Kizilirmak
Van Gölü
Lake
Urmia
Teheran
Thessaloniki
Olympus
2917
Dardanelles
2543
Uludag
A n a t o l i a
Tuz Gölü
K u r d i s t a n
Tigris
Zagros
Mountains
H
Mts
nassos
2457
Aegean Sea
İzmir
Menderes
Erciyas Dağları
3916
Al-Mawsil
Athina
(Athens)
Peloponnesus
Sporades
Bey Dağları
3069
Taurus Mountains
İskenderun
Körfezi
Adana
Euphrates
S y r i a
Aleppo
r. Ténaro
an
s
e
a
Crete
F Idi
2456
Cyclades
30°
Cyprus
Nicosia
1953
G
Beirut
Damascus
40°
15
4433
4450

Europe: Political

ICELAND
Reykjavik

Arctic Circle

Faroe Islands
(Den.)
Tórshavn

Rockall
(U.K.)

Shetland Islands

NORWAY
Trondheim

SWEDEN

Narvik

Scandinavia

Bergen
Oslo

Uppsala
Stockholm

Vänern
Göteborg
Vättern
Öland

Hebrides

Scotland

Orkney Islands

Aberdeen

North Sea

Aalborg

DENMARK
København
(Copenhagen)

Odense
Sjælland
Malmö

Baltic Sea

Kiel

Bornholm

Gdańsk

Edinburgh
Glasgow

Northern Belfast
Ireland
Man

UNITED KINGDOM

Leeds
Liverpool
Manchester
Nottingham

Gotl

Szczecin

Dublin
IRELAND

Irish Sea

Cork

Celtic Sea

Birmingham
Wales
Cardiff
Bristol
Southampton

Le Havre

NETHERLANDS
s-Gravenhage
(The Hague)
Amsterdam

Frisian Islands
Bremen
Hamburg

Hannover
Berlin
Magdeburg

Poznań

PO

London
Thames

Rotterdam
Antwerpen
BELGIUM
Köln
(Cologne)
Essen
Leipzig

Dresden
Wrocław

Channel Islands
(U.K.)

English Channel

Lille

Brest

Caen

Paris

Brussel
Brussels
(LUXEMBOURG)
LUXEMBOURG
Luxembourg

Bonn
Frankfurt
am Main

GERMANY

Stuttgart
Nürnberg

Praha
(Prague)
CZECH REPUBLIC

Krak

Ostr

Nantes

Seine

Loire

Tours

Dijon

Metz

Strasbourg

Basel

Munich

Danube

Wien
(Vienna)

SLOVA

Bratisla

Bay of Biscay

La Coruña
Gijón

León

FRANCE

Limoges

Geneva
Lyon

Berne
SWITZERLAND

4807
Mt. Blanc

Zürich
Vaduz
LIECHTENSTEIN

AUSTRIA

Salzburg

Graz

SLOVENIA

Ljubljana

Budapest

HUN

Pé

Zagreb

A

L

P

S

Porto
Valladolid

Bilbao

Bordeaux

Toulouse

Pyrénées
3404
Pico
de Aneto

Torino
(Turin)
Milano
(Milan)

Venezia
(Venice)

Po

Trieste

CROATIA

Drava

BOSNIA AND
HERZEGOVIN

Sava

Douro

PORTUGAL

Madrid

ANDORRA
Andorra

MONACO
Nice

Génova
(Genoa)

Bologna

Ligurian
Sea

Firenze
(Florence)

S. MARINO

Adriatic Sea

Sarajevo

Split

Lisboa
(Lisbon)
Tagus

Badajoz

SPAIN

Córdoba

Barcelona

València

Marseille

Corsica
(Fr.)

Elba

ITALY

Roma
(Rome)

Podgo

ALBAN

Duero

Ebro

Guadiana

Sevilla

Faro

Gibraltar
Granada

Málaga

Cartagena

Balearic Islands

Alicante
Ibiza

Palma
Mallorca

Menorca

Ajaccio

Sassari

VATICAN
CITY

Napoli
(Naples)

Bari

Taranto

Tiran

Vlor

Sardinia

Tyrrhenian Sea

Tangier
Tétouan

Ceuta
(Sp.)

Melilla
(Sp.)

Oran

Cagliari

Palermo
Messina

Sicily
Catania

Ionian Sea

Kenitra
Rabat
Casablanca

Ar-Rif
Fès
2456
Oujda

MOROCCO

Tlemcen

ALGIERS

Ech-Chellif

ALGERIA

Béjaïa

Annaba

Constantine

Tunis

Mediterrane

Sousse

MALTA
Valletta

Tébessa

TUNISIA

Sfax

Norwegian Sea

Glomma

Indalsälv

ATLANTIC OCEAN

1 : 20 000 000

0   200   400   600 km

West 0° East

16

1 : 5 000 000   0   50   100   150 km

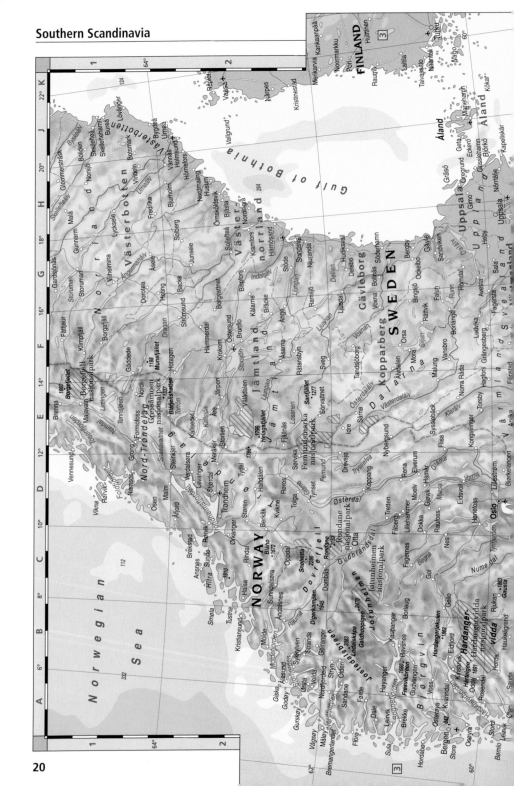

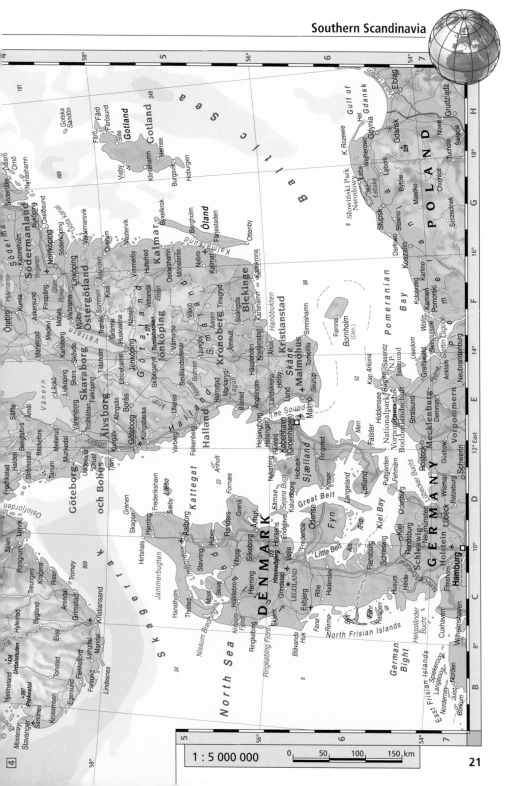

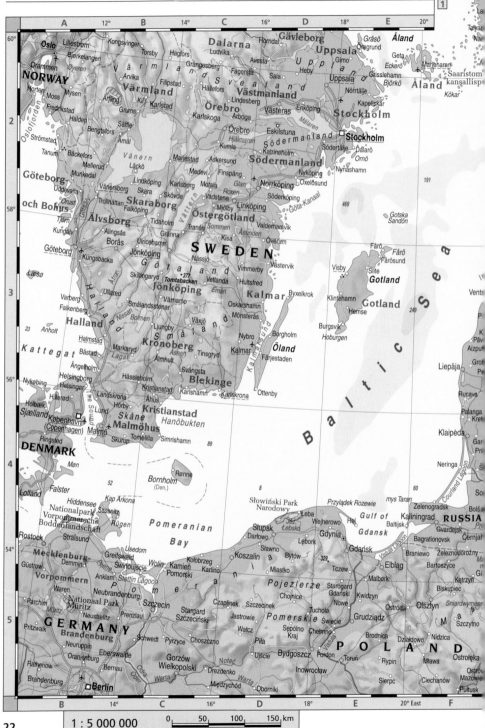

1 : 5 000 000

0   50   100   150 km

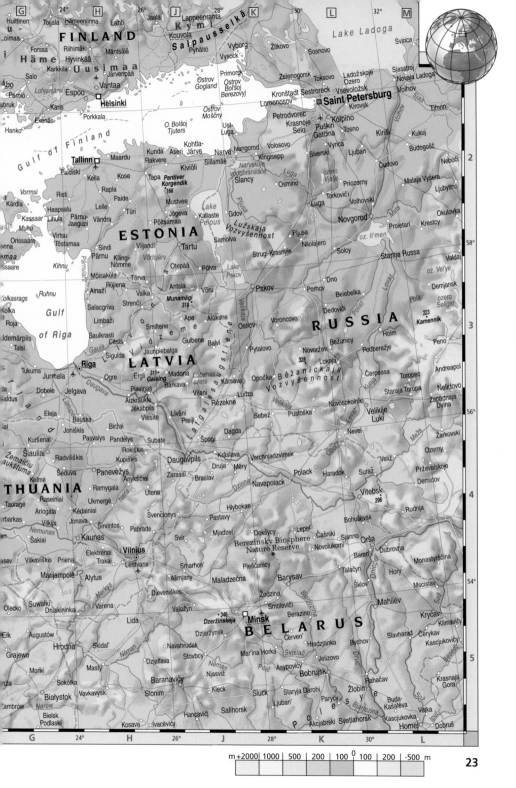

FINLAND

Huittinen · Toijala · Hämeenlinna · Lahti · Jaala · Kouvola · Lappeenranta · Pyhältö · Vyborg · Žitkovo · Sosnovo · Svirica
Forssa · Riihimäki · Mäntsälä · Häme · Hyvinkää · Järvenpää · Primorsk · Vysock · Zelenogorsk · Toksovo · Ladožskoje Ozero · Novaja Ladoga
Salo · Karkkila · Uusimaa · Vantaa · Ostrov Gogland · Ostrov Bol'šoj Berezovyj · Sestrorečk · Vsevoložsk · Sjasstroj
Åbo · Perniö · Espoo · Kronštadt · Lomonosov · Saint Petersburg · Kirovsk · Volhov · Tihvin
bruk · Karis · **Helsinki** · Porkkala · Ostrov Moščnyj · Petrodvorec · Krasnoje Selo · Puškin · Kolpino · Tosno · Kiriši · Kukuj
Ekenäs · Ust-Luga · Gatčina · Budogošč
Hanko · Volosovo · Vyrica · Ljuban · Nebolči
Tallinn · Maardu · Kunda · Aseri · Järve · Narva · Ivangorod · Kingisepp · Siverski · Priozerny · Malaja Vyšera
Paldiski · Keila · Kose · Tapa · Kiviõli · Sillamäe · Slancy · Osmino · Luga · Torkoviči · Volhovski · Ljubytino
Vormsi · Risti · Rapla · Paide · Jõgeva · Gdov · Pljusa · Novgorod · Proletari · Okulovka · Krestcy
Kärdla · Haapsalu · Lihula · Pärnu-Jaagupi · Vändra · Põltsamaa · Lake Kallaste Peipus · Nikolajero · Solcy · Staraja Russa · Valdaj
ESTONIA · Tartu · Samolva · oz. Il'men'
Kihnu · Kilingi-Nõmme · Viljandi · Võrtsjärv · Strugi-Krasnyje · oz. Vel'ye
Ruhnu · Mõisaküla · Tõrva · Otepää · Põlva · Lake Pskov · Dno · Demjansk · ozero Seliger
Gulf of Riga · Ainaži · Rūjiena · Antsla · Võru · Pskov · Porhov · Belebelka · Peno
Ape · Alūksne · Ostrov · Voroncovo · Dedoviči · Holm
RUSSIA · Kamennik
Riga · Sigulda · Cēsis · Gulbene · Balvi · Pytalovo · Novoržev · Bežanicy · Podberez'e
LATVIA · Madona · Barkava · Rēzekne · Opočka · Lokpla · Čerpessa · Toropec · Nelidovo
Gaising · Plaviņas · Viļāni · Ludza · Bežanickaja Vozvyšennost · Novosokol'niki · Staraja Toropa · Zapadnaja Dvina
Aizkraukle · Jēkabpils · Viesīte · Līvāni · Preiļi · Sebež · Pustoška · Velikije Luki
LITHUANIA · Joniškis · Birži · Subate · Dagda · Spogi · Nevel · Veliž · Žarkovski
Kuršėnai · Pasvalys · Pandėlys · Rokiškis · Daugavpils · Krāslava · Verchnjadzvinsk · Ozerny
Radviliškis · Kupiškis · Zarasai · Druja · Mёry · Polack · Haradok · Suraž · Prževalskoje
Žemaičių aukštuma · Šeduva · Panevėžys · Anykščiai · Braslav · Navapolack · Vitebsk · Demidov
Kelmė · Ramygala · Utena · Hlybokae · Bohušeusk · Rudnja
Raseiniai · Ukmergė · Svenčionys · Pastavy · Mjadzel · Dokšycy · Lepel · Čašniki · Sjanno · Orša · Monastyrščina
Ariogala · Kėdainiai · Jonava · Širvintos · Pabradė · Smarhon' · Novolukoml · Baran · Dubrovna
Šakiai · **Kaunas** · Elektrėnai · Trakai · **Vilnius** · Ašmjany · Maladzečna · Barysau · Talačyn · Hory · Mscislau
Vilkaviškis · Prienai · Lentvaris · Plešanicy · Sklou
Marijampolė · Alytus · Dieveniškės · Žodzina · Mahilёu
Suwałki · Varena · Valožyn · Smolevičy · Berazino · Kryčau · Klimaviči
Olecko · Druskininkai · Lida · Dzjaržynskaja · **Minsk** · Cёrven · Byhov · Slavharad · Čerykau · Kascjukoviči
Ełk · Augustów · Hrodna · Skidal' · Navahrudak · Dzjaržynsk · **BELARUS** · Hradzjanka · Bychov · Krasnaja Gora
Grajewo · Mońki · Masty · Stoubcy · Mar'ina Horka · Svislač · Jelizovo · Bobrujsk · Žlobin · Buda-Kašaleva · Vetka
Białystok · Sokółka · Vawkavysk · Slonim · Njasviž · Kleck · Asipovičy · Staryja Darohi · Rahačeu · Homel
Bielsk Podlaski · Baranavičy · Paryčy · Svetlahorsk · Dobruš
Kosava · Ivacevičy · Hancavičy · Salihorsk · Ljuban' · Akcjabrski

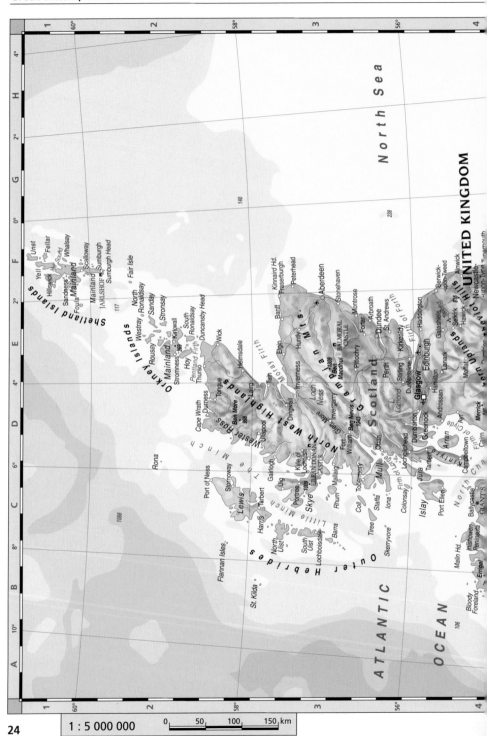

North Sea

UNITED KINGDOM

NEVIS HILLS

4°
2°
0°
2°
4°
6°
8°
10°

H
G
F
E
D
C
B
A

1
2
3
4

60°
58°
56°

Yell
Unst
Fetlar
Hillswick
Sandness
Whalsay
Foula
Mainland
Scalloway
Sumburgh
JARLSHOF
Sumburgh Head
117
Shetland Islands

Fair Isle

North Ronaldsay
Westray
Rousay
Sanday
Stronsay
Kirkwall
Mainland
South Ronaldsay
Stromness
Hoy
Pentland Firth
Duncansby Head
Orkney Islands

Kinnaird Hd.
Fraserburgh
Peterhead
Aberdeen
Stonehaven
Montrose
Arbroath
Forfar
Dundee
St. Andrews
Pitlochry
Firth of Forth
Banff
Huntly
Elgin
BALMORAL CASTLE
1309
Macduff
Perth
Stirling
Dunfermline
Kirkcaldy
Edinburgh
Haddington
Inverness
Loch Ness
Ben Nevis 1343
Fort William
Grampian Mts.
Scotland
Glasgow
Hamilton
Lanark
Moffat
Greenock
Dumbarton
Androssan
Arran
Firth of Clyde
Merrick
Cairn
Dumfries
Gatashiels
Berwick-upon-Tweed
Selkirk 816
Hawick
CHEVIOT HILLS
Newcastle-upon-Tyne
Alnwick
Southern Uplands
Duness
Cape Wrath
Wester Ross
Ben More 998
Lairg
Tongue
Ullapool
Dingwall
Glen More
Nairn
Moray Firth
Helmsdale
Wick
Thurso
North West Highlands
Kyle of Lochalsh
EILEAN DONAN CASTLE
Portree
Skye
Mallaig
Invergarry
140
238

Port of Ness
Rona
Stornoway
Lewis
Harris
Tarbert
The Minch
Gairloch
Uig
Rhum
Coll
Tobermory
Staffa
Iona
Mull
Oban
Lochgilphead
Firth of Lorn
Jura
Kintyre
Tarbert
Campbeltown
Islay
Colonsay
Port Ellen
North Channel
GIANTS
Ballycastle
Inishowen Peninsula
Malin Hd.
Errigal
Bloody Foreland

Flannan Isles
St. Kilda
Skerryvore
Barra
South Uist
North Uist
Lochboisdale
Outer Hebrides
Little Minch
Tiree
1068
1088
106

ATLANTIC
OCEAN

1 : 5 000 000

0   50   100   150 km

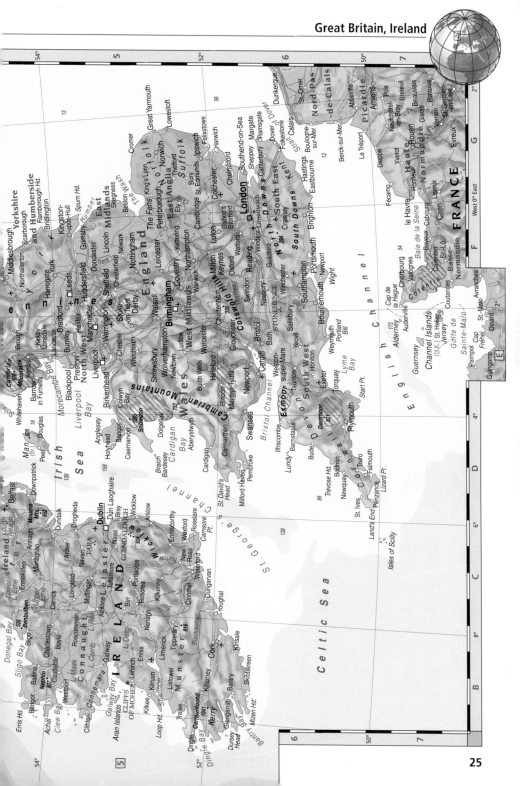

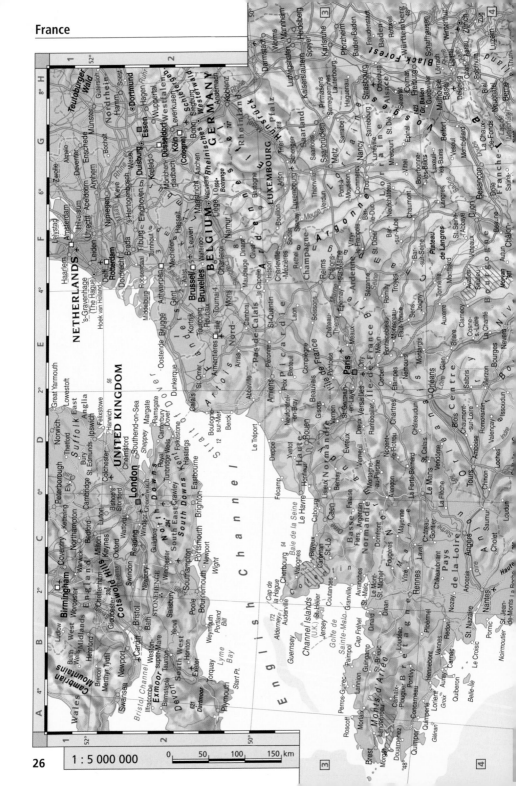

France

1 : 5 000 000

0 50 100 150 km

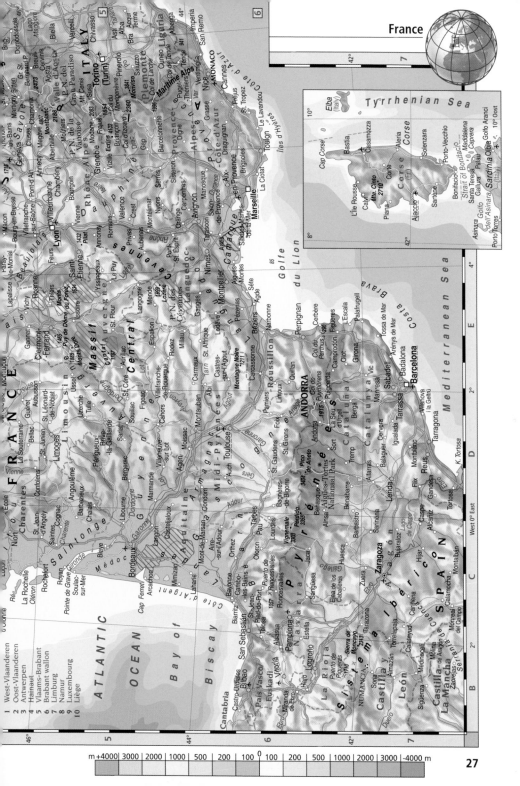

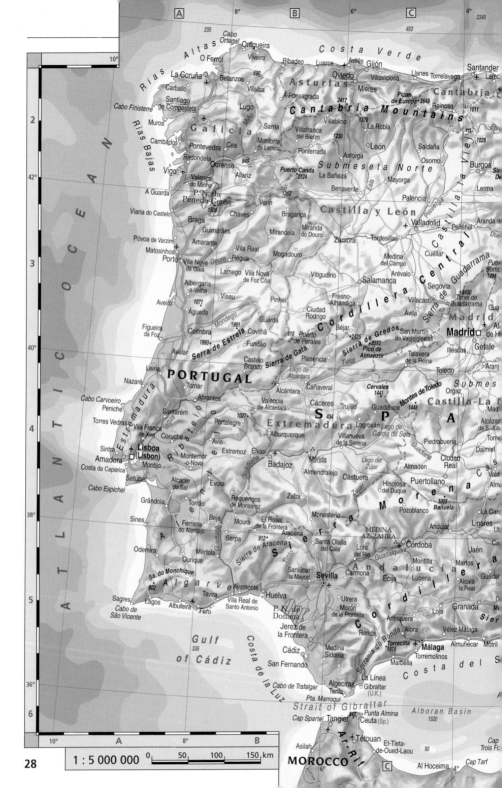

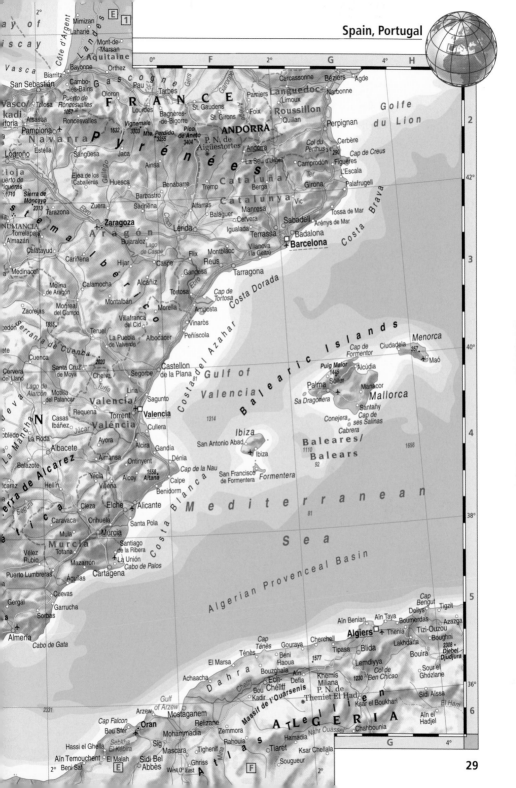

E 1

ay of
iscay

Mimizan
Laharie
Mont-de-
Marsan
Côte d'Argent

F   0°   2°   G   4°   H

Vasca
San Sebastián
Bayonne
Biarritz
Cambo-
les-Bains
Oloron
Orthez

Tarbes
Lourdes
St. Gaudens
Pau
Bagnères-
de-Bigorre
St. Girons
Foix

Carcassonne   Béziers   Agde
Languedoc-   Narbonne
Pamiers   Roussillon
Limoux
Quilian   Perpignan   Cerbère

Golfe
du Lion

2

Vasco
kadi
itoria

Tolosa
Alsasua
Atsasua

Puerto de
Roncesvalles
1087
Roncesvalles

Vignemale
3303
Mte. Perdido
1632   3355
Pico
de Aneto
3404

P. N. de
Aigüestortes
Andorra
La Seu d'Urgell

Col du
Perthus   Cap de Creus
290
Camprodón   Figueres
L'Escala

42°

Pamplona
Navarra

Jaca

ANDORRA

Ter

Girona

Palafrugell

Logroño
ioja
uerto de
igueras
1710
Sierra de
Moncayo

Estella

Sangüesa

Ejea de los
Caballeros
Huesca

Ainsa

Benabarre

Barbastro

Tremp

Berga

Cataluña/
Catalunya

Vic

Manresa

La Seu d'Urgell

Sabadell   Arenys de Mar

Tossa de Mar

Costa Brava

a
2313
Tarazona
NUMANCIA
Torrelapaja
Almazán

Zuera

Alfarras

Balaguer

Cervera

Zaragoza
Aragón

Lérida

Igualada

Terrassa

Badalona

Barcelona

Calatayud

Bujaraloz
Lago
de Caspe

Caspe

Vilanova
i la Geltrú

Costa Brava

3

a
Medinaceli

Cariñena

Hijar

Alcañiz

Flix

Gandesa

Reus

Tarragona

Costa Dorada

Zaorejas
Monreal
del Campo
1855
Serranía de Cuenca

Calamocha

Montalbán

Tortosa

Morella

Cap de
Tortosa

Amposta

Villafranca
del Cid

Vinaròs

cedo
Cuenca

Teruel

La Puebla
de Valverde

Albocácer

Peñíscola

Costa del Azahar

Cervera
del Llano

Santa Cruz
de Moya
2020
Chelva
Motilla
del Palancar

Castellon
de la Plana

Gulf of

Balearic Islands

Cap de
Formentor   Ciudadela   Menorca
357.   Maó

40°

Lago de
Alarcón

N

Liria
Segorbe

Turia

Valencia
Valencia

Sagunto

Valencia

Puig Major
1445
Palma   Sóller

Alcúdia

Manacor

Mallorca

Casas
Ibáñez

Requena

Júcar

Torrent
València

Cullera

1314

Sa Dragonera

Santañy
Conejera   Cap de
ses Salinas

La Mancha
obledo

La Roda
Albacete
Balazote

Ayora

Alcira
Gandía

Almansa

Dénia

San Antonio Abad
Ibiza
Ibiza

Cabrera
Baleares/
Balears
92   1110

1656

4

caret

Hellín

Yecla

Villena

Alcoy
1558
Altana

Cieza

Elche

Benidorm

Cap de la Nau

San Francisco
de Formentera   Formentera

Santa Cruz
Mula
Murcia

Orihuela

Alicante

Santa Pola

Costa Blanca

Mediterranean

81

38°

Vélez
Rubio

Totana

Santiago
de la Ribera
La Unión

Cabo de Palos

Sea

Puerto Lumbreras

Aguilas

Mazarrón

Cartagena

Algerian Provenceal Basin

5

Gergál
a

Cuevas

Garrucha

Sorbas

Almería   Cabo de Gata

Cap
Bengut   Delilys

Aïn Benian   Aïn Taya
Boumerdas
Algiers   Thenia

Tizit
Tizi-Ouzou
Azazga
Boughni
2308
Djebel
Djudjura

Cherchell   Tipasa   Blida
Cap   Gouraya
Ténès   Béni
El Marsa   Haoua
Achaacha   1577
Bouzghaia   Aïn
Echi-   Defla
Bou Chéliff   Kadir   Khemis
Miliana   1230   Col de
Ben Chicao

Lakhdaria

Bouira
Lemdiyya

Sour el
Ghózlane

Sidi Aïssa

Gulf
of Arzew
2331   Arzew
Bou Sfer
Cap Falcon
Mostaganem
Relizane
Oran
Mohammádia

P. N. de
l'Ouarsenis
Theniet El Had

Ksar el Boukhari
El Ham

Aïn el
Hadjel

6

Hassi el Ghella
Aïn Temouchent
Beni Saf
2°
El Malah
Sidi Bel
Abbès
West 0° East
E

Sig
Mascara
Tighenif
Ghriss
F

Zemmora
Rahouia
Mina
Tiaret

Massif de

Atlas

ALGERIA

Hamadia
Chahbounia
Nahr Ouassel
Ksar Chellala

Sougueur

2°

G

4°

29

NETHERLANDS
1 Friesland
2 Groningen
3 Noord-Holland
4 Flevoland
5 Drenthe
6 Overijssel
7 Zuid-Holland
8 Utrecht
9 Gelderland
10 Zeeland
11 Noord-Brabant
12 Limburg

BELGIUM
1 West-Vlaanderen
2 Oost-Vlaanderen
3 Antwerpen
4 Hainaut
5 Vlaams-Brabant
6 Brabant wallon
7 Limburg
8 Namur
9 Luxembourg
10 Liège

1 : 5 000 000

0   50   100   150 km

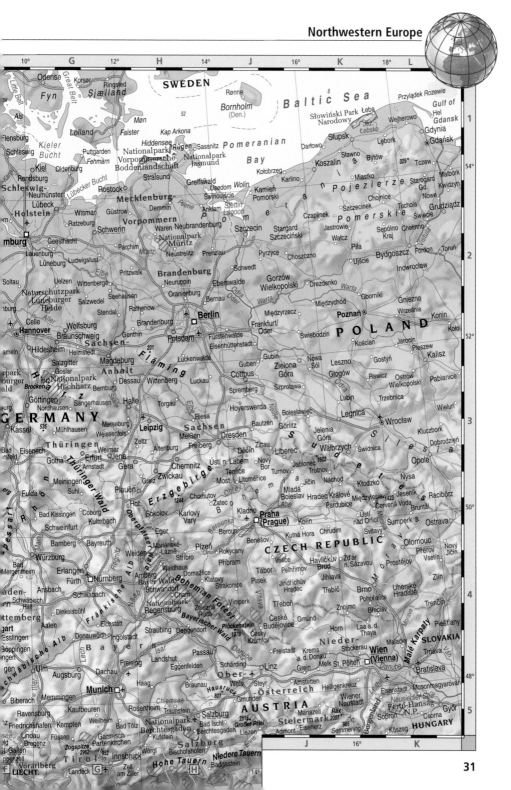

GERMANY
SWITZERLAND
LIECHT.
AUSTRIA
CZECH REPUBLIC
SLOVAKIA
HUNGARY
SLOVENIA
CROATIA
BOSNIA AND HERZEGOVINA
SAN MARINO
MONACO
Munich
Wien (Vienna)
Bern
Milano (Milan)
Torino (Turin)
Genova (Genoa)
Venezia (Venice)
Firenze (Florence)
Ljubljana
Zagreb
Gulf of Venice
Gulf of Genoa
Ligurian Sea

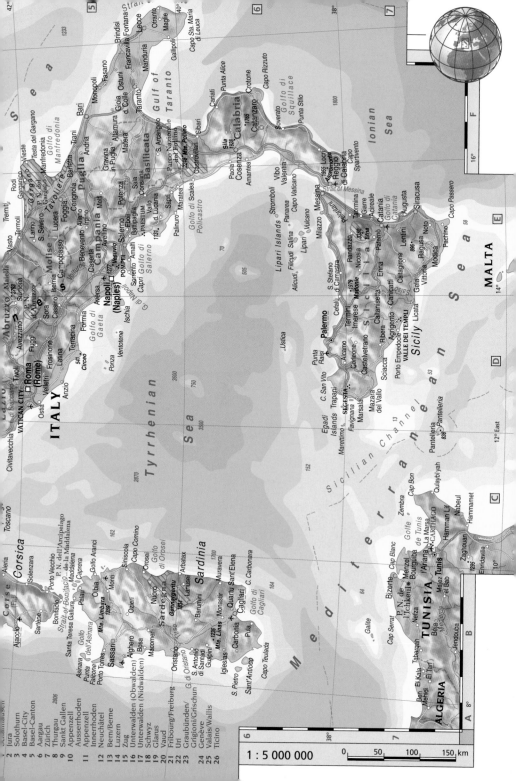

A 14° B 16° C 18° D 20°

B a l t i c   S e a

Møn
Rønne
Bornholm (Den.)
Hiddensee
Kap Arkona
Sassnitz
Rügen
Nationalpark Jasmund
Stralsund
Greifswald
Usedom
Słowiński Park Narodowy
Łeba
Przylądek Rozewie
115
mys Taran
Zelenogradsk
Sovetsk
Pomeranian Bay
Darłowo
Słupsk
Łebsko
Wejherowo
Hel
Baltijsk
Gdynia
Gulf of Gdańsk
Kaliningrad
Gvardejsk
RUSSIA
Pregoła
Mecklenburg
Anklam
Wolin
Kamień Pomorski
Karlino
Kołobrzeg
Koszalin
Sławno
Bytów
329
Gdańsk
Braniewo
Bartoszyce
Bagrationovsk
Černjahovsk
Železnodorožny
Jezioro Mamry
Vorpommern
Demmin
Stettin Lagoon
Miastko
Tczew
Elbląg
Ketrzyn
Gižycko
Neubrandenburg
Szczecin
Czaplinek
Szczecinek
Chojnice
Starogard Gdański
Malbork
Biskupiec
Orzysz
N.P. Müritz
Stargard Szczeciński
Nowe
Kwidzyn
Ostróda
Olsztyn
Jezioro Śniardwy
Neustrelitz
Prenzlau
Jastrowie
Pomerskie
Tuchola
Świecie
Grudziądz
Masuria
Szczytno
Pisz
GERMANY
Ebeswalde
Oranienburg
Schwedt
Choszczno
Wałcz
Piła
Sępólno
Chełmno
Brodnica
Działdowo
Nidzica
Łomža
Bernau
Gorzów Wielkopolski
Noteć
Ujście
Bydgoszcz
Fordon
Toruń
Rypin
Mława
Ostrołęka
Berlin
Fürstenwalde
Frankfurt/Oder
Międzyrzecz
Drezdenko
Warta
Inowrocław
Sierpc
Ciechanów
Płońsk
Pułtusk
Ostrów Mazowiecki
Potsdam
Brandenburg
Eisenhüttenstadt
Świebodzin
Międzychód
Oborniki
Gniezno
Płock
Wyszków
Luckenwalde
Gubin
Nowa Sól
Września
Konin
Sochaczew
Legionowo
Sieradz
Cottbus
Zielona Góra
Leszno
Kościan
Jarocin
Koło
Kutno
Łowicz
Warszawa (Warsaw)
Siedlce
Spremberg
Szprotawa
Głogów
Gostyń
Pleszew
Kalisz
Łęczyca
Zgierz
Skierniewice
Pruszków
Żyrardów
Otwock
Biesa
Hoyerswerda
Rawicz
Ostrów Wielkopolski
P O L A N D
Pabianice
Łódź
Radz Podla
Sachsen
Meißen
Dresden
Bautzen
Bolesławiec
Lubin
Trzebnica
Tomaszów Mazowiecki
Kozienice
Deblin
Freiberg
Zittau
Görlitz
Legnica
Piotrków Trybunalski
Radom
Zwolen
Puławy
Liberec
Jelenia Góra
Świdnica
Wrocław
Wieluń
Opoczno
Kazimierz Dolny
Ústí n. Labem
Teplice
Nový Bor
Jablonec
Wałbrzych
Kluczbork
Radomsko
Kielce
Starachowice
Most
Litoměřice
Turnov
Trutnov
Nachod
Kłodzko
Nysa
Dobrodzień
Częstochowa
Opatów
Stalowa Wola
Zatec
Mladá Boleslav
Jičín
Hradec Králové
Jeseník
Opole
Jędrzejów
Busko Zdrój
Tarnobrzeg
Praha (Prague)
Kladno
Kolín
Pardubice
Międzylesie
1423
Raciborz
Bytom
Zawiercie
Miechów
Leżajsk
Rokycany
Benešov
Kutná Hora
Chrudim
Ústí nad Orlicí
Červená Voda
Bruntál
Gliwice
Sosnowiec
Olkusz
Tarnów
Mielec
Rzesz
Příbram
Votice
CZECH REPUBLIC
Olomouc
Šumperk
Opava
Rybnik
Auschwitz
Katowice
Kraków
Dębica
Jaros
Strakonice
Tábor
Pelhřimov
Žďár n. Sázavou
Přerov
Ostrava
Frýdek Místek
Bielsko Biała
Żywiec
Myślenice
Brzesko
Galic
Pisek
Jindřichův Hradec
Jihlava
Prostějov
Vsetín
Nový Jičín
Cieszyn
Gorlice
Krosno
Sanok
Vimperk
Třeboň
Třebíč
Brno
Uherské Hradiště
Zlín
Čadca
Jablonka
Zakopane
Nowy Targ
Nowy Sącz
Bardejov
Dukelský priesmyk
Plöckenstein
1378
České Budějovice
Gmünd
Znojmo
Pohořelice
Dolný Kubín
Tatra Mountains
Tatranská
2655
Stará Ľubovňa
Bieszcz
P.N.
Český Krumlov
Horn
Laa a.d. Thaya
Břeclav
Kráľovany
Národný park
Žilina
2043
Nízke Tatry
Poprad
Prešov
Nieder-
Freistadt
Krems a.d. Donau
Stockerau
Malacky
Trenčín
Prievidza
Piešťany
Topoľčany
Banská Bystrica
Zvolen
Košice
Michalovce
Trebišov
Linz
Wels
Melk
St. Pölten
Wien (Vienna)
Trnava
Nová Baňa
SLOVAKIA
Slovenské rudohorie
Rožňava
Tornaľa
Sátoraljaújhely
Steyr
Amstetten
Heiligenkreuz
Bratislava
Nitra
Levice
Krupina
Lučenec
Ozd
Kazincbarcika
Sárospatak
Tokaj
Kisvárda
AUSTRIA
Mariazell
Wiener Neustadt
Eisenstadt
Mosonmagyaróvár
Nové Zámky
Komárno
Salgótarján
Pásztó
Bükk N.P.
Eger
Miskolc
Mátészalka
Nyíregyháza
Österreich
Rax
2007
985
Semmering
Burgenland
Neusiedler See
Ferto-Hanság N.P.
Győr
Csorna
Esztergom
Vác
Gyöngyös
1015
Mátra
HUNGARY
Ujfehértó
Nyírbát

1 : 5 000 000
0   50   100   150 km
22° East

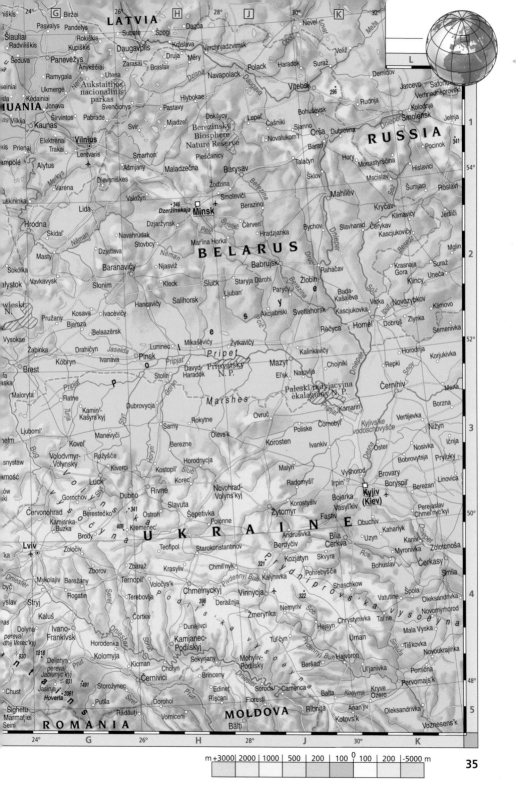

1 : 5 000 000

0   50   100   150 km

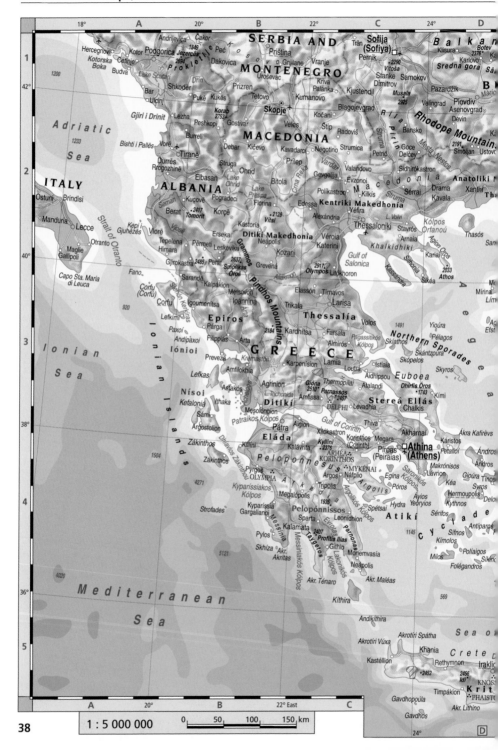

ITALY

Adriatic Sea

Ostuni
Brindisi
Manduria
Lecce
Otranto
Maglie
Gallipoli
Capo Sta. Maria di Leuca

Ionian Sea

Mediterranean Sea

Hercegnovi
Kotorska Boka
Cetinje
Budva
Bar
Ulcinj

Andrijevica
Cakor
1849
Jezerca
2694
Prokletije
Podgorica
Kotor

Shkoder
Puke
Kukes

Gjiri i Drinit
Lezha
Peshkopi
Gostivar

Bishti i Pallës
Vore
Tiranë
Durrës
Rrogozhinë

Seman
Berat
2417
Tomorrit
Kuçovë
Pogradeci

Vlorë
Ypsi
Tepelena
Permeti
Leskoviku
Himara
Gjirokastra
2485
Perat
Smolikas
Oros

Sarandë
Kalpakion

Corfu (Corfu)
Corfu
Paxoi
Andipaxoi
Lefkimi

Fano

920

1233

1200

SERBIA AND MONTENEGRO

Pec
Pristina
Gnjilane
Vranje
Dakovica
Urosevac
Kriva Palanka
Prizren
Tetovo
Kumanovo

Korab
2753
Skopje
Kočani
Veles
Štip
Radoviš

MACEDONIA

Debar
Kičevo
Kavadarci
Negotino
Strumica
Prilep

Struga
Ohrid
Lake Ohrid
Lake Prespa
Bitola
Crna Reka
Gevgelija

Florina
Edessa

2128
Vitsi
Kastoria
Alexándria
Véroia

Ditiki Makedhonia
Neápolis
Kozani
Grevená
Katerini

Elassón
Tírnavos
Larisa
Trikala

Metsovon
Ioánnina
Arta

Igoumenitsa
Epiros
Parga
Filippias
Arta
2184
Kardhítsa
Farsala
Almirós

Trän
Sofija (Sofiya)
Pernik
2290
Vitoša
Stanke Dimitrov
Samokov
Kjustendil
Dimitrov
Musala
2925

Blagojevgrad

Sofija (Sofiya)

Balkan
Klisura
Botev
2376
Karlovo
Srednagora
Sa
Pazardžik
Velingrad
Plovdiv
Asenovgrad
Devin

Rhodope Mountain.
2191
Smoljan
Ustovc

Bansko
Goce Delčev
Petrič

Valandovo
Sidhirókastron

Evzonoi
Polikastron
Kilkis
Serrai

Kentriki Makedhonia
Yéfira

Thessaloniki
Stavrós
Arnaía
Áyion Óros
Khalkidhiki
Kassándra
Sikéa

Kólpos Orfanoú
Thasós
Sam

Simón
Kariaí
2033
Athos

Drama
Kavala
Xánthi

Anatoliki
Th

L. Volvi
Gulf of Salonica
2917
Ólympos
Litókhoron

Ma
c
e
d
o
n
i
a

Thessalía

Volos
1491
Yioúra
Pagassitikós
Kólpos
Skiathos
Pélagos
Skántzoura
Skópelos

Northern Sporades

Skyros
Ag
Efst

GREECE

Karpenísion
Lamia
Istiaia
Loutrá
Aidhipsou
Euboea

Agrinion
Thermopilai
Atalandi

Gióna
2510
Parnassos
2457
Ámfissa
DELPHI
Levadhia
Chalkis

Dhirfís Óros
1743
Kimi

Stereá Ellás

Thiva

Akharnaí
Káristos

Áthina (Athens)
Pireas (Peiraias)
Petalioí
Ándros

Áthina

Ákra Kafirévs

Makrónisos
Lávrion
Kéa
Tínos
Syros
Hermoupolis
Kythnos
Delo
Sérifos

Atikí

Kyllíni
Kalávrita
2376
ARHEA KORINTHOS

Xilókastron
Korinthos (Corinth)
Megara

Aigion
Gulf of Corinth

Patraikós Kólpos
Pátra
Eláda

Peloponnesus

Pyrgos
OLYMPIA

Kyparissiakós Kólpos
Kyparissía
Gargalianoi

Argos
Náfplio
Tripolis
1935
Megalópolis

Peloponnissos
Sparta

Messini
Kalamata
2407
Profitis Ilias
Pylos
Skhíza
Akr. Akritas

Taygetos
Githio

Leonidhion
Spétsai

Egina
Póros

MYKENAI

Ar
k
a
d
i
a

Argolikós Kólpos
Ayios Yeoryios
Hydra

Saronikós Kólpos
Egina

Evrótas
Lakonikós Kólpos

Monemvasía
Neápolis

Akr. Maléas

Kíthira

Andikíthira

Akrotíri Spátha
Akrotíri Voúxa
Kastéllion

Khaniá
Rethymnon
2452
2456
Idi
Timpákion

Crete
Iraklio

KNOS
Kríti
PHAISTO
Akr. Lithino

Gavdhopoúla
Gavdhos

Sea o

Argolis

Cyclades
1145
Sifnos
Kímolos
Milos
Polláigos
Folégandros

Antíparos
Síkin

Páros

Makrónisos
Ándros
Gioúra

Strofades

Zákinthos
Zákinthos

Dhrvanis Zákinthou

4271

5121

4020

Nísoi
Kefaloniá
Sámi
Argostolion

Lefkas
Astakós
Ithaka
Mesolongion

Préveza
Amfilokhia
L. Kremastón
L. Trichonida

Ditikí

I
o
n
i
a
n

I
s
l
a
n
d
s

1504

P
i
n
d
h
o
s

M
o
u
n
t
a
i
n
s

Grammos

2637

Aliákmon

Vardar

Strumá

Pirin
Mesta-Nestos

Rila

1 : 5 000 000

0   50   100   150 km

18°   A   20°   B   22°   C   24°   D

42°

40°

38°

36°

A   20°   B   22° East   C   24°   D

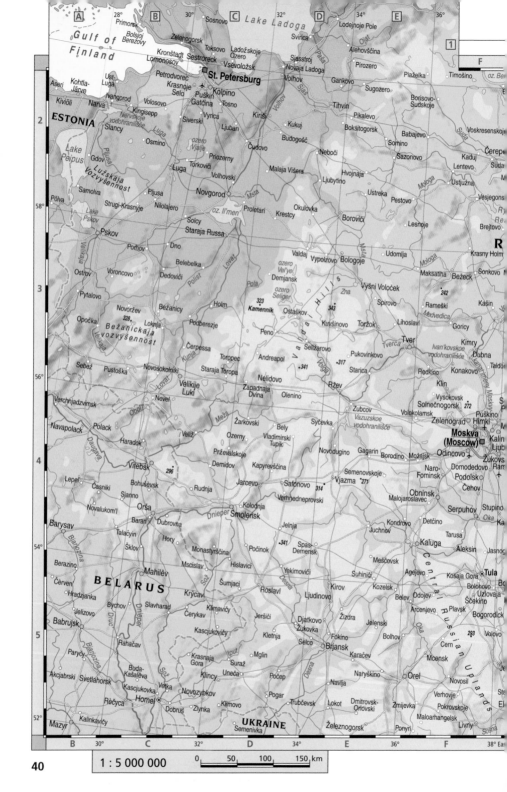

1 : 5 000 000

0   50   100   150 km

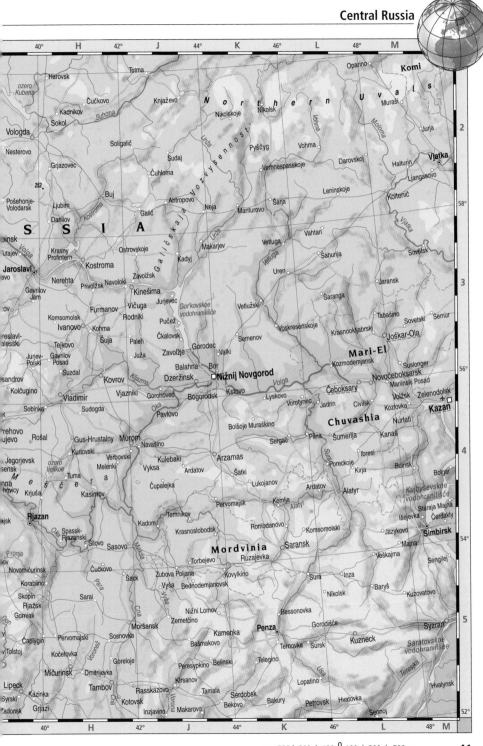

40° **H** 42° **J** 44° **K** 46° **L** 48° **M**

Komi

Harovsk
Tolma
Oparino

ozero
Kubena
Čučkovo
Knjaževo
N o r t h e r n
U v a l s
Muraši

Kadnikov
Suhona
Nikolskoje
Nikolsk
Jчhma
Moloma
Jurja
2

Sokol
Vologda
Pyšćyg
Vohma

Nesterovo
Soligalič
Sudaj
Darovskoj
Halturin
Vjatka

Grjazovec
Čuhloma
Verhnespasskoje
Ljangasovo

252
Buj
Ahtropovo
Leninskoje
Koltenič

Pošehonje-
Volodarsk
Ljubim
Galič
Neja
Manturovo
Šarja
58°

Danilov

S Ostrovskoje **S** **I** **A**
Vahtan
Vjatka

binsk
Makarjev
Vetluga

utajev
Krasny
Profintern
Volga
Kadyj
Unza
Vetluga
Šahunja
Sovetsk

Jaroslavl
Kostroma
Zavolžsk
Uren
Jaransk
3

evo
Nerehta
Privolžsk Navoloki
Kinešima
Jurjevec
Gor'kovskoe
vodohranilišče
Vetlužski
Šaranga

Gavrilov
Jam
Furmanov
Vičuga
Rodniki
Pučež
Voskresenskoje
Tabašino
Sovetski
Semür

Komsomolsk
Ivanovo
Kohma
Čkalovsk
Valki
Krasnooktjabrski
Joškar-Ola

reslavl-
alesski
Tejkovo
Šuja
Paleh
Zavolžje
Gorodec
Semenov
Mari-El

Jurjev-
Polski
Gavrilov
Posad
Juža
Balahna
Bor
Kozmodemjansk
Suslonger

sandrov
Suzdal
Kovrov
Dzeržinsk
Nižnij Novgorod
Volga
Novočeboksarsk
56°

Kolčugino
Vladimir
Vjazniki
Gorohovec
Bogorodsk
Kstovo
Lyskovo
Čeboksary
Mariinski Posad

Sobinka
Sudogda
Oka
Pavlovo
Vorotynec
Jadrin
Civilsk
Volžsk
Kozlovka
Zelenodolsk

rehovo
ujevo
Rošal
Gus-Hrustalny
Murom
Navašino
Bolšoje Muraškino
Chuvashia
Nurlati
Kazan

Jegorjevsk
sensk
ozero
Velikoe
Kurlovski
Verbovski
Melenki
Kulebaki
Vyksa
Sergač
Plina
Šumerlja
Kanaš
Ibresi
Buinsk
4

M Tuma *e* *š* *č* *e* *r* *a*
Ardatov
Šatki
Poreckoje
Kirja
Bolgar

nna
hovicy
Krjuša
Kasimov
Čupalejka
Lukojanov
Ardatov
Alatyr
Kujbyševskoe
vodohranilišče

Rjazan
Oka
Spassk-
Rjazanski
Silovo
Sasovo
Moksa
Kadom
Temnikov
Pervomajsk
Kemlja
Alatyr
Staraja Majna
Čerdakly

Pronja
Krasnoslobodsk
Romodanovo
Komsomolski
Išejevka
Jazykovo
Simbirsk
54°

ov
Novomičurinsk
Čučkovo
Para
Sack
Zubova Poljana
Kovylkino
Mordvinia
Saransk
Ružajevka
Veškajma
Majna

Korablino
Vyša
Bednodemjanovsk
Sura
Inza
Baryš
Sengilej

Skopin
Rjažsk
Sarai
Nikolsk
Kuzovatovo

Gorniak
Nižni Lomov
Zemetčino
Bessonovka
Gorodišče
Syzran
5

Don
Caplygin
Pervomajski
Sosnovka
Cna
Moršansk
Kamenka
Penza
Kuzneck
Saratovskoe
vodohranilišče

Kočetovka
Voronež
Bašmakovo
Ternovka
Sursk

Mičurinsk
Dmitrijevka
Goreloje
Peresypkino
Belinski
Telegino
Usa
Tereška
Hvalynsk

Lipeck
Tambov
Kirsanov
Lopatino

Syrski
Kazinka
Rasskazovo
Tamala
Serdobsk
Bakury
Petrovsk
Hvatovka

adonsk
Grjazi
Kotovsk
Inzavino
Vorona
Makarovo
Bekovo
Sennoj
52°

40° **H** 42° **J** 44° **K** 46° **L** 48° **M**

Ukraine

1 : 5 000 000

0   50   100   150 km

42

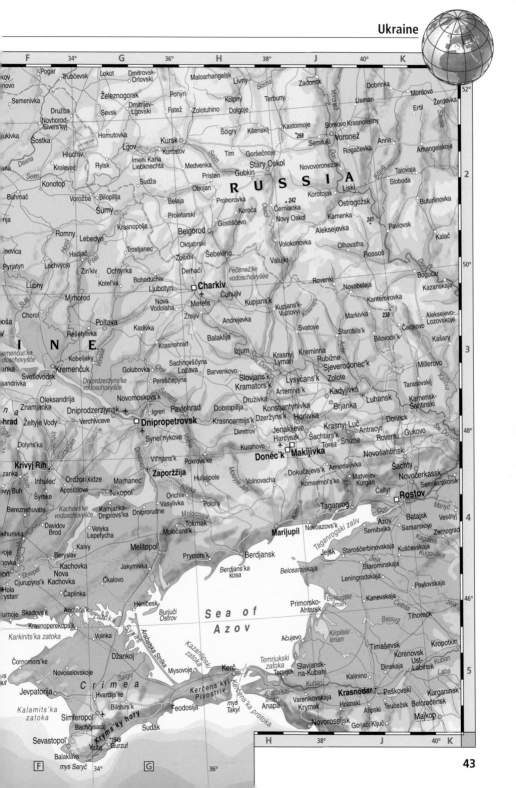

Iceland

A 24° B 22° C 20° D 18° East E 16° F 14°

1

Arctic Circle · Straumnes · Horn (North Cape) · Grímsey · Rifstangi · Fontur · Kópasker · Thórshöfn

Drangajökull 925 · Bolungarvík · Ísafjördhur · Unadhsdalur · Nordhurfjördhur · Skagatá · Siglufjördhur · Gjögurtá · Flatey · Húsavík · Thjódhgardhurinn í Jökulsárgjúfrum

66°

Djúpavík · Dalvík · Hrísey · DETTIFOSS · Bjarnarey

Gláma 920 · Hólmavík · Húnaflói · Skagaströnd · Saudhárkrókur · Myrkárjökull 1387 · Akureyri · Reykjahlídh · Grímsstadhir · Vopnafjördhur

2

Hvallátur · Bjargtangar 58 · Vatneyri · Eyri · Thingeyrar · Skútustadhir · Mývatn · Modhrudalur

Brekkuvellir · Hvammstangi · Saurbær · Mýri · Egilsstadhabær · Seydhisfjördhur · Neskaupstadhur

Breidhafjördhur · Grímstunga

65°

Stykkishólmur · Búdhardalur · Arnavatn · Eskifjördhur

Hellissandur · Ólafsvík · Grundarfjördhur · I C E L A N D · 1510 Askja · Snæfell 1833 · Djúpivogur

1448 · Akrar · Húsafell · Langjökull 1355 · Hofs-jökull 1765 · 2000 · Bárdarbunga · Hof · Hvalnes

3

Borgarnes · Grund · Hvítárvatn · Vatnajökull · Stokksnes

Faxaflói · Midhsandur · Akranes · Thjódhgardhurinn í Thingvellir · Thórsvatn · Langisjór · Höfn

Reykjavík · Thingvellir · Geysir · GULLFOSS · Thjódhgardhurinn í Skaftafell · 2119 · Jökulsárlón · Hvannadalshnúkur

64°

Gardhskagi · Keflavík · Hafnarfjördhur · Búrfell · Hekla 1491 · Kálfafell · Skaftafell

Reykjanes · Grindavík · Eyrárbakki · Selfoss · Hella · Kirkjubæjarklaustur

4

183 · Hvolsvöllur · Eyjafjallajökull 1666 · Langholt · 118

Heimaey · Vík

63°

A T L A N T I C   O C E A N

0 ___ 50 km

Small European states

FINLAND

NORWAY · SWEDEN · ESTONIA · RUSSIA

IRELAND · LATVIA

DENMARK · LITHUANIA

UNITED KINGDOM · RUSSIA · BELARUS

NETHERLANDS · POLAND

BELGIUM · GERMANY

LUX. · CZECH REPUBLIC · UKRAINE

FRANCE · LIECH. · SLOVAKIA

SWITZERLAND A · AUSTRIA · MOLDOVA

HUNGARY

SLOVENIA · CROATIA · ROMANIA

PORTUGAL · ANDORRA C · SAN MARINO B · BOSNIA AND HERZEGOVINA

MONACO · D · SERBIA AND MONTENEGRO

SPAIN · BULGARIA

VATICAN CITY E · MAC.

ITALY · ALB. · GREECE · TURKEY

MOROCCO · ALGERIA · TUNISIA · F MALTA

m+2000 | 1000 | 500 | 200 | 100 0 100 | 200 | 500 | -1000 m

A

Kriessern
Hohenems
Appenzell
Oberriet
Götzis
1640
Wasserauen
Rankwell
Damüls
Altmann
Ruggell
Feldkirch
Laterns
2436
Wildhaus
Gams
Bendern
Thüringen
AUSTRIA
SWITZERLAND
Nendeln
Schaan
Nenzing
Bludenz
Walensee
Walenstadt
Buchs
Vaduz
Galinakopf
•2198
Triesenberg
Flums
Alvier
Malbun
Fundkopf
2343
Triesen
2401
Mels
LIECHTENSTEIN
Sargans
Balzers
2964
Schruns
2552
Schesaplana
Lünersee
Falknis
Weisstannen
Maienfeld
R *ä* *t* *i* *k* *o* *n*
Bad
Ragaz
Grüsch
Weisstannental
Landquart
0   10 km
Madrisahorn *2826*

B

Bon-Voyage
FRANCE
Saint-Roman
Punte de la Veille
Mont des Mules
Monte-Carlo-Beach
La Turbie
La Rousse
Beausoleil
Monte-Carlo
Malbousquet
Casino
Moneghetti
MONACO
Port
La Condamine
Musée Océanographique
Fontvieille
Monaco
M e d i t e r r a n e a n
Cap-d'Ail
S e a
0   1 km
Punte Mala
Cap-d'Ail

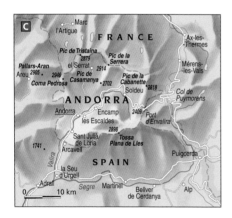

C

•Marc
l'Artigue
FRANCE
Ax-les-
Thermes
Pic de Tristaina
2879
Pic de la
Serrera
Pallars-Aran
el Serrat
2914
Mérens-
les-Vals
Areu *2905* *2946*
Pic de
Coma Pedrosa
Casamanya •*2702*
Col de
Soldeu
•*2818*
Puymorens
ANDORRA
2409
Andorra
Encamp
Port
les Escaldes
d'Envalira
2896
Sant Julià
Tossa
1741
de Lòria
Plana de Lles
Arcavell
Puigcerdà
SPAIN
la Seu
d'Urgell
•Adrall
Segre
Martinet
Alp
0   10 km
Bellver
de Cerdanya

D

Rimini
Santarcangelo
di Romagna
A d r i a t i c
S e a
Spadarolo
Miramare
Marecchia
Borghi
San Paolo
Riccione
Torriana
San Lorenzo
in Carreggiano
Misano
Verucchio
Ausa
Adriatico
ITALY
Serravalle
Coriano
Borgo
Domagnano
Marano
Monte
Maggiore
Annibolina
167
Faetano
San Marino
San Clemente
Fiorentino
SAN MARINO
M o n t e f e l t r o
Sassofeltrio
Morciano
di Romagna
Conca
Montefiore
Conca
Saludecio
0   5 km
Piandicastello

E

VIA
RIALTO C.PRO
PIAZZA DI
VIA
DELLA MELORIA
S. MARIA
CANOIA
VIA
DELLE GRAZIE
VIA MOCENIGO
VIA
VENERIO
VESPASIANO
VIA
S. Maria
VIALE
VATICANO
GERMANICO
VIA MELORIA
delle Grazie
VIA
OTTAVIANO
ENO
PIAZZA DEL
RISORGIMENTO
VIA MILLELIRE
Musei
VIA DELLA
Vaticani
VIA PORTA ANGELICA
VIA
ANGELO
VATICAN
VIA
POSTA VECCHIA
VIA
CITY
MASCHERINO
DEL FALCO
Cappella
Sistina
Stanze
VIA DEI CORRIDORI
VIALE VATICANO
Governatorio
di Raffaello
Collegio
PIAZZA
Etiopico
S. PIETRO
Pontificio
San Pietro
VIA D. CONCILIAZIONE
Sem.Romano
Radio
Stazione
Minore
Vaticana
Vaticana
Santo Spirito
VIA NICOLÒ V.
in Sassia
VIA
AURELIA
VIA DELLA
0   250 m
VIA DI PORTA CAVALLEGGERI
PORTA
STAZIONE
CAVALLEGGERI

F

M e d i t e r r a n e a n   S e a
C. S. Dimitri
Gozo
162
Victoria
Mgarr
Xewkija
Comino
Cominotto
Marfa
Comino Channel
St. Paul's Bay
St. Paul's
Ghajn
Bahar
Sliema
Tuffieha
239
Birkirkara
Valletta
Ras ir-Raheb
Nadur
Tower
Rabat
Qormi
Zejtun
MALTA
Birzebbuga
Zurrieq
Marsaxlokk Bay
C. Benghisa
Fifla
0   10 km

Asia: Physical

1 : 70 000 000

0   700   1400   2100 km

46

120° F 140° G 160° H 180° J

160°

Laptev Sea

New Siberian Islands

pack ice limit in summer

East Siberian Sea

pack ice limit in winter

20

2389

Lena

2389

Verkhoyanskiy Mountains

I   A

Pobeda
3147

Chersky Range

Jakutsk

Mus Chaia
2959

Viljui

Aldan

Okhotsk

Magadan

Kolyma Range

Anadyrskoye
Ploskogor'ye

2320

Wrangel
Island

50

NORTH

Bering Strait

AMERICA

60°

Stanovoy Range

2412

Khrebet Dzhugdzhur

Amur

*Sea of
Okhotsk*

Kamchatka Peninsula

4750
Kljucev

508

Bering Sea

Aleutian Islands

Alaska Peninsula

2

3

Amur

Greater Hinggan Range

Harbin

Manchuria

Sakhalin

Sikhote-Alin

Kuril Islands

Obruchev Rise

940

Kuril Trench

10542

Aleutian Trench

7822

*Sea of
Japan*

Hokkaido

Northwest

Pacific

Basin

40°

Liaodong

Pyongyang

Honshu

Korea

Soul
(Seoul)

Fujisan

Tokyo

Japan Trench

Shandong
Peninsula

67

Osaka

3776

Shanghai

Korea Strait

Kyushu

Shikoku

1962

P A C I F I C   O C E A N

4

Fuzhou

*East China
Sea*

Okinawa

Bonin Trench

9810

Hawaiian Ridge

Midway
Islands

Taiwan Strait

Taipei

Ryukyu Islands

Ryukyu Trench

Bonin
Islands

Mid-Pacific-Seamounts

20°

Formosa

Philippine
Basin

West
Mariana
Basin

Mariana Trench

Wake

Luzon

*Philippine
Sea*

Mariana
Islands

East
Mariana
Basin

Eniwetok-
Atoll

Marshall Islands

1811

Central
Pacific
Basin

Manila

Kyushu-Palau Ridge

10497

M

11034

Yap
Islands

Ulithi-Atoll

Bikini-Atoll

5

Palawan

Philippines Trench

Palau Islands

Hall
Islands

Ratak Chain

Dalap-Uliga-Darrit

Mindanao

Koror

Woleai-Atoll

Senyavin
Islands

Palikir

Polynesia

5540

nabalu

4101

Caroline Islands

Helen

Caroline Basin

Gilbert Islands

Bairiki

Bandar Seri
Begawan

l   a   y   s   i   a

M   e   l   a   n   e   s   i   a

6112

o

Celebes
(Sulawesi)

Molucca Islands

Bismarck
Archipelago

New Ireland

Yaren

0°

Maoke Mountains
5029°
Puncak Jaya

Bismarck Sea

Solomon Islands

Sea

Flores

Timor

**New
Guinea**

New Britain

Bougainville

6

Sumba

Arafura Sea

Cape York

Port Moresby

Guadalcanal

Phoenix Islands

Timor Sea

H   180°   J

rthwest
stralian
asin

120°   F   **AUSTRALIA**   140°   G

Coral Sea

160°

Asia: Political

FINLAND
Helsinki
Tallinn
St. Petersburg
ESTONIA
Riga
LATVIA
LITHUANIA
Vilnius
Minsk
BELARUS
POLAND
Kyjiv
(Kiev)
UKRAINE
MOLDOVA
Chişinău
ROMANIA
Bucureşti
(Bucharest)
Sofija
(Sofiya)
BULGARIA
GEORGIA
istanbul
Ankara
ARMENIA
Yerevan
Athina
(Athens)
GREECE
TURKEY
Nicosia
CYPRUS
Beirut
LEBANON
Damascus
Jerusalem
SYRIA
Amman
JORDAN
Cairo
ISRAEL
Aleppo
Al-Mawsil
Baghdad
IRAQ
Al Basrah
Abadan
Kuwait
KUWAIT
EGYPT
Medina
SAUDI
ARABIA
Mecca
Riyadh
Al Manama
BAHRAIN
Doha
QATAR
Abu Dhabi
UNITED
ARAB
EMIRATES
Muscat
OMAN
Khartoum
SUDAN
ERITREA
Asmara
Sanaa
YEMEN
Aden
DJIBOUTI
Addis
Ababa
Djibouti
ETHIOPIA
SOMALIA
UGANDA
KENYA
Kampala
Mogadishu
Kigali
RWANDA
Bujumbura
Nairobi
BURUNDI
Dodoma
TANZANIA

Mediterranean Sea

Barents Sea
Novaya Zemlya
North Land

Murmansk
Dikson
Gyda
Hatanga
Vorkuta
Norilsk
Salehard
Tura
Arhangel'sk
Sergino
Surgut
Nizjnevartovsk

R U S S

Moskva
(Moscow)
Jaroslavl
Perm
Yekaterinburg
Bratsk
Nižnij
Novgorod
Kazan
Ufa
Čeljabinsk
Omsk
Novosibirsk
Krasnojarsk
Samara
Magnitogorsk
Barnaul
Irkutsk
Volgograd
Astana
Lake Ba
Don
Rostov
Atyrau
Karaghandy
Semej
Krasnodar
Aral
Kyzylorda
Altaj
MONGOLIA
Grozny
Aktau
Ulan B
Astrakhan
Ural
Aral Sea
KAZAKHSTAN
Balkhash
Lake Balkhash
Bishkek
Almaty
Ürümqi
Ba
Volga
Caspian Sea
Black Sea
Tibilisi
Baki
(Baku)
UZBEKISTAN
Tashkent
KYRGYZSTAN
Tabriz
Turkmenbaşy
Samarkand
Kashi
CHINA
AZERBAIJAN
TURKMENISTAN
Dushanbe
TAJIKISTAN
Lanzhou
Teheran
Ashgabad
Mashhad
Tianshui
Kabul
Islamabad
Kerman
Herat
Peshawar
Rawalpindi
IRAN
Isfahan
Lhasa
Chengdu
Baghdad
Shiraz
Kandahar
New Delhi
Lahore
AFGHANISTAN
Chongqing
Guiy
Bandar-e
Abbas
Quetta
Multan
Faisalabad
Delhi
NEPAL
Brahmaputra
BHUTAN
Kunming
Kathmandu
Thimpu
Jaipur
Agra
Lucknow
PAKISTAN
Hyderabad
Kanpur
Varanasi
BANGLADESH
Karachi
Ganges
Dhaka
Hanoi
Ahmadabad
INDIA
Nagpur
Calcutta
MYANMAR
Mumbai
(Bombay)
Hyderabad
Pune
Vishakhapatnam
Yangon
Vientiane
Chiang Mai
Bangalore
Chennai
(Madras)
Andaman
Islands
(India)
Krung Thep
(Bangkok)
THAILAND
CAMB
Lakshadweep
(India)
Cochin
Madurai
Phnom Penh
Trivandrum
Trincomalee
SRI LANKA
Colombo
Nicobar Islands
(India)
Kuala
Lumpur
Medan
MAL
SINGAPO
Pont
Male
Padang
MALDIVES
Sumatra
Sem
Palembang
INDIAN OCEAN
SEYCHELLES
Mahé
Victoria
Jakarta
Bandur
Chagos Archipelago
(U.K.)
Cocos Islands
(Australia)

48
1 : 70 000 000
0   700   1400   2100 km

80°
60°
100°
40°
80°
60°
80° East
40°
0°
20°
60°
20°
40°
A   B   C   D   1   D

120°   F   140°   G   160°   H   180°   J

160°

New Siberian Islands

East Siberian
Sea

Wrangel
Island

2

Verkhoyansk

Arctic Circle

UNITED

Anadyr

STATES

Jakutsk

60°

Lensk

Magadan

Korf

Okhotsk

Tommot

Ajan

Bering Sea

Petropavlovsk-
-Kamčatskij

Sakhalin

Aleutian Islands

3

Poronajsk

Habarovsk

Južno-
Sahalinsk

Kuril Islands

Harbin

Sapporo

Jilin

Shenyang   Vladivostok

Jinzhou

NORTH KOREA

40°

Anshan

Pyongyang

Sendai

in   Lüda   Soul
SOUTH   (Seoul)   Kyoto   Tokyo   JAPAN

han   Qingdao   KOREA   Kobe   Nagoya   Yokohama

hou   Pusan   Osaka

Nanjing   Kitakyushu   Hiroshima

4

anchang   Shanghai

ha   Wenzhou
Fuzhou

Bonin
Islands
(Japan)

Marcus Island
(Japan)

Hawaii
(U.S.)

ou   Taipei

TAIWAN

Tropic of Cancer

ng Kong   Kaohsiung

PACIFIC OCEAN

20°

Wake
(U.S.)

Quezon City

Northern Mariana Islands
(U.S.)

PHILIPPINES

MARSHALL
ISLANDS

Manila

Guam
(U.S.)

Roxas   Cebu

M i c r o n e s i a

5

Davao

Koror

Dalap-Uliga-Darrit

Kota Kinabalu

Palikir

PALAU

MICRONESIA

RUNEI

Manado

Bairiki

M e l a n e

Equator   0°

Balikpapan

Yaren

KIRIBATI

asin

N E S I A

NAURU

6

Ujung Pandang

PAPUA
NEW GUINEA

SOLOMON
ISLANDS

TUVALU

aya   East
Timor   Timor

Port Moresby

Honiara

a

H   180°   J

A U S T R A L I A

VANUATU

120°   F   140°   G   160°

49

Western Russia

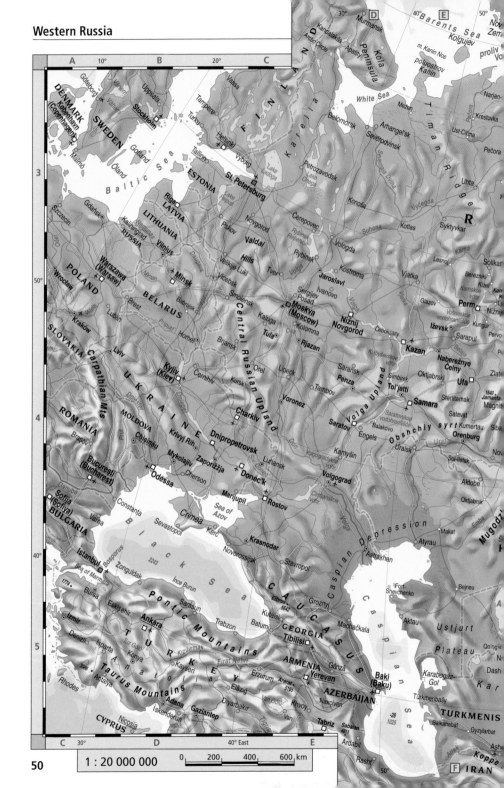

1 : 20 000 000

0   200   400   600 km

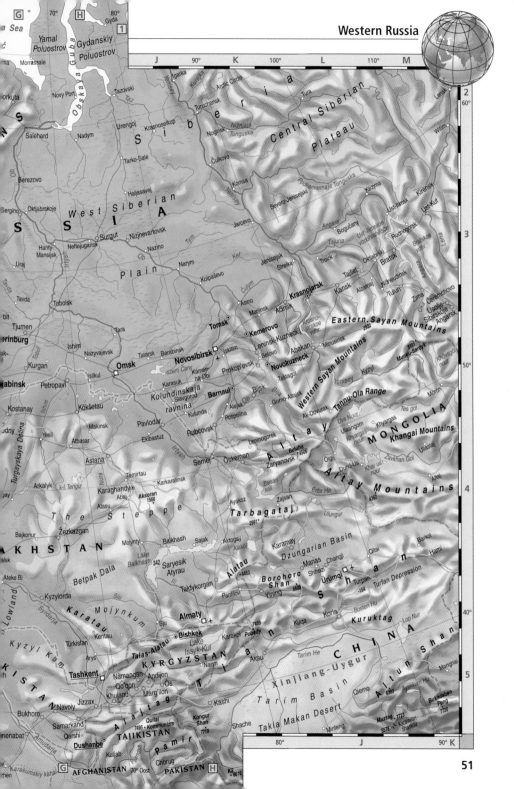

Eastern Russia

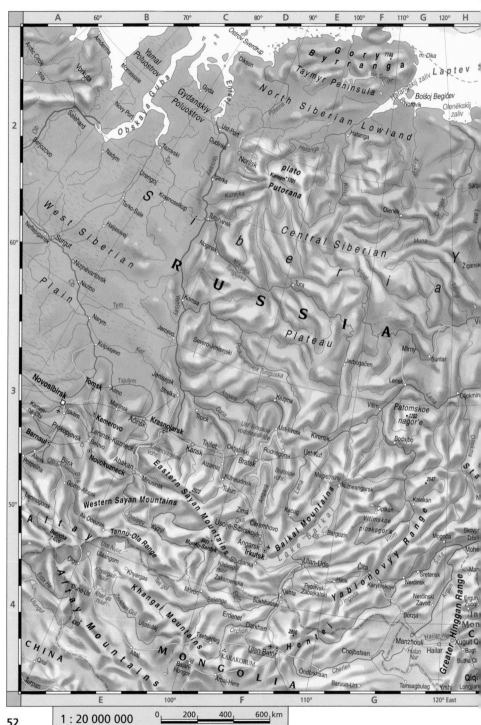

1 : 20 000 000

0 200 400 600 km

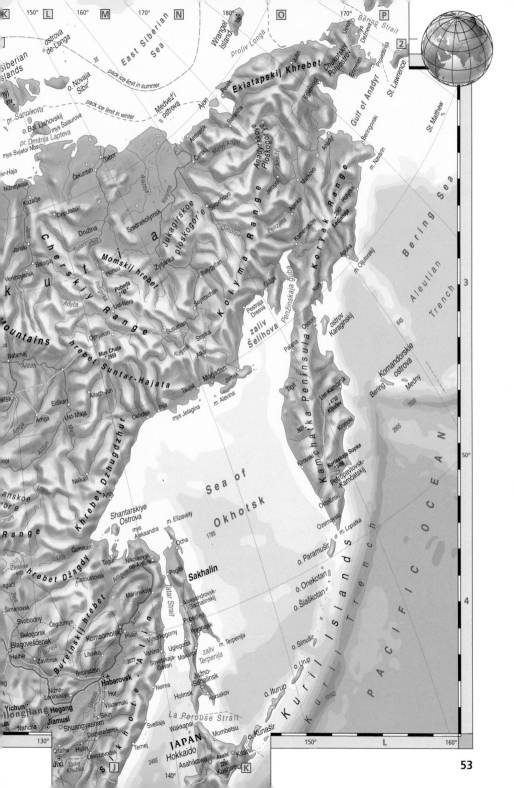

1 : 20 000 000

0   200   400   600 km

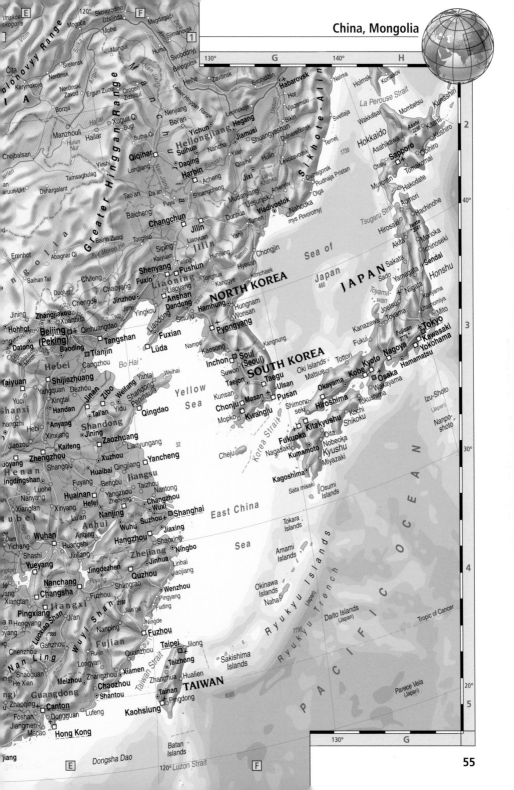

E skogore
Ilmskoe

120° Skovorodino

F

1

130° G 140° H

A
I
A

Čita
Karymskoje
Nerčinsk
Nerčinskij
Zavod
Borzja
Chojbalsan

Mogoča
Sretensk
Mone
Mangui
Hallar
Xuguit Qi
Manzhouli
Hulun
Nur
Hailar
Tamsagbulag
Dshargalant

Skovorodino
Džalinda
Mogoča
Svobodnyj
Belogorsk
Huma
Nenjiang
Bei'an
Yichun
Hegang
Jiamusi
Shuangyashan
Yilan

Habarovsk
Hot
Vjazemskij
Bikin
Lesozavodsk
Krsenovj
Olga
mys Povorotnyj

Nelma
Holmsk

La Perouse Strait
Wakkanai
Mombetsu
Rebun

Korsakov
Kunashiri

Oroqen
Zizhiqui
Nan Jiang
Heihe
Zavitinsk
Birobidžan
Ussuri

Hokkaido
Asahikawa
Otaru Sapporo
Muroran
Hakodate

Asahi
2290
Kitami
Kushiro
Obihiro
Tomakomai

Greater Hinggan Range
Qiqihar
Daqing
Harbin
Acheng
Sungari
Jixi
Mudanjiang
Ussurijsk
Vladivostok
Nahodka

Suihua
Nancha
Tao'an
Da'an
Fuyu
Shuangcheng
Duniua
Tumen

Aomori
Hachinohe
Morioka
Ichinoseki

Sikhote-Alin
Hirosaki
Akita

Iwate
2041

40°
Changchun Jilin
Bairin Zuoqi
Xar Moron He
Siping
Liaoyuan
Tieling
Yanji
Chongjin
Hyesan

Sendai
Tsugaru Strait
Yamagata Honshu
Niigata

Erenhot
Abagnar Qi
Kaiyuan
Tonghua
Kanggye
Kimchaek

Sea of
Japan
460

Sado
Toyama-
wan
Joetsu

Koriyama
Utsunomiya
Mito

Shenyang
Fushun
Chifeng
Chaoyang
Fuxin
Anshan
Dandong
Liaoning
Liaoyang
Yingkou
Hamhung
Hungnam
Wonsan

NORTH KOREA
Pyongyang
Nampo

JAPAN
Fukui
Kanazawa
Toyama

Fujisan
3776
Tokyo
Kawasaki
Yokohama

Zhangjiakou
Xuanhua
Hohhot
Beijing
(Peking)
Datong
Baoding
Tianjin
Tangshan
Lüda

Qinhuangdao
Fuxian

Kaesong
Soul
(Seoul)
Inchon

Kangnung

Nagoya
Kyoto Hamamatsu
Kobe
Osaka

Izu-Shoto
(Japan)

Hebei
Shijiazhuang
Taiyuan
Yangquan Dezhou
Yuci
Xingtai

Cangzhou
Bo Hai
Yantai
Weifang
Shandong
Peninsula

Suwon
Taejon
Taegu
Ulsan

Tottori
Oki Islands
Matsue

Okayama
Hiroshima

Wakayama

Nanpo-
shoto

Handan
Shanxi
Jinan
Zibo
Tai'an
Yidu
Qingdao

Kunsan
Chonju
Masan
Pusan

Shimono-
seki

Tokushima
Shikoku
Kochi

Anyang
Xinxiang
Kaifeng
Zaozhuang
Jining
Shandong

Mopko
Kwangju

Fukuoka
Kitakyushu
Oita
Nobeoka

Zhengzhou
Xuzhou
Yancheng
Lianyungang
32
Cheju

Nagasaki
Kumamoto
Kyushu
Miyazaki

Henan
Shangqiu
Huaibai
Qingjiang
Jiangsu

Kagoshima
Sata misaki

Osumi
Islands

Luohe
Nanyang
Fuyang
Bengbu
Taizhou
Nantong

Hefei
Xinyang
Zhenyjang
Changzhou
Wuxi
Shanghai

East China

Tokara
Islands

Wuhan
Anhui
Wuhu Suzhou
Nanjing Tai Hu
Jiaxing

Hubei
Anqing
Huangshi
Hangzhou
Shaoxing

Sea

Amami
Islands

Yueyang
Jiujiang
Zhejiang Ningbo
Jinhua Linhai

Yichang

Nanchang
Jingdezhen
Quzhou
Wenzhou

Okinawa
Islands
Naha

Ryukyu Islands
(Japan)

Changsha
Jiangxi
Fuzhou
Pingyang
Fuding

Xiangtan
Pingxiang
Luoxiao Shan
Ji'an
Nanping
Ningde

Tropic of Cancer

Hengyang
Ganzhou
Fuzhou

Daito Islands
(Japan)

Nan Ling
Chenzhou
Ruijin
Longyan
Xiamen
Fujian
Taipei
Jilong
Taizhong
Hualien

Sakishima
Islands

Meizhou
Zhangzhou
Shaoguan
He Xian
Chaozhou
Shantou
Zhanghua
TAIWAN

Guangdong
Canton
Foshan
Dongguan
Hong Kong

Lufeng
Kaohsiung
Tainan
Pingdong

Macao

Batan
Islands

Jiang
E Dongsha Dao
120° Luzon Strait
F

G

20°

PACIFIC OCEAN

55

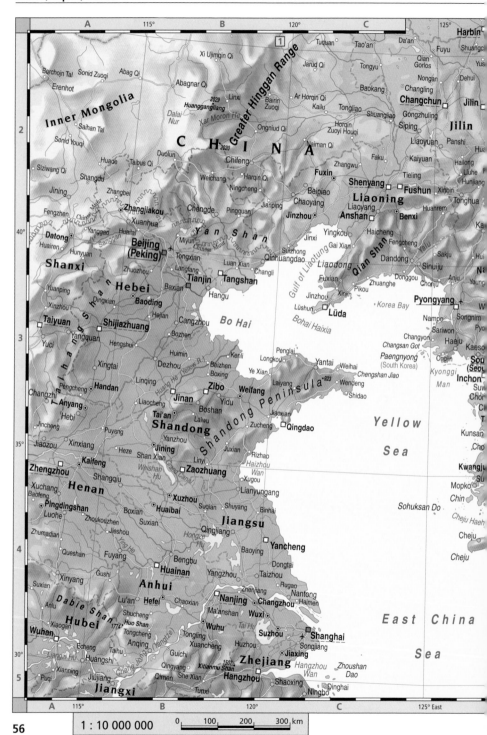

1 : 10 000 000

0   100   200   300 km

China, Japan, Korea

Turkey

BULGARIA

26° A 28° B 30° C 32° D

42°

Harmanli Malko Tárnovo

B l a c k

Kerempe Burnu

Kırklareli *1031 İğneada 70 **S e a** Cide İn

Krumovgrad Orestiás Edirne Pınarhisar Zonguldak Bartın Uluş Az

Babaeski Lüleburgaz Saray Karacaköy Çaycuma K

GREECE Souflíon Uzunköprü Kilyos Bosporus Pazarbaşı Baba Burnu Kozlu Safranbolu Arı

Komotiní Férai Hayrabolu Çorlu Sarıyer Şile Burnu Karasu Ereğli Devrek 1976 Karabük

Alexandroupolis Keşan Tekirdağ Silivri Yeşilköy İstanbul Kandıra Akçakoca Yığılca

Enez Malkara 1221 Kartal İzmit Hendek Düzce Gerede Çerkeş Kurşunl

Samothraki Saros Körfezi Şarköy Marmara **S e a o f M a r m a r a** Gebze Hereke Adapazarı Bolu

Gelibolu Yarımadası M. P. Erdek Yalova Gölcük Geyve Köroğlu Dağları Camlidere Sabanözü

Kilitbahir Biga Mudanya İznik Gölü Osmaneli Mudurnu Kıbrıscık Kızılcahamam

Gökçeada Çanakkale Gönen Kuş Gölü Karacabey Gemlik İznik Nallıhan Beypazarı Çubuk

40° Dardan TROY Çan Ulubat Gölü 2543 İnegöl Bilecik Sarıyal Brj. Ayaş İdris Dağı 1992

Bayramiç Mustafakemalpaşa Uludağ Sincan Ankara Elmadağ

Bozcaada Ezine **Kaz dağı** Balya Orhaneli Bozüyük Porsuk 1786 Sançakaya Mihalıçcık Gölbaşı

Ayvacık 1774 Edremit Balıkesir Kepsut Eskişehir Alpu **GÖRDION**

Baba Burnu Edremit Körfezi Savaştepe Tavşanlı Polatlı

Míthimna Ayvalık Bigadiç Emet Kütahya Seyitgazi Sakarya Haymana

PERGAMON Soma Akdağ Sındırgı Simav 2089 Çavdarhisar Çifteler Sivrihisar

Mytilíni Dikili **T U R K E Y**

Lesvos (Lesbos) Çandarlı Körfezi Bergama Akhisar Demirci Gediz Murat Dağı 2309 İhsaniye Emirdağ Celtik Kulu

Karaburun Foçea Gördes Afyonkarahisar İscehisar Eber- meer Yunak Sülüklü Şerefl

Volissós İzmir Körfezi Manisa Kum Selendi Uşak Banaz Sinanpaşa Bolvadin Çay Cihanbeyli Toz Gölü

Chíos 1218 Menemen Gediz Kula **A** Eber Gölü n a

Çeşme İzmir Turgutlu Salihli Alaşehir Eşme Çivril Sultandağı Turgut Akşehir Kadınhanı

Seferihisar Urla Boz Dağı 2159 Kiraz Sandıklı Ilgın

Bayındır Ödemiş Sangöl Egridir Gölü 2800 Sarkikaraağaç Ala Dağ 2305 Aşağı Pınarbaşı

EPHESOS Selçuk Tire Aydın Dağları 1828 Buldan Çal Dinar Kızıldağ M. P. Beyşehir Gölü Kızılören **Konya** Karap

Kuşadası Körfezi **Aydın** Nazilli Menderes **PAMUKKALE** Dazkırı Burdur Gölü Aci- göl Isparta Burdur 2980 Dedegöl Dağı Beyşehir Cumra

Samos Germencik Denizli Çardak Yeşilova 2334 Bucak Bozburun Dağı Suğla Gölü 2271

Sámos Söke Koçarlı Karacasu 2528 Acıpayam Katrancık Dağı Köprülü Kanyon M. P. 2504 Kara Dağ

Ikaría Foúrnoi MILET Çine Kale Boz Dağ 2421 Tefenni Gölhisar Korkuteli Akseki Çarşamba Karan

Pátmos Yenihisar Güllük Milás Muğla Köyceğiz Kızılca Dağı 2598 **Antalya** Geyik Dağı 2877 M

Dhonoúsa **HALIKARNASSOS** Gökova Çameli Serik Manavgat

Amorgós Kálimnos Bodrum Gökova Körfezi Ortaca Elmalı **Olimpos** **SIDE** Gündoğmuş Ermenek

Kos Knidos Datça Bozburun Kemer Bey Dağları 3069 Beydağları M. P.

Astypálea Nísiros Symi Fethiye Körfezi Fethiye **Ak Dağ** 3014 Kemer Alanya Gökdere 2257

Síma Tílos Alimiá Rhodes **B a t ı T o r o s l a r** Kumluca **Gulf of** Gazipaşa Aydıncık O

Khálki 1215 **Rhodes** Kalkan Kaş Kale Finike Yardımcı Burnu **A n t a l y a** Anamur Anamur Burnu

Saría Atáviros Megísti Kekova Adasi 3064 1122

Kárpathos 2295 4433

Kásos 973

3100 C. Kormakitis

Lápithos Girne

M e d i t e r r a n e a n S e a Morfou Bay Güzelyurt 1023 Kythrea SAI

Cape Arnaoutis Morfou Lefke **CYPRUS** Nico

Peyia 1953 Troódos Larnaka Mari

Pólis Pafos Pakhna AMATHUS

1559 Episkopi Limassol

Peyia Cape Gata Akrotiri (U.K.)

36°

38°

40°

2 3 4 5

A e g e a n S e a **S o u t h e r n D o d e c a n e s e S p o r a d e s**

58 1 : 5 000 000 0 50 100 150 km

A 28° B 30° C 32° East D

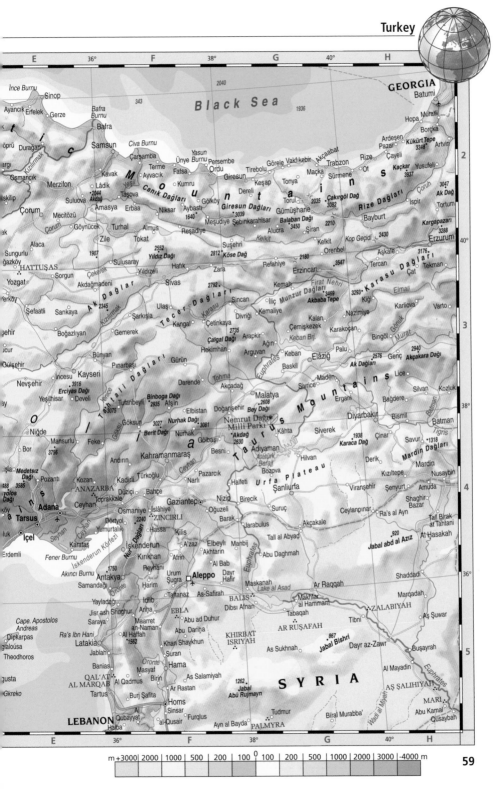

E   36°   F   38°   G   40°   H

İnce Burnu
Sinop
GEORGIA
Batumi

2040
B l a c k   S e a
343
1936

Ayancık Erfelek
Gerze
Bafra
Burnu
Hopa, Muratlı
Borçka
öprü Durağan
Bafra
Ardeşen
Pazar
Kükürt Tepe
3348
Artvin

argı
Samsun
Civa Burnu
Çarşamba
Terme Ayvacık
Yasun
Ünye Burnu Persembe
Görele Vakfıkebir Akçaabat
Trabzon
Rize
Çayeli
Kızılırmak
Osmancık
Kavak
Fatsa
Ordu
Giresun
Tirebolu
Keşap
Tonya
Maçka
Sürmene
Of
Kaçkar
3937
Yusufeli

İskilip
Merzifon
Lâdik
2044
Akdağ
Taşova
Kumru
Gölköy
Dereli
Giresun Dağları
3039
Torul
Çakırgöl Dağ
2035
3082
Rize Dağları
İspir
Çoruh
3047
Ak Dağ
Tortum

Çorum
Suluova
Amasya
Erbaa
Niksar
Aybastı
1640
Meşudiye Şebinkarahisar
Gümüşhane
Balaban Dağı
3450
2210
Bayburt
Kargapazarı
3288
Erzurum

ak
Mecitözü
Göynücek
Turhal
Almus
Reşadiye
Alucra
Şiran
Kop Geçidi
2430

Alaca
Zile
Tokat
Suşehri
Kelkit
Orenbel
Aşkale
3176

Sungurlu
gazköy
HATTUŞAŞ
Sülusaray
1907
2552
Yıldız Dağı
Hafık
Zara
Köse Dağ
2812
Refahiye
2180
3547
Erzincan
Tercan
Çat
3175
Tekman

Yozgat
Sorgun
Çekerek
Yıldızeli
Sivas
Kemah
Fırat Nehri
İliç Munzur Dağları
3469
Akbaba Tepe
3293
Kiğı
Karasu Dağları
Elmalı
Varto

erköy
Şefaatli
Sarıkaya
Akdağmadeni
2792
Ulaş
Sincan
Kemaliye
Nazimiye
Karlıova
Gönük

şehir
Boğazlıyan
Gemerek
2345
Şarkışla
Kangal
Divriği
Kalan
Cemişkezek
Karakoçan
Bingöl
Murat
2940

ucur
Bünyan
Pınarbaşı
Çetinkaya
Çalgal Dağı
2735
Arapkır
Ağın
Keban Brj.
Keban
Palu
Elâzığ
2576
Genç
Akçakara Dağı

Gülşehir
İncesu
Kayseri
Gürün
Hekimhan
Arguvan
Baskil
Maden
Ak Dağları
Lice

Nevşehir
Erciyas Dağı
3916
Darende
Tohma
Akçadağ
Sivrice
Ergani
Silvan
Kozluk

ay
Yeşilhisar
Develi
3075
Tufanbeyli
Binboga Dağı
2935 Alşin
Elbistan
Doğanşehir
Malatya
2608
Bey Dağı
Diyarbakır
Bismil
Batman

Niğde
Mansurlu
Feke
Göksun
3027
Nurhak Dağı
3081
Nemrut Dağı
Milli Parkı
Kâhta
Siverek
1938
Karaca Dağ
Çınar
Savur
1318
Tigris
Mardin Dağları

Bor
3756
Berit Dağı
Nurhak
Akdağ
2630
Gölbaşı
Adıyaman
Hilvan
Derik
Kızıltepe
Mardin

işla
Medetsiz
Dağı
Pozantı
Kozan
Kadirli
Türkoğlu
Besni
Atatürk
Baraji
Bozova
Viranşehir
Şenyurt
Amuda
Nusaybin

488 3585
yolos
Dağı
Kahramanmaraş
Narlı
Pazarcık
Halfeti
U r f a   p l a t e a u
Ra's al Ayn
Shaghir
at Tahtani
Tall Birak

Adana
a Tarsus
Andırın
Düziçi
Bahçe
Gaziantep
Nizip
Birecik
Şanlıurfa
Ceylanpınar

ANAZARBA
Ceyhan
Toprakkale
Osmaniye İslâhiye
Oğuzeli
Suruç
Akçakale
At Hasakah

luk
İçel
Dörtyol
2240
Hassa
Kilis
Barak
Jarabulus
Jabal abd al Azız
920

Erdemli
Karataş
Yumurtalık
İskenderun
A'zaz
Elbeyli Manbij
Tall al Abyad
Abu Daghmah
Shaddadi

Fener Burnu
İskenderun Körfezi
Kırıkhan
Akhtarin
Al Bab
Abu Dariha

Akıncı Burnu
1750
Reyhani
Urum
Sugra
Aleppo
Dayr
Hafir
Maskanah
Lake al Asad
Ar Raqqah
Marqadah

Samandağı
Antakya
Harim
Taftanaz
As-Safirah
BALIS
Makhta
al Hammam
ZALABIYAH
Aş Şuwar

Cape. Apostolos
Andreas
Yayladağı
İdlib
Dibsi Afnan
Tabaqah
Tibni

Dipkarpas
Jisr ash Shughur
Ariha
Maarret
an-Naman
EBLA
Abu ad Duhur
AR RUŞAFAH
Al Mayadin

gialousa
Theodoros
Saraya
Ra's Ibn Hani
Al Haffah
1562
Khan Shaykhun
KHIRBAT
ISRIYAH
As Sukhnah
867
Jabal Bishri
Dayr az-Zawr
Buşayrah

gusta
Gkreko
Latakia
Jablah
Banias
Masyaf
Süran
Hama
As Salamiyah

AL MARQAB
Al Qadmus
Birin
Ar Rastan
1262
Jabal
Abū Rujmayn
S Y R I A
AŞ ŞALIHIYAH
MARI

Tartus
Burj Şafita
Homs
Sinsar
Tudmur
Biral Murabba'
Abu Kamal
Qusaybah

LEBANON
Qubayyat
Halba
Furqlus
Ayn al Bayda
PALMYRA

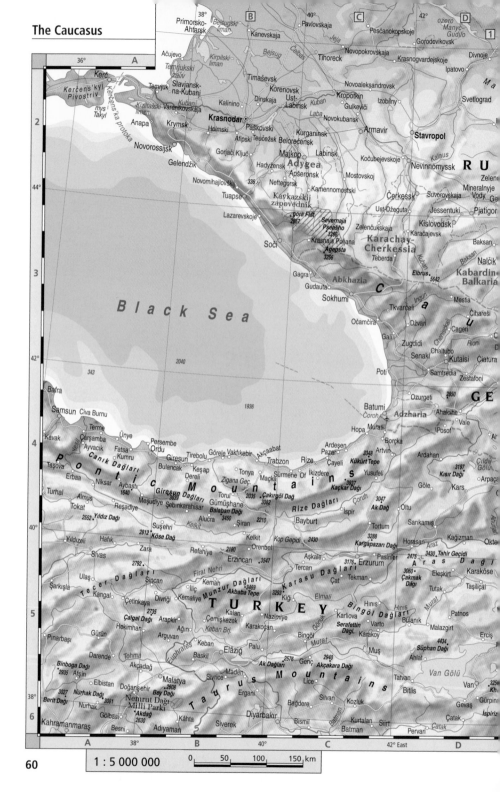

The Caucasus

60   1 : 5 000 000   0   50   100   150 km

iskoje
nr.

Kalmykia

Komsomolski   Ulan Hol   Kaspijski

Kuma

S s i o n

ovsk   Neftekumsk

Kizljarski
zaliv   Tjuleni

Kočubej

B u z a s h c h y
t ü b e g i

Tüledy
araldary

Tübkaraghan müyis

Manghystau
skyrghanaghy

Fort-
Shevchenko

Manghystau
üstirti   Taushyk

2

KAZAKHSTAN   Septe   44°

Mozdok   Kizljar   Krajnovka   Čečen

Kizljar

Chechenia

Nazran   **Groznyj**   Güdermes

Ingushetia   Argun

Šali

Terek

Kizljurt

Hasayjurt   Sulak

Sulak

Aktau   Manghystau   Zhetibai

Pesschanyj müyis   Kuryk

3

Mahačkala

Rakushechnyi müyis

Vladikavkaz

Itumkale   Botlih   Bujnaksk   Kaspijsk

Izberbaš

pereval
Krestovyi   Tebulosmta
4492   4285   Addala-
Suhgelmeer   Sergokala
3151   Karadah

Bežta

Ssetia

Mamedkala   Dagestanskije
Ogni   788

Kumuh   Derbent

4073.   Djultydag   Belidži

šeti   Ahmeta

Kaspi

Telavi

ilisi   Sagaredžo

Marneuli   Rustavi

Gardabani   Citeli-Ckaro

Hiv

Kasumkent   Xudat

Zaqatalä   Rutul   Qusar

Samur   Quba

Xaçmaz

Cnori

Kazah   Alazani

4466. Bazardüzü

Alaverdi   Tovuz   Šamkir   Vartašen

Deveç

Siyezen

Vanadzor   Dilizan   Gänzä

Mingeçevir su
anbari   Mingeçevir

3629. Babadağ

Ismayilli   Sumqayit

Mastağa   Apşeronskij poluostrov
Artyom

Sevan   Xanlar   Yevlax   Göyçay   **Baki
(Baku)**   Märdäkän

Aždahak
3597   3724   Bärdä   Ucar   Ağsu   Şamaxi   Lökbatan   Subunçu

Lake Sevan   Gamiş   Mirbäşir   Kürdämir

Suiti
burnu

Yerevan

Zärdäb   Qazlmemmed   Alät   40°

ARMENIA   Mardakert   Ağdam   Ağcabädi   Sabirabad
Imişli   Saatli   Ali Bäyramli

Ararat   Ehegnadzor   **Xankendi**

Nagorno-Karabakh   Salyan   Banka

pereval Bičanekskij
2346   Laçin   Füzüli   Parsabad
Goris   Puşkin   Neftçala

razit   Sisian   Cäbrayil   Bilehsävär   26 baki
komissarlari adina

Mäkü   3904.
Kaputjug   Kafan   Kadžaran   Mahmüdäbäd   Prişib   Masalli   Kurinskaja
zaliv Kirova

Naxçivan   Culfa   Zängilan   Oghäsh   Germi   Port-Ilïç   Kurkosa   -28
1025

Evowghi   Jolfa   Ordubad
Megri   Huränd   Razi   Kjalvaz   Lekeran

Khvoy   Araz
3347.   Meshkinshahr   Namin   Astara

Kiyämaki Dägh   Qarä Dägh   Ahar   Qareh Sü   Äştärä

otür   Zonuz   Varzaqän

Tasüj   Maränd   Herïs   **I R A N**   Kühhä-ye Sabalän   Čübar

Salmäs   Sufiän   Mehräbän   Ardabil   38°

Khän Takhti   Shabestar   **Tabriz**   Saräb   Nir   Khüshäbär

Lake   Krosrowshahr   Osku   3197.   6
Urmia   Mamaqän

Israel

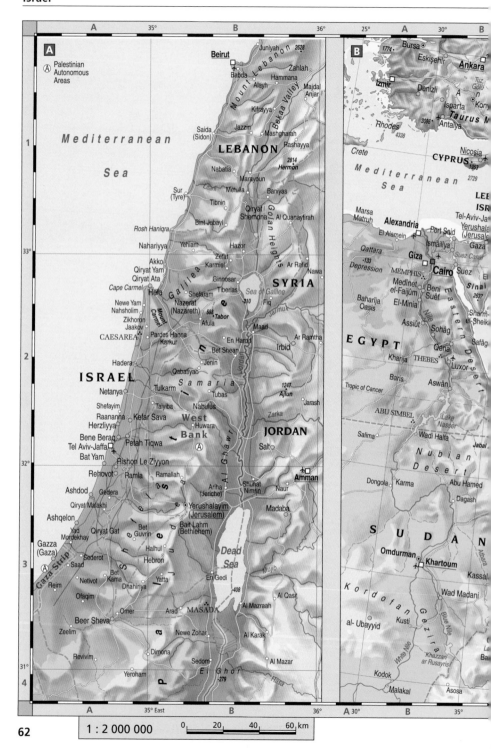

1 : 2 000 000

0 20 40 60 km

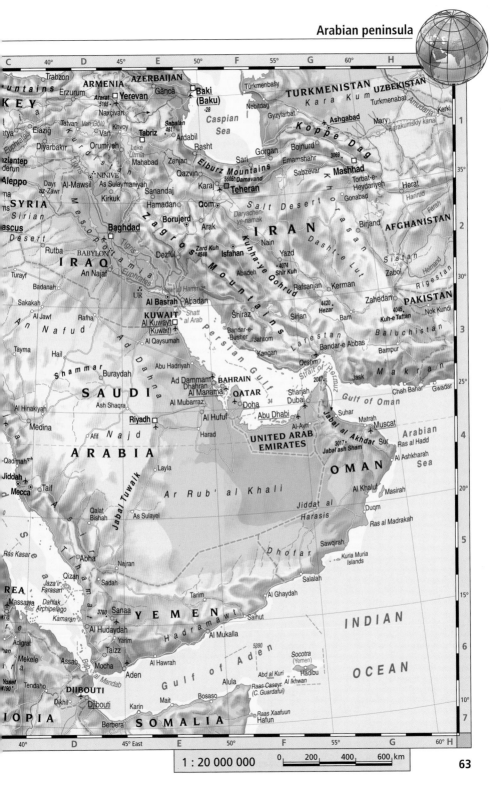

C 40° D 45° E 50° F 55° G 60° H

Trabzon
ARMENIA AZERBAIJAN
untains Erzurum Ararat Yerevan Gäncä Baki
KEY 5165 (Baku)
Naxçivan -28
Van Gölü Khvoy Tabriz Sabalan Ardabil
Tatvan Van Orumiyeh 4611
Elazig Lake Mahabad Zanjan Qazvin Rasht
Diyarbakir Urmia
az NINIVE Kirkuk
aziantep Dayr Al-Mawsil As Sulaymaniyah
derun az-Zawr Sanandaj Hamadan
Aleppo SYRIA Sirian Baghdad Borujerd
ascus Desert Rutba BABYLON Arak
IRAQ An Najaf Dezful Zard Kuh
Turayf Badanah 4548 Isfahan
Sakakah UR Al Basrah Abadan
Al Jawf Rafha Shatt al Arab Shiraz
An Nafud KUWAIT Al Kuwayt (Kuwait)
Tayma Al Qaysumah Abu Hadriyah
Hail Buraydah
Shammar SAUDI Ad Dammam BAHRAIN
Al Hinakiyah Ash Shaqra Dhahran Al Manama
Medina Al Mubarraz QATAR Doha
Riyadh Al Hufuf Abu Dhabi
Afif Najd Harad Al-Ayn UNITED ARAB
ARABIA EMIRATES
-Qadimah
Jiddah Layla
Mecca Taif
Qalat As Sulayel
Bishah
Ras Kasar Abha Najran
Qizan Sadah
REA Jaza'ir Farasan
Massawa Dahlak 3760 Sanaa YEMEN
Archipelago Kamaran Al Hudaydah Hadramawt
Adigrat Yarim Al Mukalla
Mekele Taizz Sahut
Assab Mocha Al Hawrah
Yosef Tendaho Aden Alula
4190 DJIBOUTI Gulf of Aden
Dikhil Djibouti Karin Mait Bosaso
IOPIA SOMALIA Berbera Hafun

Caspian Sea
TURKMENISTAN UZBEKISTAN
Türkmenbaşy Kara Kum Turkmenabat Amudarja Kerki
Nebitdag Gyzylarbat Ashgabat Mary arakumskiy kanal
Koppe Dag
Sari Gorgan Bojnurd
Elburz Mountains Emamshahr 3069 Mashhad
Damavand Sabzevar Torbat-e- Herat
5605 Teheran Heydariyeh Hariwd
Karaj Gonabad
Qom Salt Desert Birjand AFGHANISTAN
Daryachen- ye-namak Sistan
IRAN Nain Dasht-e Lut
Yazd Helmand
Abadeh Shir Kuh Rafsanjan Kerman Zabol Rigestan
Zahedan PAKISTAN
4074 4420 4045 Nok Kundi
Hezar Kuh-e Taftan
Sirjan Bam Baluchistan
Bandar-e- Jahrom Bampur Makran
Busher Kangan Larestan Bandar-e Abbas Jask
Qeshm Chah Bahar Gwadar
2087 Strait of Hormuz
Sharjah Gulf of Oman
34 Dubai Arabian
Suhar Matrah Sea
Jabal al Akhdar Muscat
Sur Ras al Hadd
3017 Jabal ash Sham Ras al Ashkharah
OMAN
Ar Rub' al Khali Al Khalut Masirah
Jiddat al Duqm
Harasis Ras al Madrakah
Sawqirah
Dhofar Kuria Muria Islands
Salalah
Tarim Al Ghaydah
INDIAN
5390 Socotra (Yemen)
Abd al Kuri Hadibu OCEAN
Raas Caseyr Al Ikhwan
(C. Guardafui)
Raas Xaafuun

35° 1
30° 2
30° 3
25° 4
20° 5
15° 6
10° 7

40° D 45° East E 50° F 55° G 60° H

1 : 20 000 000   0 200 400 600 km

63

1 : 10 000 000

0 | 100 | 200 | 300 km

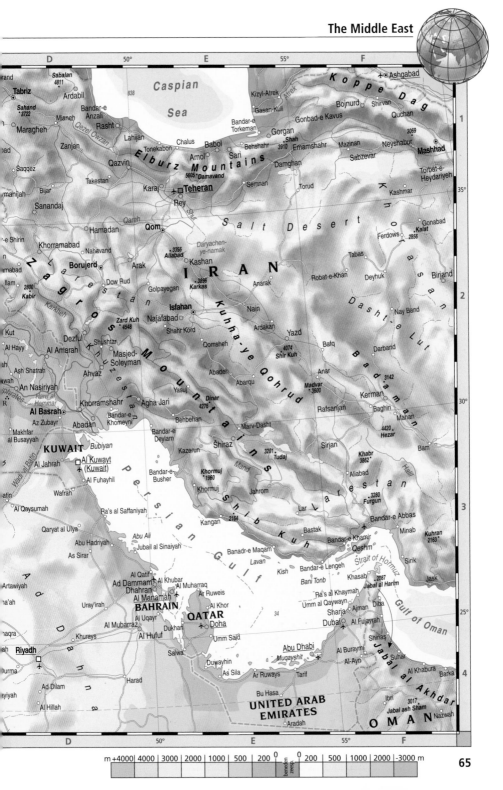

rand
Sabalan 4811
Tabriz
Sahand 3722
Ardabil
Mianeh
Maragheh
Bandar-e Anzali
Rasht
838
Caspian Sea
Kizyl-Atrek
Atrek
Gasan-Kuli
Ashgabad
Koppe Dag
Bojnurd
Shirvan
Quchan
Kvzyl-Atrek
Bandar-e Torkeman
Gonbad-e Kavus
Gorgan
Shah 3910
Mazinan
3069
Neyshabur
Mashhad
ad
Zanjan
Qezel Ozvan
Lahijan
Tonekabon
Chalus
Babol
Behshahr
Emamshahr
Sabzevar
Torbat-e-Heydariyeh
Saqqez
Qazvin
Elburz Mountains
Amol
Sari
Damghan
Teheran
Rey
5605 Damavand
Karaj
Semnan
Torud
Kashmar
35°
manijah
Bijar
Takestan
Sanandaj
Qareh
Salt Desert
Khorasan
Kalat 2856
Gonabad
-e Shirin
Hamadan
Qom
Daryachen-ye-namak
Ferdows
3356 Aliabad
Kashan
Tabas
Deyhuk
Robat-e-Khan
Birjand
Khorramabad
Nahavand
imabad
Borujerd
Arak
IRAN
Anarak
Dasht-e Lut
Nay Band
Ilam
2800 Kabir
Zagros
Larestan
Dow Rud
Golpayegan
3896 Karkas
Nain
Isfahan
Ardakan
Yazd
Darband
3142
Kut
Al Hayy
Dezful
Zard Kuh 4548
Najafabad
Shahr Kord
Qomsheh
Kuhha-ye Qohrud
4074 Shir Kuh
Bafq
Anar
Kerman
Al Amarah
Shushtar
Masjed-Soleyman
Abadeh
Abarqu
Madvar 3600
Rafsanjan
Baghin
Mahan
Ash Shatrah
Ahvaz
Khuzestan
Yasuj
Dinar 4276
4420 Hezar
awah
An Nasiriyah
Rawl al Hammar
Khorramshahr
Agha Jari
Behbehan
Marv-Dasht
Sirjan
Bam
Al Basrah
Abadan
Bandar-e Khomeyni
Shiraz
3201 Tudaj
Khabr 3862
Aliabad
Az Zubayr
Bandar-e Deylam
Kazerun
Hali
Makhfar al Busayyah
KUWAIT
Bubiyan
Persian
Bandar-e Busher
Khormuj 1960
Jahrom
Lar
3280 Furgun
Larestan
Al Kuwayt (Kuwait)
Al Jahrah
Khormuj
2164
Bandar-e Abbas
Minab
Kuhran 2163
Al Fuhayhil
Gulf
Kangan
Bastak
Bandar-e Khamir
Qeshm
atin
Wafrah
Ra's al Saffaniyah
Banadr-e Maqam
Lavan
Bandar-e Lengeh
Strait of Hormuz
Sirik
Jask
Al Qaysumah
Abu Ali
Jubail al Sinaiyah
Kish
Bani Tonb
Khasab
2087 Jabal al Harim
Qaryat al Ulya
Abu Hadriyah
As Sirar
Banadr-e Maqam
Ra's al Khaymah
Umm al Qaywayn
Sharja
Ajman
Diba
25°
Artawiyah
Al Qatif
Ad Dammam
Al Khubar
Dhahran
Al Muharraq
Ar Ruweis
Umm al Qaywayn
Dubai
Al Fujayrah
Gulf of Oman
na'ah
Uray'irah
Al Manamah
BAHRAIN
Al Uqayr
Ar Khor
34
Abu Dhabi
Al Buraymi
Shinas
Suhar
naqra
Khurays
Al Mubarraz
Dukhan
QATAR
Doha
Al-Ayn
Jabal al Khabura
Barka
Riyadh
Al Hufuf
Umm Said
Salwa
Muqayshit
As Sila
urma
Duwayhin
Ar Ruways
Tarif
Ibri
3017 Jabal ash Sham
ayiyah
Ad Dilam
Harad
Bu Hasa
UNITED ARAB EMIRATES
Nazwah
Al Hillah
Aradah
OMAN

D 50° E 55° F

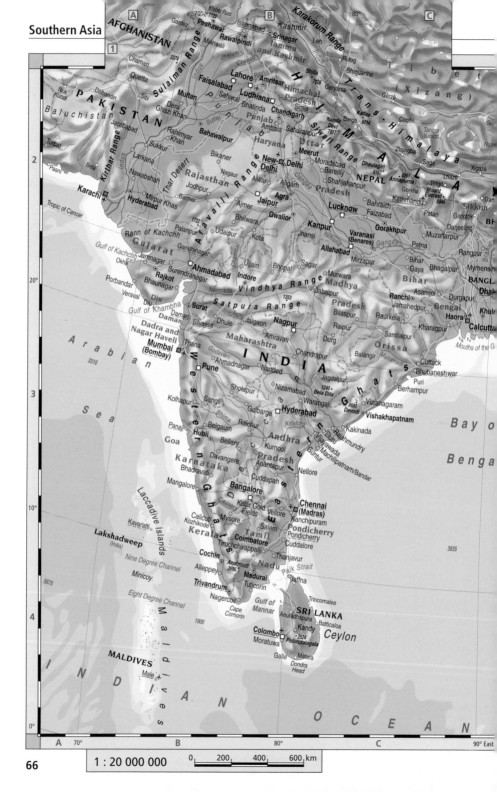

1 : 20 000 000

0   200   400   600 km

D 100° E 110° F

CHINA

Bayan Har Shan
Darlag
Yushu
Baqen
ang
Qamdo
Batang
Garzê
Juding Shan
4894
Nanchong
Chengdu
Ya'an
Leshan
Neijiang
Gongga Shan
7556
Zigong
Luzhou
Zhaotong
Yibin
Xichang
Dukou
Dongchuan
Pan Xian
Anshun
Shuicheng
Guiyang
Duyun
Zunyi
Kunming
Qujing
Luxi
Anlong
Baoshan
Chuxiong
Maotou Shan
3305
Yuxi
Kaiyuan
Tiandong
Gejiu
Shiping
Lao Cai
Pingxiang
Lincang
Jinghong
Keng Tung
Louang
Nam Tha
Luang Prabang

MYANMAR
Monywa Mandalay
Victoria
3053
Myingyan
Pakokku
Meiktila
Pyinmana
Magwe
Prome
Henzada
Toungoo
Pegu
Bassein
Yangon
Moulmein
2080
Ye

THAILAND
Chiang
Mai
Lampang
Uttaradit
Phitsanulok
Udon
Thani
Nakhon
Phanom
Savannakhet
Khon Kaen
Nakhon
Sawan
Lop Buri
Nakhon
Ratchasima
Saraburi
Ayutthaya
Thon
Buri
**Krung Thep
(Bangkok)**
Phetchaburi
Hua Hin
Prachuap
Khiri Khan
Chumphon
Ranong
Phanangan
Samui
Surat Thani
Nakhon Si Thammarat
Phattalung
Songkhla
Pattani
Hat Yai
Kota Baharu

LAOS
Vientiane
Nong Khai

VIETNAM
Hanoi
Haiphong
Nam Dinh
Thanh Hoa
Vinh
Ha Tinh
Dong Hoi
Huê
Da Nang
Quang Ngai
Qui Nhon
Tuy Hoa
Nha Trang
Da Lat
Phan Rang
Phan Thiet
Ho Chi Minh
My Tho
Bien Hoa

CAMBODIA
ANGKOR
Tonle Sap
Battambang
Pursat
Kompong Chhnang
Phnom Penh
Kompong Som
Chau Phu
Can Tho
Ca Mau
Bac Loi
Con Son
Mui Ca Mau

Gulf of
Thailand

**South China
Sea**
Paracel Islands
(China)
South China Basin
Hainan
Haikou
Zhanjiang
Hong Kong
Macao
Canton
TAIWAN
Taipei
Taizhong
Kaohsiung
Tainan
Pingdong
Hong Gai
Beihai

Guangdong
Shantou
Chaozhou
Meizhou
Zhangzhou
Xiamen
Fujian
Fuzhou
Jiling
Ningde
Putian
Nanping
Longyan
Ruijin
Ganzhou
Chuanzhou
Hualien
Zhanghua

MALAYSIA
Kota Baharu
Kuala
Terengganu
George Town
Taiping
Ipoh
Kuala
Lumpur
Kelang
Seremban
Melaka
(Malacca)
Johor Baharu
SINGAPORE
Kuantan
Rompin

**Borneo
(Kalimantan)**
Bintulu
Sibu Mukah
Kuching
BRUNEI
Bandar Seri Begawan
Weston
Beaufort
Kota
Kinabalu
Kinabalu
4101
Kudat

INDONESIA
Sumatra
Medan
Pematang
siantar
Tanjung
balai
Dumai
Singkawang
Kepulauan
Natuna
Kepulauan
Anambas
Paloh
Kaap Datu
Ukeng

67

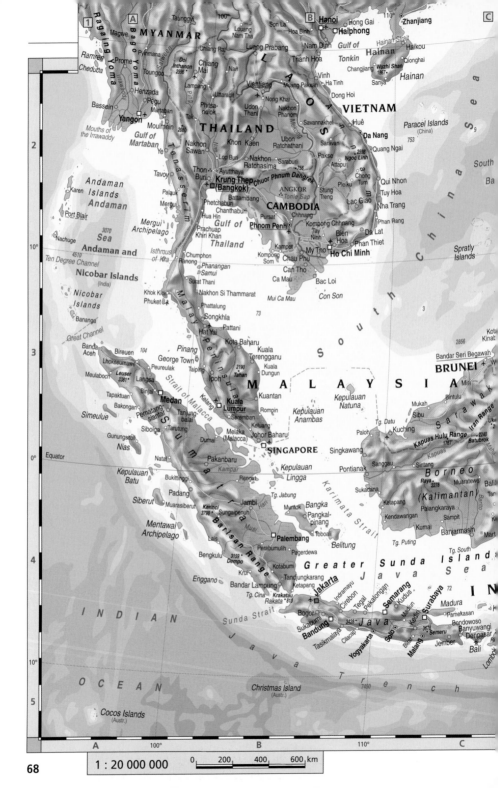

1 A B C

Taunggyi   Son La   Hanoi   Hong Gai   Zhanjiang   110°
MYANMAR   Louang   Hoa Binh   Haiphong
Magwe   Nam Tha   Gulf of   Hainan Strait   Haikou
Pyinmana   Chiang Rai   Luang Prabang   Nam Dinh   Tonkin   Hainan
Ramree   Prome   Chiang   Nan   Thanh Hoa   Changjiang   Wuzhi Shan   Qionghai
Cheduba   Toungoo   Inthanon   Mai   1867   Hainan
Doi   2595   Vinh   Sanya
Henzada   Lampang   Uttaradit   Vientiane   Muang Pakxan   Ha Tinh
Bassein   Pegu   Phisa-   Nong Khai   Nakhon   Dong Hoi
Martaban   nulok   Udon   Phanom   VIETNAM   Paracel Islands
Yangon   Moulmein   Tak   Thani   Savannakhet   Huê   (China)   753
Mouths of   Gulf of   THAILAND   Khon Kaen   Ubon   Saravan   Da Nang
the Irrawaddy   Martaban   2080   Nakhon   Ratchathani   Pakse   2598   Quang Ngai   South
Ye   Sawan   Lop Buri   Saraburi   Ngoc Linh   Attapu
Andaman   Tavoy   Thon   Ayutthaya   Ratchasima   756   Pleiku   Chong   Qui Nhon   Ba
Islands   Buri   Krung Thep   Chuor Phnum Dangrek   Tum   Tuy Hoa
Andaman   Palauk   (Bangkok)   ANGKOR   Stung   Nha Trang
Port Blair   Mergui   Phetchaburi   Battambang   Tonle Sap   Treng   Lac Giao
Nachuge   3070   Mergui   Chanthaburi   Pursat   Chhnang   Kompong Chhnang   Phan Rang
Sea   Archipelago   Hua Hin   Gulf of   Phnom Penh   Bien   Da Lat
Andaman and   Prachuap   Thailand   Tay   Hoa   Phan Thiet
4510   Khiri Khan   Kampot   Ninh   My Tho   Ho Chi Minh   Spratly
Ten Degree Channel   Isthmus   Chumphon   Kompong   Chau Phu   Islands
Nicobar Islands   of Kra   Ranong   Som   Can Tho
(India)   Phanangan   Ca Mau   Bac Loi
Nicobar   Samui   Con Son
Islands   Surat Thani   Mui Ca Mau
Bananga   Khok Kloi   Nakhon Si Thammarat   73
Great Channel   Phuket   Phattalung
Banda   104   Songkhla   S
Aceh   Bireuen   Pinang   Hat Yai   Pattani   o
Lhokseumawe   George Town   Kota Baharu   Kuala   u
Meulaboch   Peureulak   Taiping   Terengganu   t   Bandar Seri Begawan   2856
Leuser   Langsa   Ipoh   Kuala   h   BRUNEI   Kota
Tapaktuan   3381   Binjai   Tahan   Dungun   Kinab
Bakongan   Medan   2190   MALAYSIA   C   Miri
Simeulue   Pematang   Kelang   Kuantan   Mukah   Bintulu   S
siantar   Kuala   Rompin   Kepulauan   Tg. Datu   Sibu   a
Nias   Gunungsitoli   Tanjung   Lumpur   Natuna   Kuching   r   Iran Range   2240
Sibolga   balai   Seremban   h   Batubrok
Tarutung   Ketuang   Paloh   Kapuas Hulu Range   a   1767
Dumai   Melaka   Johor Baharu   Singkawang   1767   w
Equator   (Malacca)   SINGAPORE   Sanggau   a   Kapuas
Kepulauan   Pakanbaru   Kepulauan   Pontianak   Sintang   k   Borneo
Batu   Bukittinggi   Kampar   Lingga   Sukadana   Raya   Muaratewe   Balik
Padang   Rengat   2278
Siberut   Muarasiberut   Jambi   Tg. Jabung   Ketapang   (Kalimantan)   Benuo
Kerinci   Sungaipenuh   Bangka   Kendawangan   Palangkaraya   Sampit
Mentawai   3798   Muntok   Pangkal-   Kumai   Banjarmasin   Mar
Archipelago   Lais   pinang   Tg. Puting
Perabumulih   Pagardewa   Toboali   Palembang   Belitung   Tg. South
Bengkulu   3159   Kotabumi   Greater   Sunda   Island
Dempo   Tandjungkarang   Ketapang   Jakarta   Java   Java   Sea   72
Enggano   Krui   Bandar Lampung   Indramayu   Semarang   Madura
Tg. Cina   Krakatau   Tg.   Cirebon   Pekalongan   Kudus   Surabaya   Pamekasan
Rakata   818   Bogor   Tegal   Madiun   Solo   Malang   Bondowoso   Banyuwangi
Sukabumi   3428   Java   Kediri   3676   Jember   Denpasar
Bandung   Yogyakarta   Semeru   Bali
Tasikmalaya   Cilacap   Malang   Lombok
INDIAN   Sunda Strait   Java   Trench

OCEAN   Christmas Island   7450
(Austr.)

Cocos Islands
(Austr.)

1 : 20 000 000   0   200   400   600 km

A   100°   B   110°   C

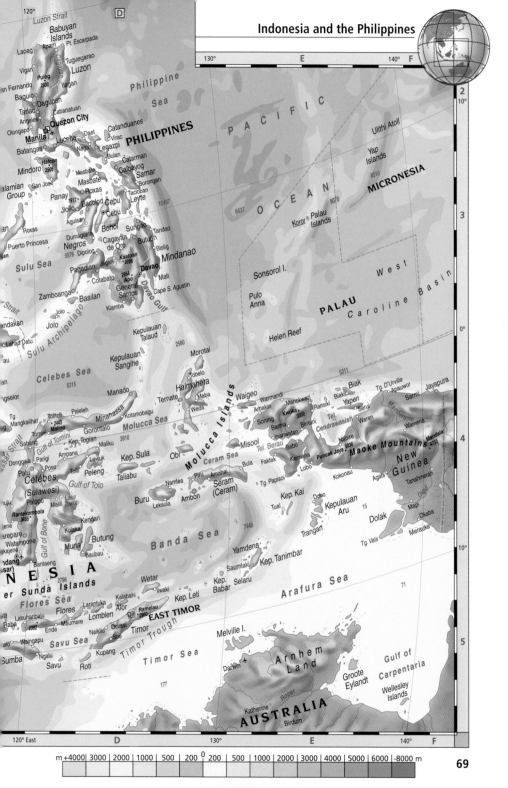

120°
Luzon Strait
Babuyan
Islands
Laoag Aparri Pt. Escarpada
Vigan Tuguegarao
Pulog Ilagan Luzon
San Fernando 2930
Baguio Dagupan
Tarlac Cabanatuan
Angeles
Olongapo Quezon City
Manila
Lucena Catanduanes
Batangas Daet Virac
Naga Legazpi PHILIPPINES
Mindoro Halcon Bulan
2505 Catarman
Calamian San Jose Masbate Calbayog
Group Masbate Samar
Panay Roxas Borongan
917 Tacloban
Jloilo Bacolod Cebu Leyte
Roxas Cebu
Aguisan
Dumaguete Bohol Surigao Tandao
Negros Cagayan Butuan
Puerto Princesa Dipolog de Oro Bislig
5576 Kaatoan
Pagadian Jilgan 2896 Mindanao
Sulu Sea Cotabato 2954 Davao
Zamboanga Apo Mati
Basilan General Cape S. Agustin
Jolo Santos
Sulu Archipelago Kiamba Davao Gulf
Jolo
Lahad Datu

Kepulauan
Talaud 2580
Kepulauan Morotai
Celebes Sea Sangihe
5315
Manado Tobelo
Halmahera
Minahassa Ternate Maba
Tg. Mangkalihat Tolitoli Paleleh Weda
Sabang Kotamobagu
Tomini Malino Gorontalo Molucca Sea
Donggala Parigi 3910 Misool
Palu Ampana Luwuk Kep. Sula Obi
Celebes Poso Peleng Maliku Ceram Sea
(Sulawesi) Toli Taliabu Piru Amahai
Palopo Gulf of Tolo Namlea Seram
Rantekombola Lake Buru (Ceram)
3455 Towuti Leksula Ambon
Kendari
Kolaka Banda Sea
Watampone Muna Butung
Baubau

NESIA Yamdena
Bantaeng Saumlaki Kep. Tanimbar
er Sunda Islands 2796
Flores Sea Wetar
Larantuka Ilwaki Kep. Selaru
Labuhanbajo Flores Alor Kep. Leti
2302 Lomblen Olli Ramelau Babar
Raba Maumere Naikliu EAST TIMOR
Ende Ocussi Timor
Waingapu Soe
Sumba Ngalu Kupang Timor Trough
Savu Savu Sea
Roti
Sumba Timor Sea
177

PACIFIC
OCEAN
6437 8070
Koror Palau
Islands
MICRONESIA
8510

Ulithi Atoll
Yap
Islands

West
Sonsorol I.
Pulo PALAU Caroline Basin
Anna
Helen Reef
5311

Waigeo
Warmandi
Tobelo Arbakin Manokwari Biak
Weda Sorong Kwoka Ranski Biak
Barma 3000 Yapen
Inanwatan Tel. Serui
Babo Cendrawasih Waren Sarmi Tg. D'Urville Apauwor Jayapura
Tel. Berau Wamena
Bintuni Nabire Mamberamo
Bula Kaimena Puncak Jaya 5030 Maoke Mountains Mandala
Faktak Lobo 4750
Tg. Papisou Kokonau Agats New
Kep. Kai Tanahmerah Guinea
Tual Dobo Diosi
Trangan Kepulauan Mapi
Dolak Okaba
Aru Merauke
15 Tg. Vals
7440

Arafura Sea
71

Melville I. Arnhem
Land Gulf of
Darwin Carpentaria
Groote Wellesley
Eylandt Islands
AUSTRALIA
Katherine Roper
Birdum

120° East D 130° E 140° F

m +4000 3000 2000 1000 500 200 0 200 500 1000 2000 3000 4000 5000 6000 -8000 m

Oceania: Physical

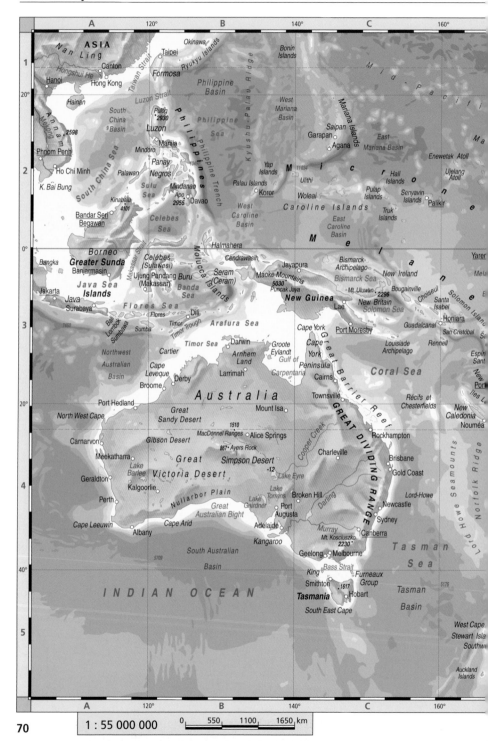

1 : 55 000 000

0 550 1100 1650 km

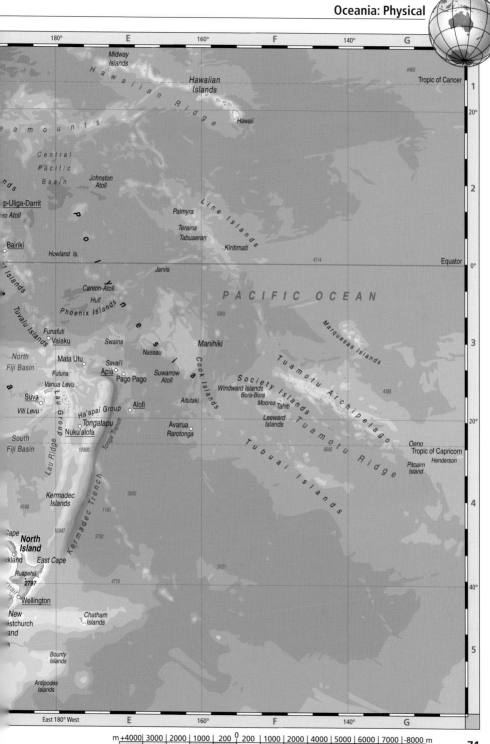

180° E 160° F 140° G

Tropic of Cancer

4465

1

20°

Midway
Islands

Hawaiian
Islands

Hawaii

H a w a i i a n   R i d g e

S e a m o u n t s

C e n t r a l
P a c i f i c
B a s i n

Johnston
Atoll

2

n d s

p-Uliga-Darrit
ro Atoll

Bairiki

Howland Is.

P o l y n e s i a

Palmyra

Teraina
Tabuaeran

Kiritimati

L i n e   I s l a n d s

4114

Equator 0°

Jarvis

PACIFIC   OCEAN

Marquesas Islands

Canton-Atoll
Hull

Phoenix Islands

5065

3

Tuvalu Islands

Funafuti
Vaiaku

Swains

Nassau

Manihiki

North
Fiji Basin

Mata Utu

Savai'i
Apia

Pago Pago

Suwarrow
Atoll

C o o k   I s l a n d s

Society Islands

Windward Islands
Bora-Bora
Moorea Tahiti

T u a m o t u   A r c h i p e l a g o

4385

Futuna

Vanua Levu

Suva

Viti Levu

Alofi

Aitutaki

Leeward
Islands

20°

Ha'apai Group
Tongatapu
Nuku'alofa

Avarua
Rarotonga

T u a m o t u   R i d g e

South
Fiji Basin

10800

4645

Oeno

Tropic of Capricorn

Henderson

Lau Ridge

Tonga Trench

L a u   G r o u p

T u b u a i   I s l a n d s

Pitcairn
Island

Kermadec
Islands

5850

4188

1143

5792

3121

4

Kermadec Trench

10047

Cape

North
Island

ckland   East Cape

4716

40°

Ruapehu
2797

Wellington

New
istchurch
and

Chatham
Islands

Bounty
Islands

5

Antipodes
Islands

East 180° West E 160° F 140° G

m +4000 | 3000 | 2000 | 1000 | 200 0 200 | 1000 | 2000 | 4000 | 5000 | 6000 | 7000 | -8000 m

Oceania: Political

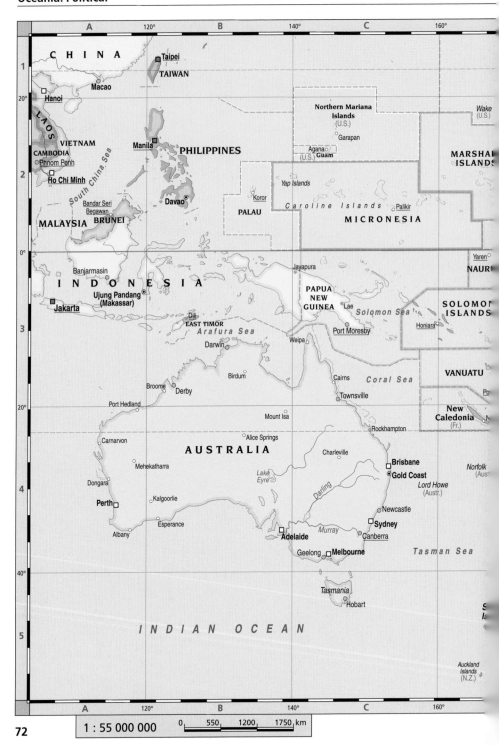

1 : 55 000 000

0 | 550 | 1200 | 1750 | km

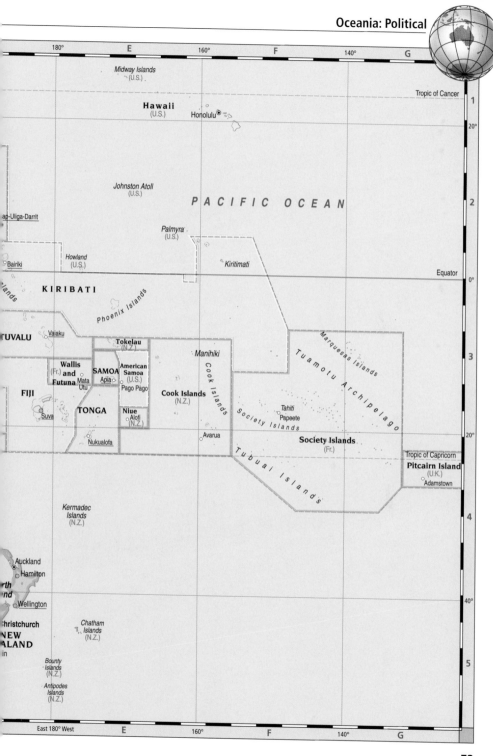

180°   E   160°   F   140°   G

Midway Islands
(U.S.)

Tropic of Cancer

1

Hawaii
(U.S.)
Honolulu

20°

Johnston Atoll
(U.S.)

P A C I F I C   O C E A N

2

ap-Uliga-Darrit

Palmyra
(U.S.)

Howland
(U.S.)

Kiritimati

Bairiki

Equator   0°

K I R I B A T I

Phoenix Islands

TUVALU   Vaiaku

Marquesas Islands

Tokelau
(N.Z.)

Manihiki

Tuamotu Archipelago

3

Wallis
(Fr.) **and**
Futuna Mata
Utu

SAMOA
Apia

American Samoa
(U.S.)
Pago Pago

Cook Islands

FIJI

Cook Islands
(N.Z.)

Tahiti
Papeete

Society Islands

Suva

TONGA

Niue
Alofi
(N.Z.)

Avarua

Society Islands
(Fr.)

20°

Nukualofa

Tubuai Islands

Tropic of Capricorn

Pitcairn Island
(U.K.)
Adamstown

Kermadec
Islands
(N.Z.)

4

Auckland
Hamilton

rth
nd

Wellington

40°

Christchurch
NEW
ALAND
in

Chatham
Islands
(N.Z.)

Bounty
Islands
(N.Z.)

5

Antipodes
Islands
(N.Z.)

East 180° West   E   160°   F   140°   G

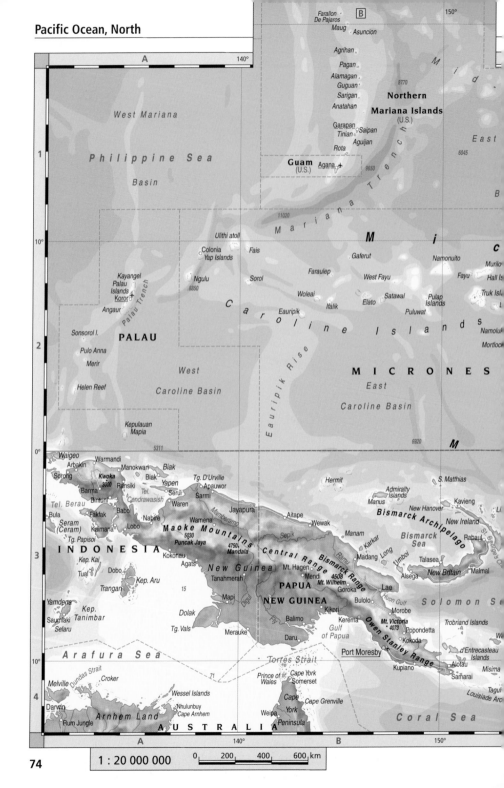

A 140°

Farallon
De Pajaros B 150°
Maug Asuncion

Agrihan

Pagan

Alamagan
Guguan
Sarigan
Anatahan

**Northern
Mariana Islands**
(U.S.)

West Mariana

8770

Garapan
Tinian Saipan
Aguijan
Rota

East

6045

Guam Agana
(U.S.) 9650

P h i l i p p i n e   S e a

M

i

d'

1

11020

B

Basin

M a r i a n a   T r e n c h

10°

Ulithi atoll

M *i*

C

Colonia
Yap Islands Fais

Gaferut

Namonuito

Murilo

Kayangel
Palau
Islands
Koror

Ngulu
6850

Sorol

Faraulep

West Fayu

Fayu Hall Is

Truk Isl.

Woleai

Satawal
Elato

Pulap
Islands

L

Angaur

C *a* *r* *o*

Italik

Puluwat

Sonsorol I.

PALAU

l *i* *n*

Euripik

Puluwat

Namolu

Mortlock

Pulo Anna

e

I *s* *l* *a* *n* *d* *s*

Merir

West

M I C R O N E S

Helen Reef

Caroline Basin

East

Caroline Basin

Kepulauan
Mapia

6920

M

0°

5311

Waigeo
Arbakin Warmandi
Sorong Manokwari Biak
Kwoka
3000 Ransiki Biak
Barma Tel.
Bintuni Cendrawasish Yapen Tg. D'Urville
Serui Apauwor
Sarmi

Hermit

S. Matthias

Admiralty
Islands
Manus Kavieng
New Hanover Li

Tel. Berau
Bula Fakfak Babo Waren Jayapura Aitape
Nabire Wamena Wewak
Seram Keimana Lobo
(Ceram)
Tg. Papisoi

Maoke Mountains
5030
Puncak Jaya

Bismarck Archipelago
New Ireland
Rabaul

INDONESIA Kokohau
Kep. Kai. Agats
Tual Dobo Kep. Aru
Trangan 15

4750
Mandala

Central Range

Manam
Karkar
Madang Long

*Bismarck
Sea*
Talasea
Alsega New Britain Malmal

Mt. Hagen
Tanahmerah
Mapi *New Guinea* Mendi 4508
Goroka

Mt. Wilhelm

Lae

Solomon Se

Yamdena
Kep.
Saumlaki **Tanimbar**
Selaru

Dolak
Tg. Vals
Merauke

Balimo
Daru

**PAPUA
NEW GUINEA**
Kikori
Kerema
*Gulf
of Papua*

Bulolo
Morobe
Mt. Victoria
4073 Popondetta
Kokoda

Huon Gulf

Trobriand Islands

Owen Stanley Range

d'Entrecasteau
Islands

10°

Arafura Sea

71

Torres Strait

Port Moresby
Kupiano

Misima

Samarai

Louisiade Arc

Melville Dundas Strait Croker
Darwin
Rum Jungle *Arnhem Land*

Nhulunbuy
Wessel Islands Cape Arnhem

Prince of
Wales Cape York
Somerset

Cape
York Cape Grenville

Weipa
Peninsula

Coral Sea

4

A U S T R A L I A

A 140° B 150°

1 : 20 000 000 0 200 400 600 km

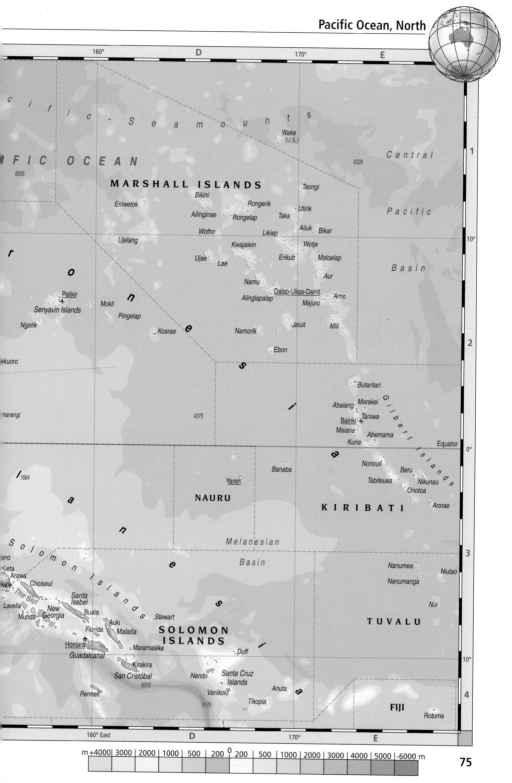

160° D 170° E

c i f i c - S e a m o u n t s
Wake
(U.S.)

C e n t r a l 1
FIC OCEAN
6035 6220

MARSHALL ISLANDS
Taongi
Bikini
Eniwetok Rongerik Utirik P a c i f i c
Ailinginae Rongelap Taka
Wotho Likiep Ailuk Bikar 10°
Ujelang Kwajalein Wotje
r Ujae Lae Erikub Maloelap
o Namu Aur B a s i n
Palikir Namu
Senyavin Islands Mokil Alinglapalap Dalap-Uliga-Darrit Arno
Ngatik n Pingelap Majuro
Kosrae Namorik Jaluit Mili
e Ebon 2

kuoro
s
marangi 4375 i Butaritari
Abaiang Marakei
Bairiki Tarawa
Maiana Abemama
Kuria Equator 0°
1664 a Nonouti Beru
Banaba Tabiteuea Nikunau
a Yaren Onotoa
NAURU KIRIBATI Arorae
n
Melanesian
S Basin Nanumea Niutao 3
ano e Nanumanga
Kieta Arawa
ville Choiseul s Nui
Lavella Santa New Isabel i Stewart TUVALU
Munda Georgia Buala
Florida Auki
Honiara Malaita SOLOMON
Guadalcanal Maramasike ISLANDS Duff
Kirakira 10°
San Cristóbal Nendo Santa Cruz
Rennell 8310 Islands Anuta a
Vanikolo
9175 Tikopia FIJI 4
Rotuma

160° East D 170° E

m +4000 3000 2000 1000 500 200 0 200 500 1000 2000 3000 4000 5000 -6000 m

75

Tonga, Samoa, French Polynesia

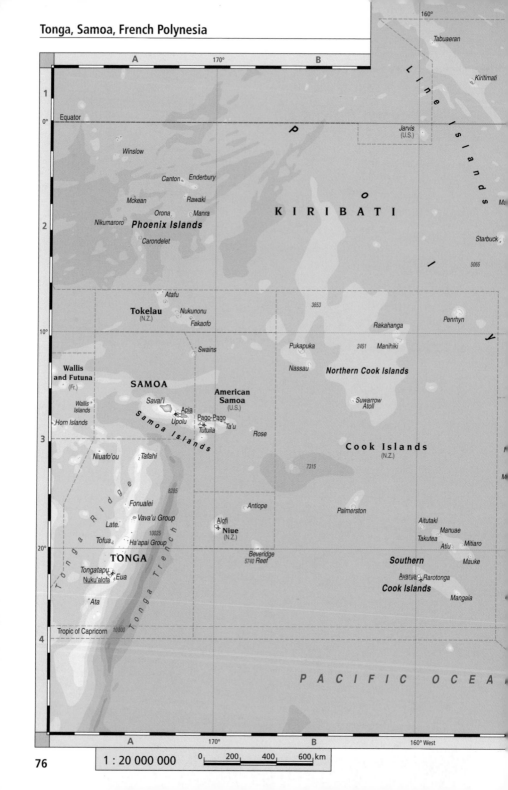

160°

Tabuaeran

Line Islands

Kiritimati

170°

A

B

1

0° Equator

P

Jarvis
(U.S.)

Winslow

Canton Enderbury

Mckean   Rawaki

O

Me

Orona   Manra

K I R I B A T I

Nikumaroro *Phoenix Islands*

2

Carondelet

Starbuck

5065

I

Atafu

3653

Tokelau Nukunonu
(N.Z.)

Rakahanga

Penrhyn

Fakaofo

10°

y

Swains

Pukapuka   2451 Manihiki

**Wallis
and Futuna**
(Fr.)

Nassau

Northern Cook Islands

SAMOA

Savai'i

**American
Samoa**
(U.S.)

Suwarrow
Atoll

Wallis
Islands

Apia

Horn Islands

Samoa Islands

Upolu   Pago-Pago
Tutuila   Ta'u

3

Rose

Niuafo'ou   Tafahi

Cook Islands
(N.Z.)

F

7315

Mi

Tonga Ridge

8285

Fonualei

Antiope

Palmerston

Aitutaki

Vava'u Group

Alofi

Manuae

Late.

10025

Niue
(N.Z.)

Takutea

Atiu   Mitiaro

Tofua   Ha'apai Group

Tonga Trench

20°

TONGA

Beveridge
5740 Reef

Southern

Mauke

Tongatapu
Nuku'alofa   Eua

Avarua Rarotonga

Cook Islands

Mangaia

Ata

Tropic of Capricorn   10800

4

P A C I F I C   O C E A

A   170°   B   160° West

76

1 : 20 000 000

0   200   400   600 km

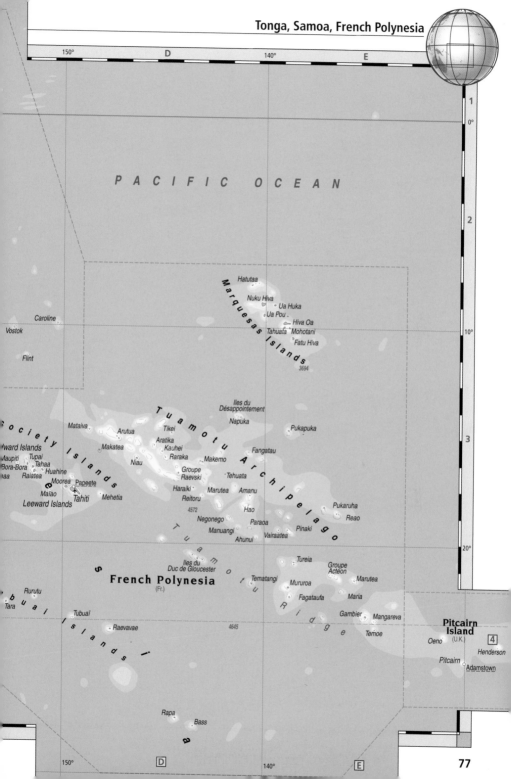

150°   D   140°   E

1

0°

P A C I F I C   O C E A N

2

Hatutaa

Marquesas Islands

Nuku Hiva
Ua Huka
Ua Pou
Hiva Oa
Tahuata   Mohotani
Fatu Hiva

Caroline

Vostok

10°

Flint

3694

Iles du
Désappointement

Tuamotu Archipelago

Napuka

Pukapuka

Society Islands

Mataiva

Arutua

Tikei

Aratika

Kauhei

ward Islands

Makatea

Raraka

Makemo

Fangatau

Maupiti   Tupai

Niau

Bora-Bora   Tahaa

aa   Raiatea

Huahine

Groupe
Raevski

Tehuata

3

Moorea   Papeete

Haraiki

Marutea

Amanu

Maïao   Tahiti

Mehetia

Reitoru

Pukaruha

Leeward Islands

4572

Hao

Reao

Negonego

Paraoa

Manuangi

Pinaki

T u a m o t u

Ahunui

Vairaatea

20°

Iles du
Duc de Gloucester

Tureia

Groupe
Actéon

French Polynesia
(Fr.)

Tematangi

Mururoa

Marutea

Ridge

Fagataufa

Maria

Rurutu

Gambier

Mangareva

Tara

Tubuaï

*Pitcairn
Island*

buai Islands

Raevavae

4645

Temoe

Oeno   (U.K.)

4

Henderson

Pitcairn

Adamstown

Rapa

Bass

a

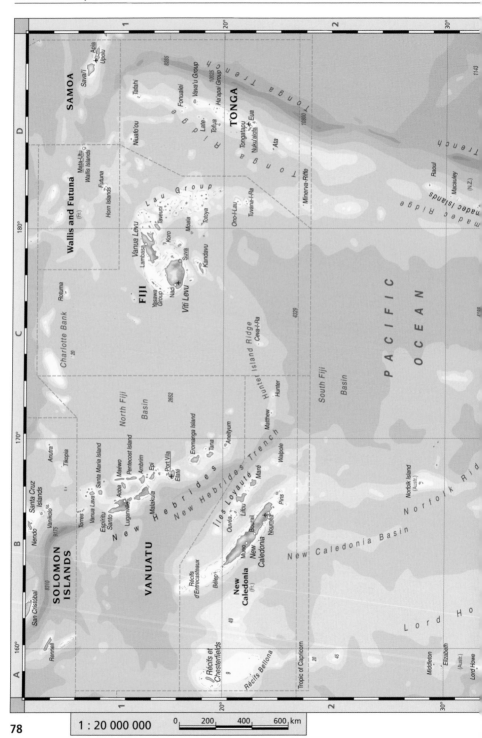

1 : 20 000 000

0 200 400 600 km

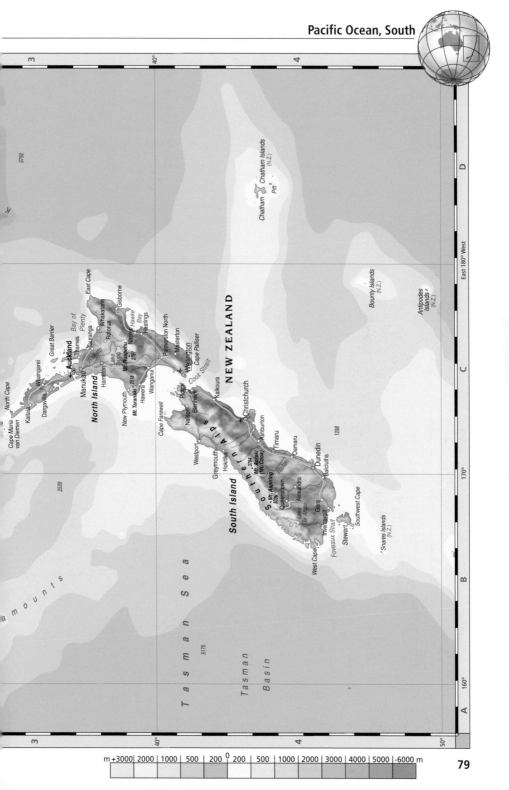

m +3000 | 2000 | 1000 | 500 | 200 0 200 | 500 | 1000 | 2000 | 3000 | 4000 | 5000 | -6000 m

Australia

1 : 20 000 000

0   200   400   600 km

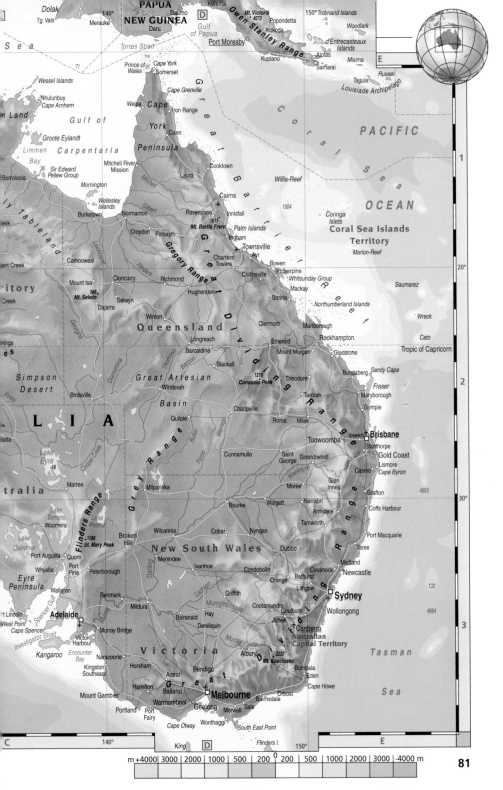

81

Hawaiian Islands

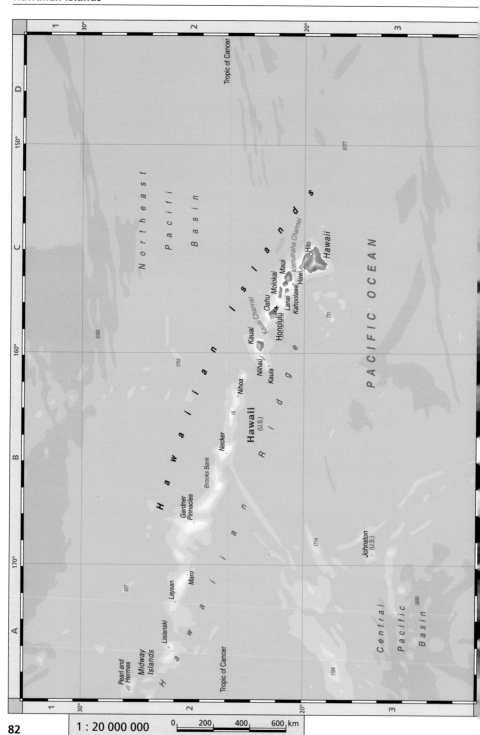

1 : 20 000 000 0 200 400 600 km

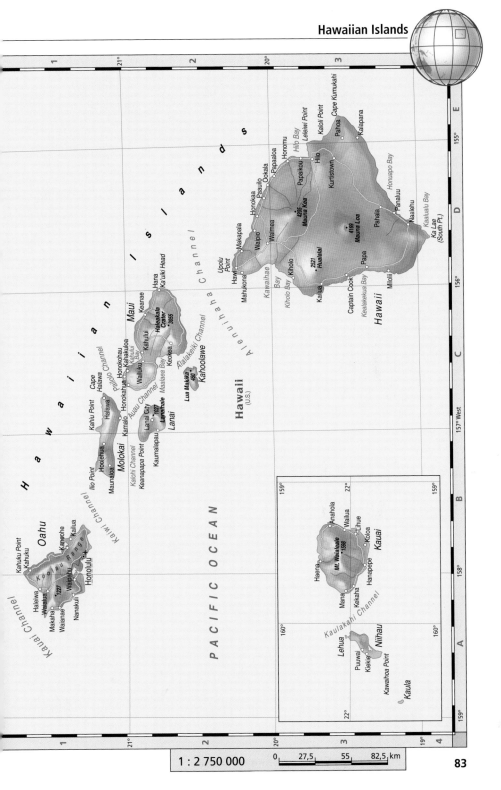

1 : 2 750 000

0 27,5 55 82,5 km

Africa: Physical

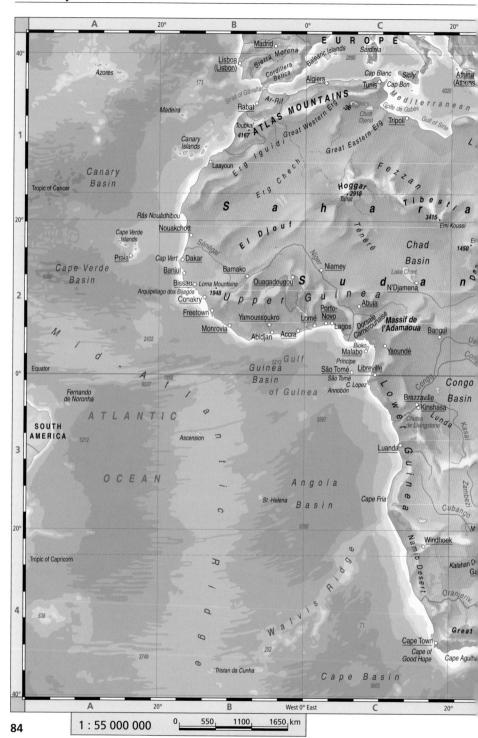

A 20° B 0° C 20°

EUROPE

Madrid
Lisboa (Lisbon)
Sierra Morena
Cordillera Bética
Balearic Islands
Sárdinia
2890
Azores
173
Algiers
Cap Blanc
Tunis
Cap Bon
Sicily
Athína (Athens)
4020
Mediterranean
Madeira
Strait of Gibraltar
Ar-Rit
Rabat
ATLAS MOUNTAINS
-36
Golfe de Gabès
Gulf of Sirte
Toubkal
4167
Great Western Erg
Chott Djerid
Tripoli
Canary Islands
Erg Iguidi
Great Eastern Erg
Canary Basin
Laayoun
Erg Chech
Fezzan
Tropic of Cancer
Hoggar
2918
Tahat
Sahara
Tibesti
Rås Nouâdhibou
3415
Cape Verde Islands
Nouakchott
El Djouf
Ténéré
Emi Koussi
Chad
1450
Praia
Cap Vert
Dakar
Sénégal
Niger
Niamey
Chad Basin
Cape Verde Basin
Banjul
Bamako
Lake Chad
Bissau
Loma Mountains
Ouagadougou
Sudan
N'Djamena
Arquipélago dos Bijagós
1948
Upper Guinea
Conakry
Freetown
Yamoussoukro
Lomé
Porto-Novo
Abuja
Monrovia
Abidjan
Accra
Lagos
Dorsale Camerounaise
Massif de l'Adamaoua
Bangui
2432
Bioko
Malabo
Yaoundé
Equator
Gulf
5212
of Guinea
Guinea Basin
Príncipe
São Tomé
São Tomé
C. Lopez
Annobón
Libreville
Congo
Congo Basin
Fernando de Noronha
7858
6537
Brazzaville
Kinshasa
Lunda
Chutes de Livingstone
SOUTH AMERICA
ATLANTIC
5212
Ascension
5697
Luanda
Lower Guinea
OCEAN
Angola
St.-Helena
Cape Fria
Basin
Zambezi
Cubango
5590
Windhoek
Tropic of Capricorn
Walvis Ridge
Kalahari D
Ga
Oranjeriv.
638
71
Namib Desert
Great
Cape Town
Cape of Good Hope
Cape Aguilh
3749
252
Tristan da Cunha
Cape Basin
5605

A 20° B West 0° East C 20°

84 1 : 55 000 000 0 550 1100 1650 km

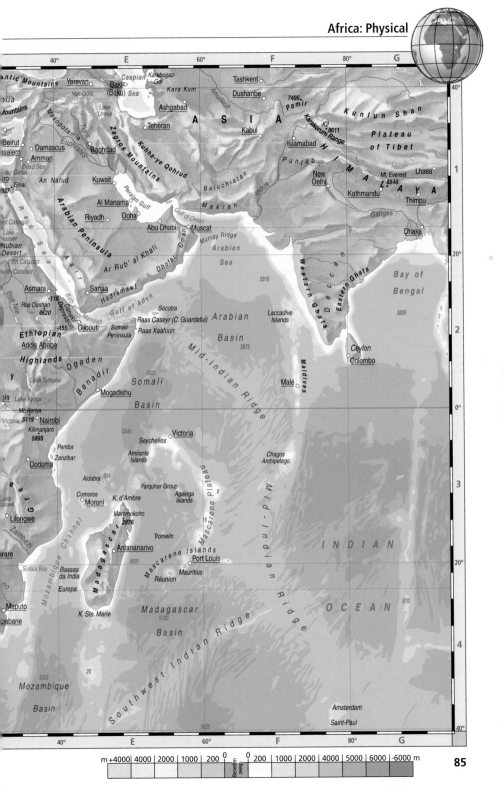

40°   **E**   60°   **F**   80°   **G**

ntic Mountains   Yerevan   Caspian   Karabogaz-Gol   Tashkent

olia   Van Gölü   Baku (Baku)   Sea   Kara Kum   Amudarja   Dushanbe

Mountains   Lake Urmia   Ashgabad   7495 Pamir   Kunlun Shan

Beirut   Mesopotamia   Teheran   A S I A   Kabul   Karakorum Range   K2 8611   Plateau

Damascus   Tigris   Euphrates   Baghdad   Islamabad   HIMA   of Tibet

salem   Amman   Zagros Mountains   Kuhha-ye Qohrud   Punjab   Lhasa

Dead Sea   An Nafud   Kuwait   Baluchistan   New Delhi   Mt. Everest 8846   LAYA

Suez Canal   Sinai   Indus   Kathmandu   Thimpu

337   Al Manama   Persian Gulf   Makran   Ganges

st Cataract   Riyadh   Doha   Gulf of Oman   Dhaka

Lake Nasser   Arabian Peninsula   Abu Dhabi   Muscat   Murray Ridge

Nubian Desert   Fifth Cataract   Asir   Ar Rub' al Khali   Dhofar   Oman   Arabian

urth Cataract   Sea   3310   Western Ghats   Deccan   Eastern Ghats   Bay of Bengal

Asmara   Sanaa   Hadramawt   3835

Blue Nile   Ras Dashan 4620   Danakil Depression   -116   Gulf of Aden   Socotra   Laccadive Islands

-155   Djibouti   Somali Peninsula   Raas Casey (C. Guardafui)   Arabian   Raas Xaafuun   Basin   5675

Ethiopian   Bab el Mandab

Addis Ababa   Ceylon

Highlands   Ogaden   Colombo

y   Lake Turkana   3023   Somali   Male   Maldives

ala   Lake Kyoga   Benadir   Basin   Mid-Indian Ridge

Mt. Kenya 5119   Nairobi

Victoria   Kilimanjaro 5895   5340   Victoria   Seychelles

Pemba   Amirante Islands   Chagos Archipelago   Mid-Indian Ridge

Zanzibar

Dodoma   Aldabra 924   Farquhar Group

ake alawi   Comoros Moroni   K. d'Ambre   Agalega Islands   I N D I A N

Lilongwe   Maromokotro 2876   Mascarene Plateau

Zambezi   Tromelin

rare   Antananarivo   Mascarene Islands   O C E A N   870

Sofala Bay   4931   Port Louis

Bassas da India   Mauritius   Mid-Indian Ridge

Europa   Réunion

Maputo   K. Ste. Marie   Madagascar 5720

babane   Basin   Southwest Indian Ridge

5322   20

Mozambique

Basin   Amsterdam   Saint-Paul   5825

m +4000 | 4000 | 2000 | 1000 | 200 | 0   0 | 200 | 1000 | 2000 | 4000 | 5000 | 6000 | -6000 m

85

Africa: Political

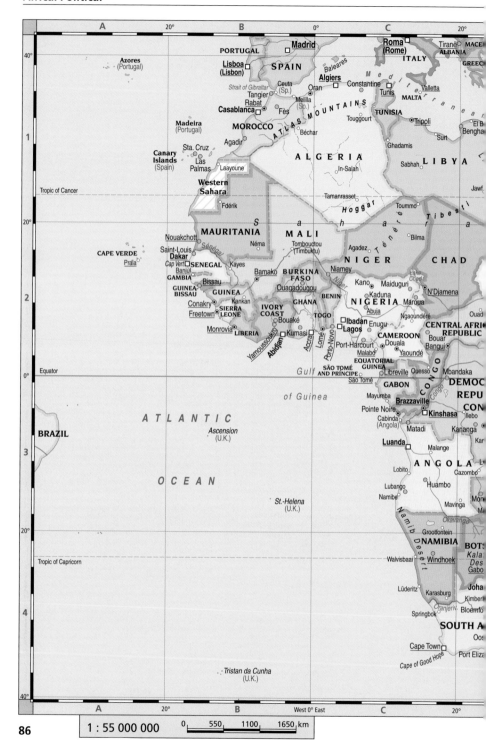

1 : 55 000 000

0 | 550 | 1100 | 1650 | km

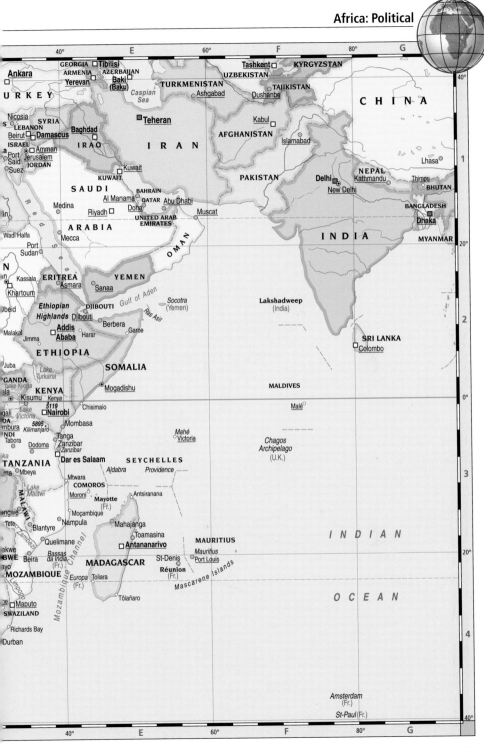

Northwestern Africa

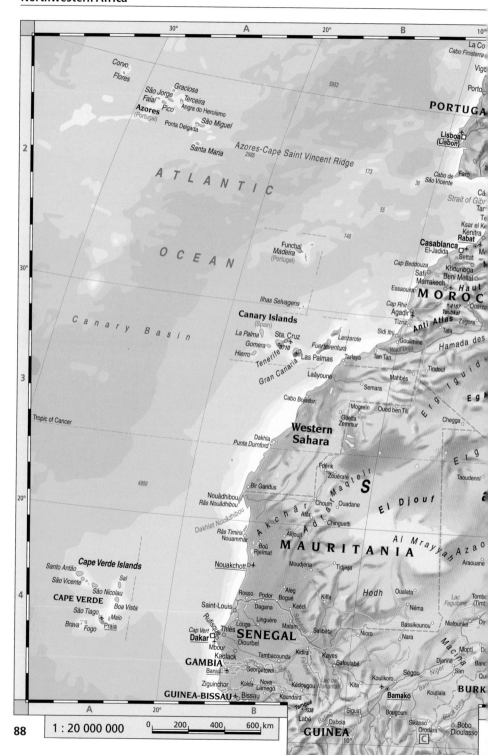

30°   A   20°   B   10°

ATLANTIC OCEAN

Corvo
Flores
Graciosa
São Jorge
Faial
Pico
Terceira
Angra do Heroísmo
Azores
(Portugal)
São Miguel
Ponta Delgada
Santa Maria

Azores-Cape Saint Vincent Ridge
2985
173

5853

La Co
Cabo Finisterra
Vigo
Porto
PORTUGA
Lisboa□
(Lisbon)

Cabo de Faro
São Vicente 36
Cá
Strat of Gibr
Tar
Te
Ksar el Ke
Kenitra
Rabat
Casablanca Me
El-Jadida
Settat
Khouribga
Safi Beni Mellal
Marrakech **Haut**
Essaouira **MOROC**
Cap Rhir *4167
Agadir Toubkal
Tiznit **Anti Atlas** Zagora
Sidi Ifni Goulimine Tata
Wadi Drâa **Hamada des**
Tarfaya Tan Tan
Tindouf
Mahbés

Canary Basin

Funchal
Madeira
(Portugal)
148
55
36

Ilhas Selvagens

Canary Islands
(Spain)
La Palma Sta. Cruz
Gomera 3710 Lanzarote
Hierro Fuerteventura
Tenerife Las Palmas
Gran Canaria

Laâyoune
Semara
Cabo Bojador
Mogrein Oued ben Tili
Guelta
Zemmur
Chegga

Cap Beddouza

Western
Sahara
Dakhla
Punta Durnford

Tropic of Cancer

Fdérik
Zoüérate
Bir Gandus
Choum Ouadane
Nouâdhibou Atâr
Râs Nouâdhibou
Chinguetti
Dakhlet Nouâdhibou
Râs Timiris
Nouamrhâr
Akjoujt
Boû
Rjeimat
MAURITANIA

Taoudenni
El Djouf
Al Mrayyah Azao
Araouane

4900

Cape Verde Islands
Santo Antão
São Vicente Sal
São Nicolau
CAPE VERDE
São Tiago Boa Vista
Brava Maio
Fogo Praia

Nouakchott
Moudjéria Tidjikja

Rosso Podor Aleg
Bogué Kiffa
Saint-Louis Dagana Kaédi
Louga Linguère
Thiès Matam
Cap Vert Diourbel Selibabi
Dakar
Mbour **SENEGAL** Nioro
Kaolack Nara
GAMBIA Tambacounda Kidira Kayes
Banjul Georgetown Bafoulabé
Ziguinchor Kolda Nova Kédougou Kita
GUINEA-BISSAU Lamego Koundara
Bissau Tamgué
1538
Siguiri
Labé Dabola
GUINEA
10°

Hodh
Oualata
Néma
Lac
Faguibine
Bassikounou Niafounké
Macina
Djenné
Koulikoro Ségou Niger
Bamako
Koutiala
Bougouni
Sikasso
Orodara Bobo
Dioulasso

Tombo
(Timb
Dir
Mopti
Banc
San
Qu
BURK
Do

Black Volta

88   1 : 20 000 000   0   200   400   600 km

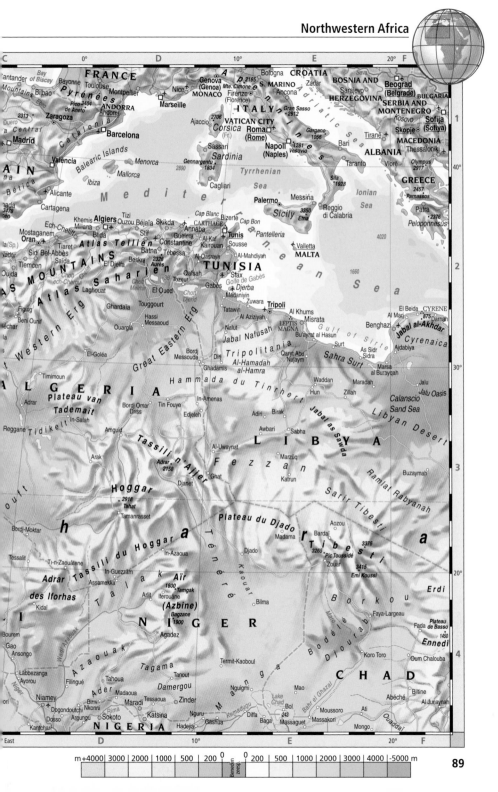

m +4000 | 3000 | 2000 | 1000 | 500 | 200 | 0 | Beneden zeep. | 0 | 200 | 500 | 1000 | 2000 | 3000 | 4000 | -5000 m

Northeastern Africa

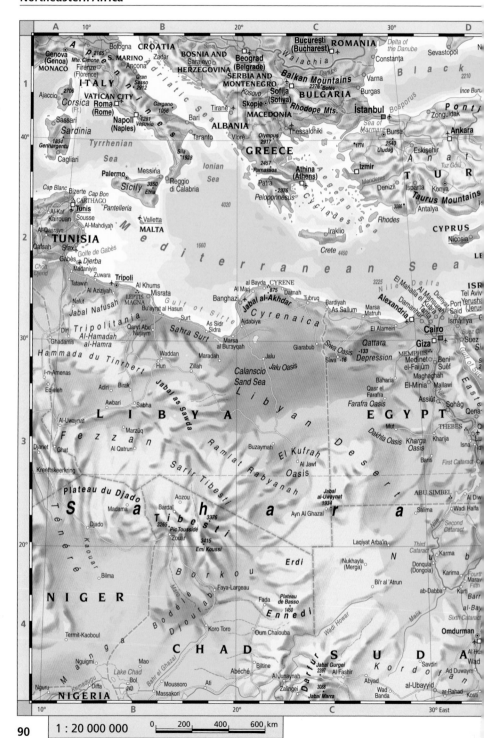

1 : 20 000 000

0 200 400 600 km

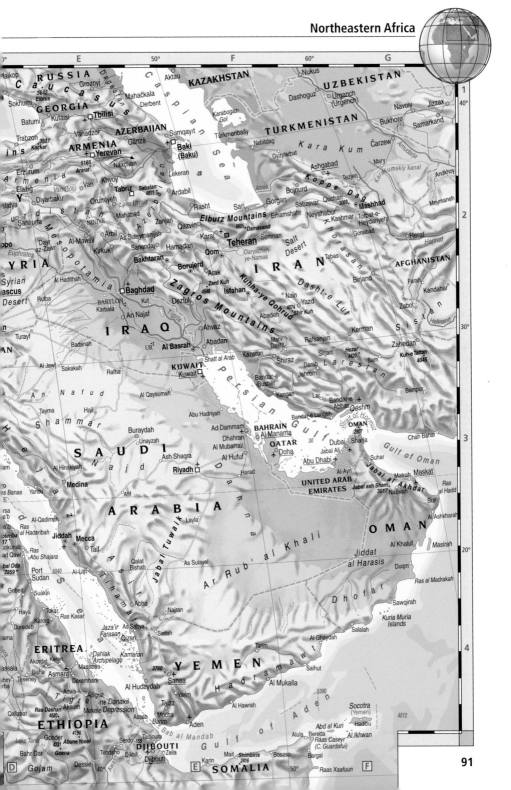

Western Africa

Santo Antão
Cape Verde
Islands
São Vicente
Sal
São Nicolau
CAPE VERDE
Boa Vista
São Tiago
Maio
Brava
Fogo
Praia
1

Nouakchott
Moudjéria
Tidjikja
Araouane

MAURITANIA
Rosso
Podor
Aleg
Kiffa
Hodh
Oualata
M A
Bogué
Lac
Faguibine
Saint-Louis
Dagana
Kaédi
Néma
Tombouctou
(Timbuktu)
Linguère
Matam
Bassikounou
Niafounké
Diré
Louga
Selibabi
Cap Vert
Thiès
Nioro
Nara
Hombori
An
Dakar
Mbour
Diourbel
SENEGAL
Kidira
Kayes
Batoulabé
Mopti
Douentza
Lab
Kaolack
Tambacounda
Djenne
Bandiagara
Djibo
GAMBIA
Georgetown
Koulikoro
Ségou
San
Quahigouya
Kongouss
Banjul
Koleda
Nova
Koulian
Kita
BURKINA F
Ziguinchor
Lamego
Kédougou
Bamako
Koutiala
Koundara
GUINEA-BISSAU
Bafatá
Gaoual
Siguiri
Bougouni
Koudougou
Ouagadou
Bolama
Fouta
Labé
Sikasso
Bobo
Tenk
Arquipélago
Boké
Djalon
Dabola
Orodara
Dioulasso
U
dos Bijagós
Kamsar
Fria
Kouroussa
Tengrela
Banfora
Bolgatanga
Dubreka
Kindia
Mamou
GUINEA
Kankan
Kérouane
Odienné
Boundiali
Ferkéssédougou
Gaoua
Sansa
Coyah
Kissidougou
Korhogo
Bouna
Wa
Conakry
Loma Mountains
Béyla
Tamale
1948
Guéckédou
Touba
Dabakala
Salaga
SIERRA LEONE
Koindu
Nzérékoré
Bondoukou
Freetown
Bo
IVORY COAST
Sunyani
GHANA
Moyamba
Kenema
Mt. Nimba
Biankouma
Bouaké
At
Sherbro
Bonthe
1752
Ganta
Man
Yamoussoukro
Lake
Pujehun
Gbarnga
Luc de
Dimbokro
Kumasi
Volta
Kpa
Kossou
Robertsport
Daloa
Issia
Adzope
Koforidua
Monrovia
LIBERIA
Gagnoa
Abidjan
Buchanan
Adzope
Gold Coast
Acc
Greenville
Ivory Coast
Grand
Cape Coas
Sierra Leone
Sassandra
Bassam
Sekondi-
Cape Coas
Basin
Harper
San Pedro
Cape Three
Takoradi
Cap Palmas
Points

2432

Gulf o

Guinea

Equator
Basin

5212

7856

M
i
d

6537

ATLANTIC

A
t
l
a
n
t
i
c

OCEAN

R
i
d
g
e

Equator
0°

2

3

4

A
20°
B
10°
C
West 0

92
1 : 20 000 000
0   200   400   600 km

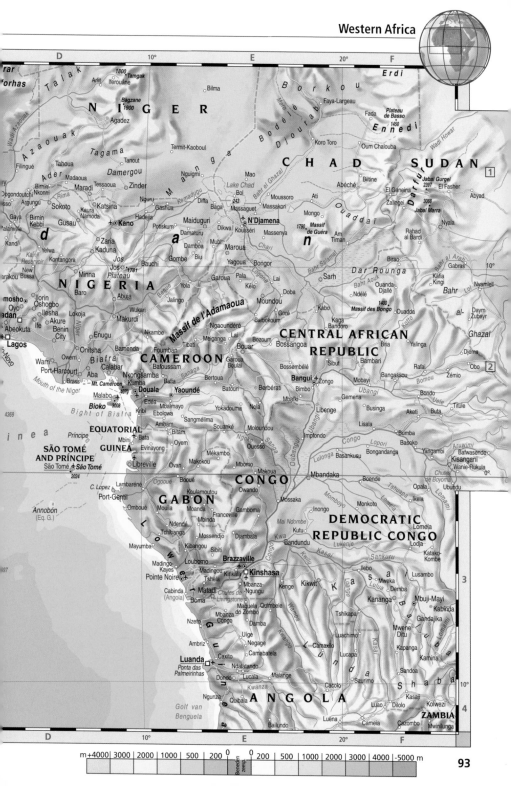

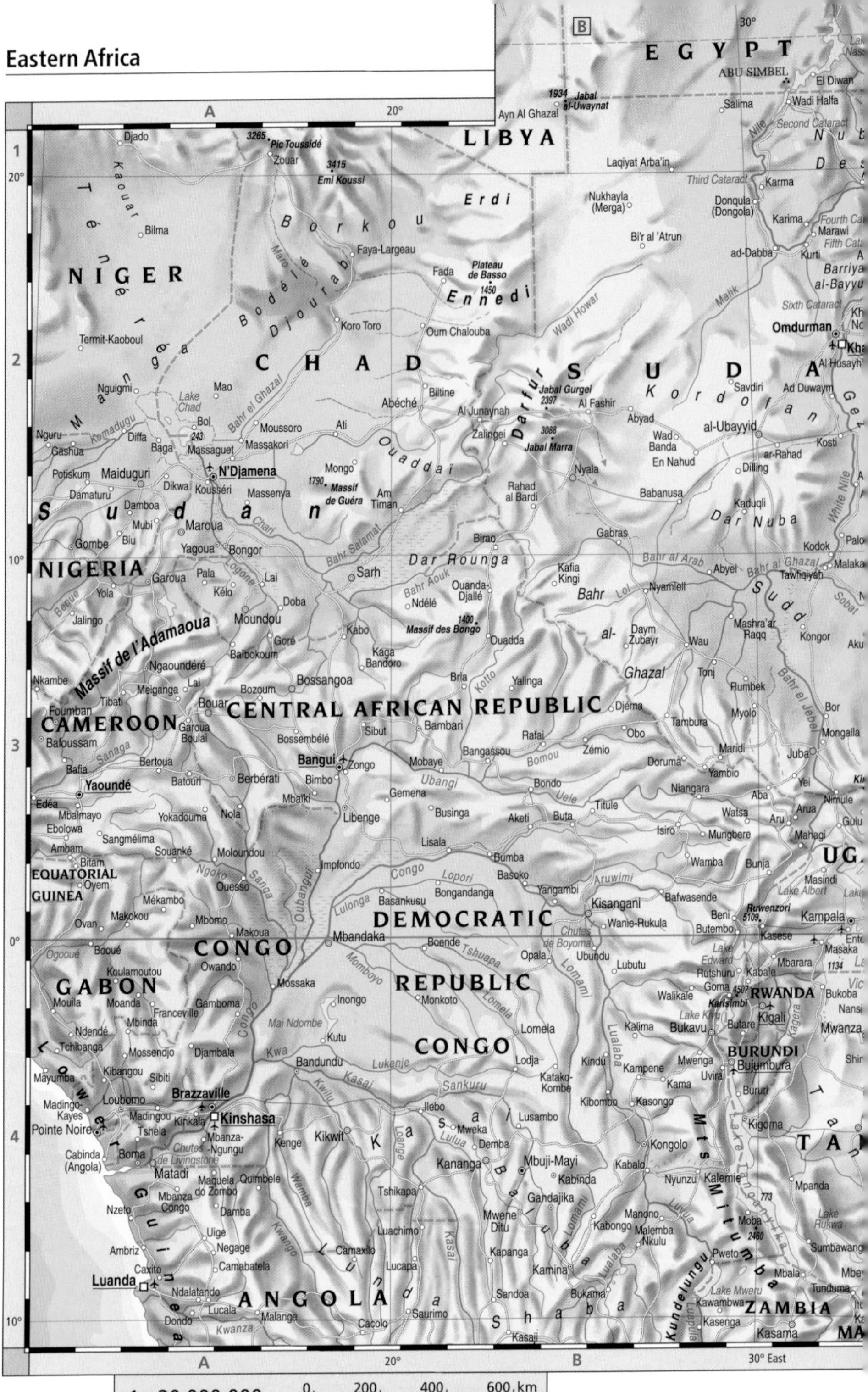

LIBYA

EGYPT

ABU SIMBEL
El Diwan
Wadi Halfa
Second Cataract

NIGER

CHAD

SUDAN

NIGERIA

CAMEROON

CENTRAL AFRICAN REPUBLIC

EQUATORIAL GUINEA

GABON

CONGO

DEMOCRATIC REPUBLIC

CONGO

RWANDA

BURUNDI

UGANDA

TANZANIA

ZAMBIA

ANGOLA

Yaoundé
N'Djamena
Bangui
Brazzaville
Kinshasa
Luanda
Kigali
Bujumbura
Kampala

1 : 20 000 000

0 200 400 600 km

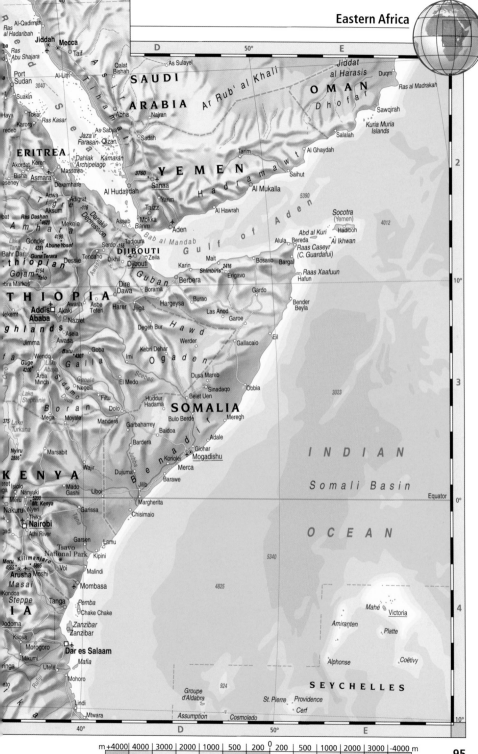

SAUDI
ARABIA
OMAN

Al-Qadimah
Ras al Hadaribah
Jiddah Mecca
Taif
Ras
Abu Shajara
Port Sudan
Al-Lith
3040
Suakin
Haya
Tokar
Karora
redeb

As Sulayel
Qalat Bishah
Abha
Najran
Sadah

50°

Jiddat al Harasis Duqm
Ras al Madrakah
Dhofar
Sawqirah
Kuria Muria Islands
Salalah

D
E
2

ERITREA
Akordat Keren
Bisha Asmara
aseney
Massawa
Dexemhare

Dahlak Archipelago
Kamaran
3760
Sanaa
Al Hudaydah
Taizz
Mokka
Barim

YEMEN

Tarim
Saihut
Al Mukalla

Al Ghaydah

5390

Socotra
(Yemen)
Hadiboh
4012

Abd al Kuri
Bereda
Al Ikhwan

Adwa Adigrat
Aksum
-116
Ras Dashan
4620 Mekele
4190
Guna Terara
Abune Yosef
4231
Serdo -155
Tadjoura

Amhara

Jaza'ir Farasan
Qizan
As Sabya

Assab

Al Hawrah
Bab al Mandab

Gulf of Aden

Alula Raas Caseyr
(C. Guardafui)

Lake Tana
Bahr Dar
Gonder
Dessie
Dikhil
Tendaho
DJIBOUTI
Djibouti
Zeila
Karin
Mait
Bosaso Bargal
Raas Xaafuun
Hafun
3023

t h i o p i a n
Gojam 4154
Telo
ebra Markos
Guba n
Berbera
Shimbiris 2416
Erigavo

THIOPIA
Dire Dawa Borama
Burao
Gardo
Bender Beyla

Addis
Ababa
Akaki
Nazret
Awash
Asbe Tefери
Harer Jijiga
Hargeysa
Las Anod
Garoe

g h l a n d s
Asela
Degeh Bur
Werder
Eil

Jimma
Awasa

H a w d

Nekemt
Wendo
Batu 4307
Goba
Kebri Dehar
Gallacaio

f a
Guge
4200
Lake Abaya
Imi

G a l l a
O g a d e n

Arba Minch
Negeli
El Medo
Dusa Mareb

Lake Stephanie

Huddur
Hadama
Sinadaqo Obbia

B o r a n
Dolo
Belet Uen

375 Lake Turkana
Mega Moyale
Mandera
SOMALIA

Nyiru
2886
Marsabit
Garbaharrey
Baidoa
Bardera
Adale

Wajir
Gichor
Koriolei
Mogadishu
Merca
Meregh

KENYA
Dujuma
Jilib
Barawe

oret Isiolo
ga Nanyuki
Meru Mado Gashi
Liboi

5200
Mt. Kenya
Margherita
Chisimaio

INDIAN

Somali Basin
Equator

Nakuru Nyeri
Thika
Nairobi
Athi River

Garissa

3

0°

Meru
4565
Kilimanjaro
5895
Tsavo National Park
Voi
Garsen
Lamu
Kipini

OCEAN

Arusha Moshi

M a s a i
Steppe
Tanga
Pemba

Malindi
Mombasa
5340

Mahé
Victoria
Amiranten
Platte

4

I A
Kondoa
Dodoma
Kilosa
Chake Chake
Zanzibar
Zanzibar
4825
Alphonse
Coëtivy

Morogoro
Mikumi
Dar es Salaam
Mafia

SEYCHELLES

ringa Utete
Mohoro

924

Lindi
Mtwara

Groupe d'Aldabra
St. Pierre Providence
Cerf

ato
Assumption
Cosmoledo

10°

40°
D
50°
E
10°

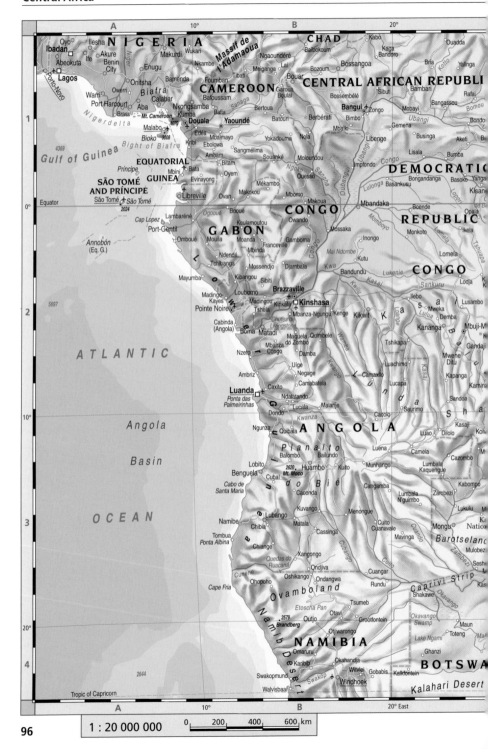

1 : 20 000 000

0 200 400 600 km

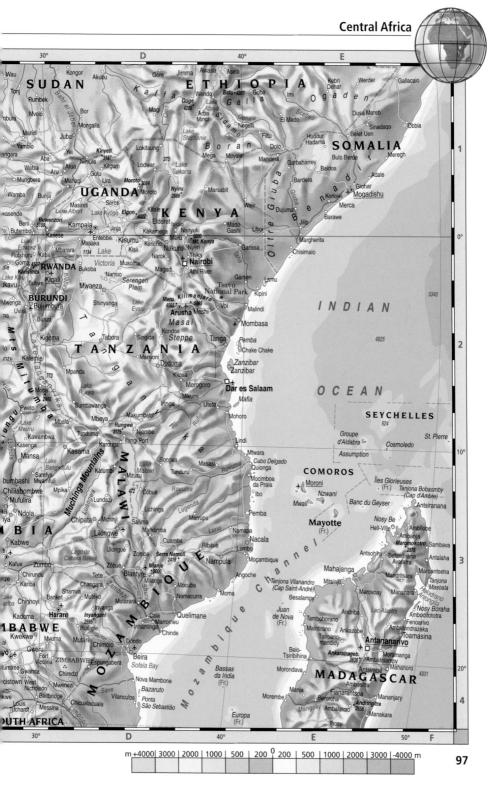

Southern Africa

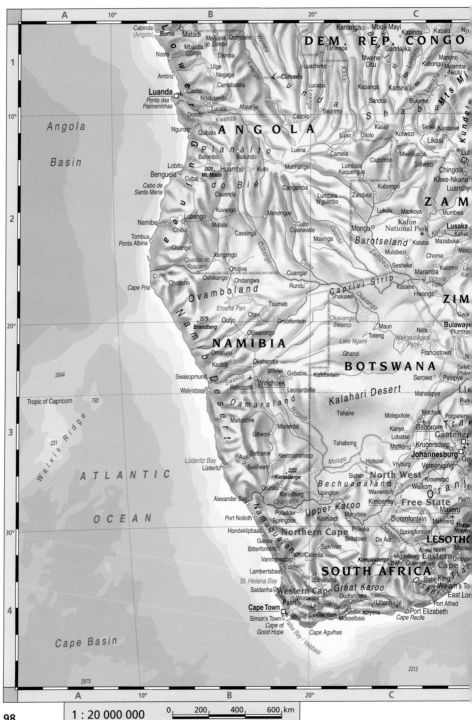

1 : 20 000 000

0 200 400 600 km

T A N Z A N I A

panda

Manyoni Dodoma

Kilosa Morogoro

Lake
Rukwa

Mikumi

Zanzibar
Zanzibar

Dar es Salaam

Amirante
Islands

Alphonse Group 1

Sumbawanga

Iringa Utete

Mafia

Makumbato

Mbeya Rungwe
3175

Mohoro

S E Y C H E L L E S

924

Njombe

Tunduma Itungi Port

St. Pierre Providence

Kasama Karonga

Lindi

Mtwara

Cabo Delgado

Cerf

10°

Songea Masasi

Katumbi Mzuzu

Quionga

Assumption Cosmoledo Farquhar Group

Lake
Malawi Tunduru

Ruvuma

Mocimboa
da Praia

COMOROS

Îles Glorieuses
(Fr.)

Agalega Islands
(Mauritius)

Cóbué Rovuma

Ibo

Moroni

Tanjona Bobaomby
(Cap d'Ambre)

Lundazi

Lichinga

Marrupa

Nzwani

Mwali

Banc du Geyser

Antsiranana

Chipata Mchinji

Salima Mandimba

Namana

Mayotte
(Fr.)

Nosy Be
Hell-Ville

Amblobe

Ambanja

Sambava

M a s c a r e n e

Lilongwe

Cuamba

Ribáuè Lumbo

Nacala

Antsohihy

Maromokotro
2876

Befandriana
Avaratra

Antalaha

Ulongué Zomba Serra Namúli
2419

Nampula

Moçambique

Mandritsara Marqantsetra

B a s i n 2

Tete Mt. Mulanje
3000

Blantyre

Angoche

Mahajanga

Mitsinjo

Tanjona Masoala

Belodrano

Tromelin
(Fr.)

Changara Mocuba

Milange

Namacurra

Moma

Marovoay Mananara

Nosy Boraha

Ambodifototra

Inyanga Mutoko

Inyangani
2595

Marromeu

Quelimane

Besalampy

Andriba Lac Alaotra

Fenoarivo

Ambatondrazaka

Toamasina

M a s c a r e n e   I s l a n d s

Rusape Inhaminga Chinde

Juan
de Nova
(Fr.)

Tambohorano

Ankazobe

Antananarivo

20°

Mutare Chimoio Dondo

Maintirano

Tsiroano-
mandidy

Moramanga

MAURITIUS

Port Louis

BABWE Espungabera

Beira

Sofala Bay

Belo-
Tsiribihina

Ankaratra
2638 Ambatolampy

Mahanoro

Saint Denis

Mauritius

redzi ezi

Nova Mambone

Bassas
da India
(Fr.)

Morondava

MADAGASCAR

Antsirabe 4931

Ambositra

Réunion
(Fr.)

Saint-Pierre

Bazaruto

Chicualacuala Vilanculos

Ponta
São Sebastião

Manja

Morombe Beroroha

Fianarantsoa

Andringitra
2658

Mananjary

Ponta da
Barra Falsa

Europa
(Fr.)

Mangoky Ambalavao

Manakara

P.

Ponta da Barra
Inhambane

Sakaraha

Ihosy

Farafangana

Marão

Inharrime

Toliara Betioky

Betroka

Mo omba Xai Xai

Maputo

Baía de Maputo

Ampanihy

Beraketa

ane Bela Vista

Amboyombe

Tôlañaro

VAZILAND

Tanjona Vohimena
(Cap Sainte-Marie)

5120

ulu- Mbatuba

Richards Bay

M a d a g a s c a r

al ritzburg

I N D I A N

B a s i n

pstone

M o z a m b i q u e

O C E A N

1928

30°

5322

B a s i n

3

4

m +4000| 3000 | 2000 | 1000 | 500 | 200 0 200 | 500 | 1000 | 2000 | 3000 | 4000 | -5000 m

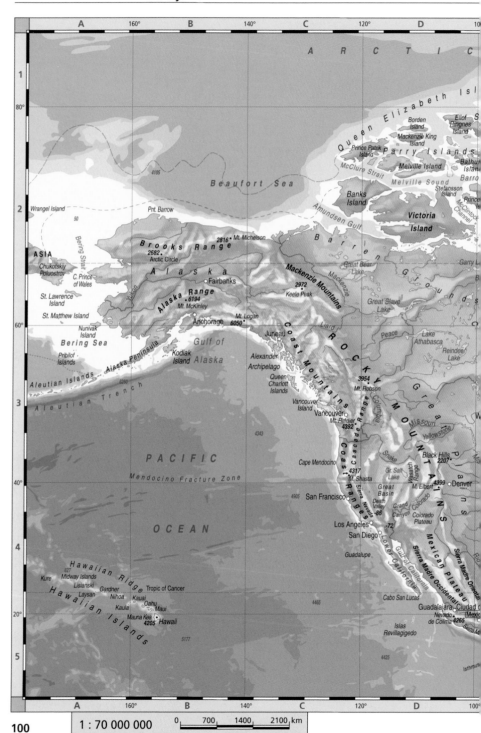

1 : 70 000 000

0 — 700 — 1400 — 2100 km

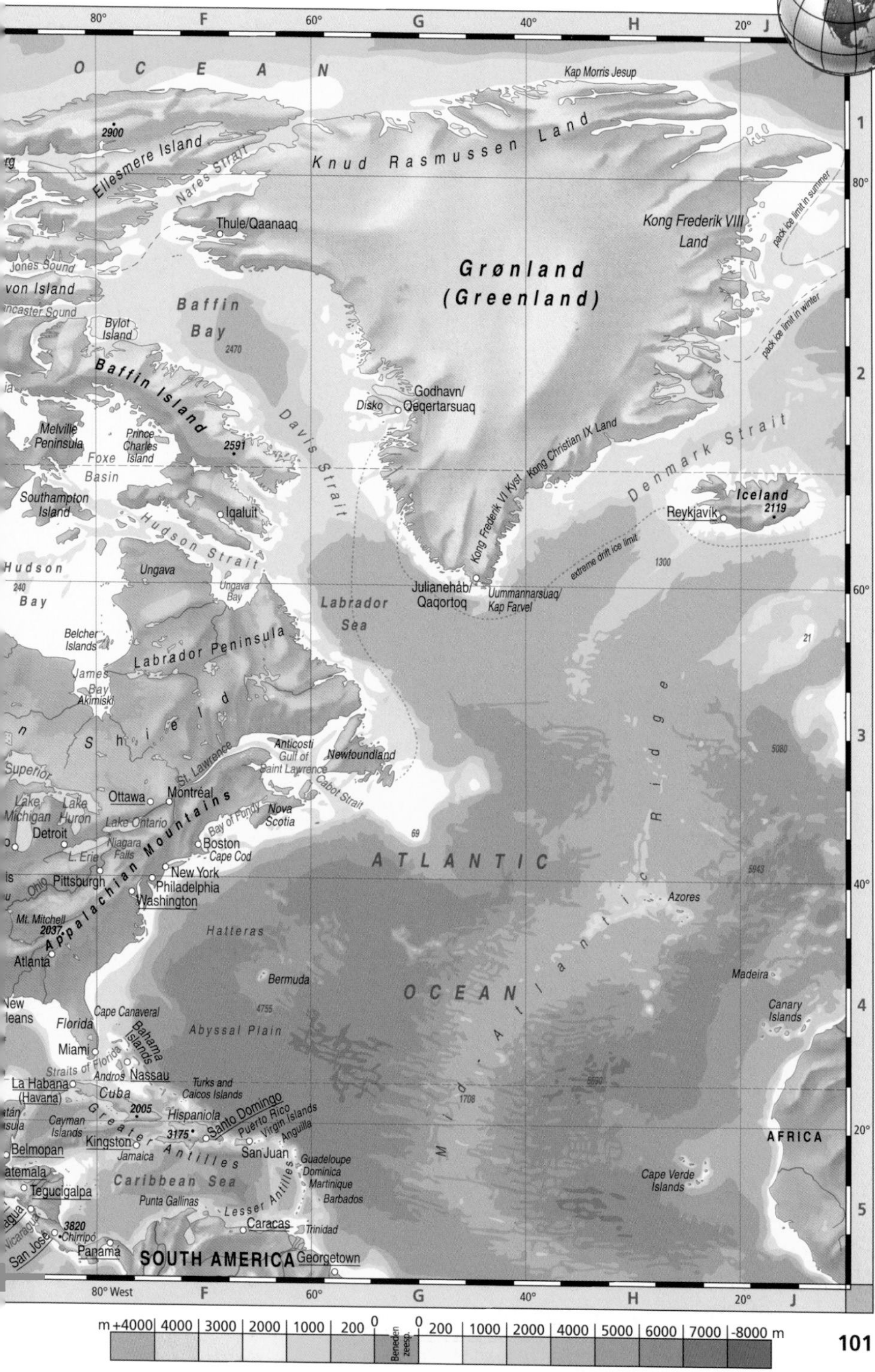
80°
F
60°
G
40°
H
20°
J
O C E A N
Kap Morris Jesup
1
2900
Ellesmere Island
Nares Strait
Knud Rasmussen Land
80°
Thule/Qaanaaq
Kong Frederik VIII Land
pack ice limit in summer
Grønland
(Greenland)
Jones Sound
von Island
ncaster Sound
Baffin Bay
Bylot Island
2470
pack ice limit in winter
Baffin Island
2
Godhavn/
Qeqertarsuaq
Disko
Davis Strait
Melville Peninsula
Prince Charles Island
2591
Kong Christian IX Land
Denmark Strait
Foxe Basin
Kong Frederik VI Kyst
Southampton Island
Iqaluit
Iceland
2119
Reykjavik
Hudson Strait
extreme drift ice limit
1300
Hudson Bay
240
Ungava
Ungava Bay
Julianehåb/
Qaqortoq
Uummannarsuaq/
Kap Farvel
60°
Labrador Sea
Belcher Islands
21
Labrador Peninsula
James Bay
Akimiski
Shield
3
Anticosti
Gulf of Saint Lawrence
Newfoundland
5080
Superior
St. Lawrence
Cabot Strait
Lake Michigan
Lake Huron
Ottawa
Montréal
Lake Ontario
Nova Scotia
Bay of Fundy
Detroit
Niagara Falls
Boston
Cape Cod
69
L. Erie
Appalachian Mountains
New York
ATLANTIC
Mid-Atlantic Ridge
Ohio
Pittsburgh
Philadelphia
Washington
5943
40°
Azores
Mt. Mitchell
2037
Hatteras
Atlanta
Madeira
Bermuda
OCEAN
4
New Orleans
Cape Canaveral
4755
Canary Islands
Florida
Abyssal Plain
Bahama Islands
Miami
Straits of Florida
Andros
Nassau
Turks and Caicos Islands
5560
La Habana
(Havana)
Cuba
1708
Cayman Islands
2005
Hispaniola
Santo Domingo
Puerto Rico
Virgin Islands
Anguilla
Greater Antilles
3175
20°
AFRICA
Belmopan
Kingston
Jamaica
San Juan
Guadeloupe
Dominica
Martinique
Cape Verde Islands
Tegucigalpa
Caribbean Sea
Barbados
Lesser Antilles
Punta Gallinas
5
3820
Chirripó
Caracas
Trinidad
San José
Panamá
SOUTH AMERICA
Georgetown
80° West
F
60°
G
40°
H
20°
J
m +4000
4000
3000
2000
1000
200
0
Beneden zeesp.
0
200
1000
2000
4000
5000
6000
7000
-8000 m

North and Central America: Political

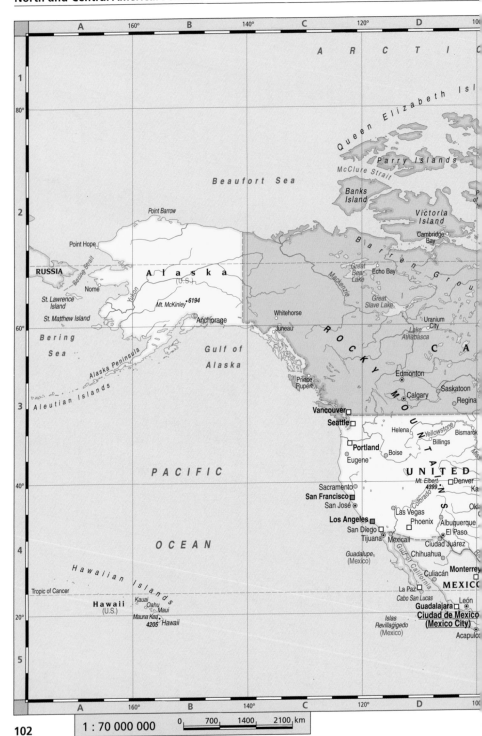

1 : 70 000 000

0   700   1400   2100 km

80°   F   60°   G   40°   H   20°   J

O C E A N

Ellesmere Island

1

80°

Thule/Qaanaaq

Grønland
(Greenland)
(Den.)

Devon Island

Baffin

Bay

Baffin Island

2

Godhavn/
Qeqertarssuaq

Denmark Strait

Davis Strait

Arctic Circle

Foxe
Basin

ICELAND

Southampton
Island

Iqaluit

Reykjavik

Ivujivik

Hudson Strait

Godthåb/Nûk

Hudson

60°

Bay

Labrador
Sea

Uummannarsuaq/
Kap Farvel

D A

Labrador Peninsula

Schefferville

Moosonee

Goose Bay

Sept-Îles

3

der Bay

Gander

Superior

Québec

Gulf of
Saint Lawrence

Newfoundland

Saint John's

olis

Lake
Huron

Montréal

Fredericton

Sydney

St. Pierre et Miquelon
(Fr.)

Lake
Michigan

Ottawa

Toronto

Nova Scotia

ee

L. Ontario

Detroit

L. Erie

Halifax

Boston

S

Buffalo

New York

apolis

Pittsburgh

Philadelphia

ATLANTIC

ouis

Cincinnati

Baltimore

40°

Ohio

Washington

Azores

Memphis

Raleigh

Atlanta

Bermuda

Madeira

Savannah

Hamilton (U.K.)

New
Orleans

Jacksonville

OCEAN

Canary Islands

4

Tampa

Orlando

of

Miami

BAHAMAS

Western
Sahara

co

Nassau

Turks and

La Habana
(Havana)

Santiago
de Cuba

Caicos Islands
(U.K.)

DOMINICAN REPUBLIC

tán

CUBA

Santo Domingo

Puerto Rico (U.S.)

Virgin Islands (U.S./U.K.)

20°

Chetumal (U.K.)

Cayman Islands

HAITI

Anguilla (U.K.)

ANTIGUA AND BARBUDA

BELIZE

JAMAICA

Port-

San Juan

Guadeloupe (Fr.)

MAURITANIA

Belmopan

Kingston

au-Prince

ST KITTS AND NEVIS

DOMINICA

HONDURAS

Caribbean

Martinique (Fr.)

SAINT LUCIA

CAPE VERDE

SENEGAL

Tegucigalpa

Sea

Netherlands (Nl.)

SAINT VINCENT AND THE GRENADINES

NICARAGUA

Antilles

BARBADOS

5

Barranquilla

Caracas

GRENADA

GUINEA

Managua

Maracaibo

Valencia

TRINIDAD
AND TOBAGO

San José

Orinoco

Ciudad

COSTA RICA

Panama

Guayana

PANAMA

San Cristóbal

VENEZUELA

Georgetown

80° West   F   60°   G   40°   H   20°   J

Alaska

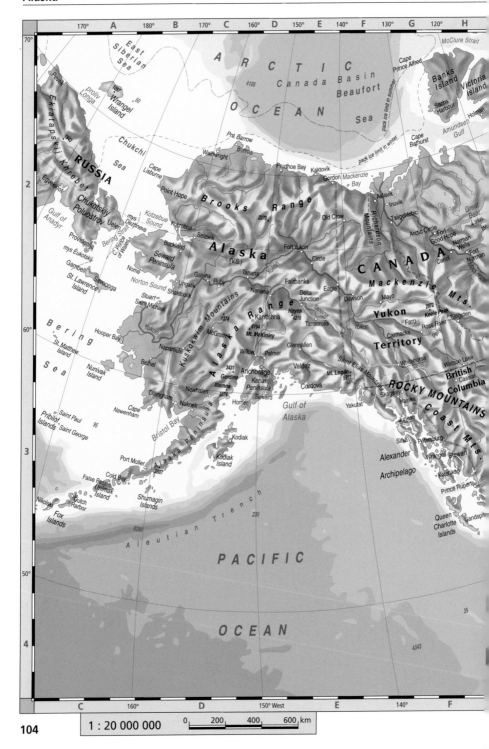

East
Siberian
Sea

A　R　C　T　I　C

McClure Strait

Cape
Prince Alfred

Canada Basin

Beaufort

Banks
Island

Victoria
Island

4105

Povek

Proliv
Longa

1067　50

Wrangel
Island

O　C　E　A　N

Sea

Sachs
Harbour

Holman

Amundsen
Gulf

pack ice limit in summer

Chukchi

Sea

Pnt. Barrow

Barrow

Cape
Bathurst

Cape
Lisburne

Prudhoe Bay　Kaktovik

Great
Bear
Lake

Gordon　Mackenzie
Bay

Ekiarlapskiy Korebel

1548

RUSSIA

Point Hope

B　r　o　o　k　s　　R　a　n　g　e

Aklavik

Inuvik

Tsilgehtchic

pack ice limit in winter

2

Egyekinot

Chukotskiy
Poluostrov　Uelen

Kotzebue
Sound

2370

Old Crow

Richardson
Mountains

Arctic Circle

Fort
Good Hope

Norman
Wells

159

Gulf of
Anadyr

mys
Dezhneva

C. Prince
of Wales

Kotzebue

Selawik

A　l　a　s　k　a
(V.S.)

Fort Yukon

Canol

Fort
Norman

Providenija

mys Eukolski

Bering Strait

Buckland

Seward
Peninsula

Circle

C　A　N　A　D　A

Gambell

St. Lawrence
Island

Savoonga

Nome

Norton Sound

Ungalik

Galena

Ruby

Tanana

Yukon

Fairbanks

Eagle

M　a　c　k　e　n　z　i　e

Dawson

Mayo

2972

M　t　s.

Keele Peak

Stuart
Saint Michael

Shaktoolik

Nenana

Delta
Junction

Tanana

Yukon

Faro

Ross River

Tungsten

60°

B　e　r　i　n　g

Hooper Bay

Yukon

Napamute

Kuskokwim Mountains

1374

McGrath

R. Kantishna

Hayes

6194

Mt. McKinley

4216

A

Tanacross

Carmacks

Territory

Keno Peak

St. Matthew
Island

Bethel

l　a　s　k　a

R　a　n　g　e

Willow

Glennallen

Whitehorse

Watson Lake

S　e　a

Nunivak
Island

3431
Gerdine

Palmer

Anchorage

Valdez

Mt. Logan
5951

Saint Elias Mountains

British

Cassiar

Columbia

Dillingham

Newhalen
Iliamna

3074

Kenai
Peninsula

Cordova

Skagway

Haines

ROCKY MOUNTAINS

Pribilof
Islands

Saint Paul

Saint George

85

Cape
Newenham

Naknek

Homer

Seward

Gulf of
Alaska

Yakutat

Juneau

C　o　a　s　t　　M　t　s.

Bristol Bay

Kodiak

Sitka

Petersburg

3

Port Moller

Alaska Peninsula

Kodiak
Island

Alexander

Archipelago

Wrangell　Stewart

Ketchikan

Cold Bay

2507

False Pass

Unimak
Island

Shumagin
Islands

Prince Rupert

Nikolski

Dutch
Harbor

Fox
Islands

6280

A　l　e　u　t　i　a　n　　T　r　e　n　c　h

230

Queen
Charlotte
Islands

Sandspit

P　A　C　I　F　I　C

50°

35

O　C　E　A　N

4343

4

1 : 20 000 000　　0　200　400　600 km

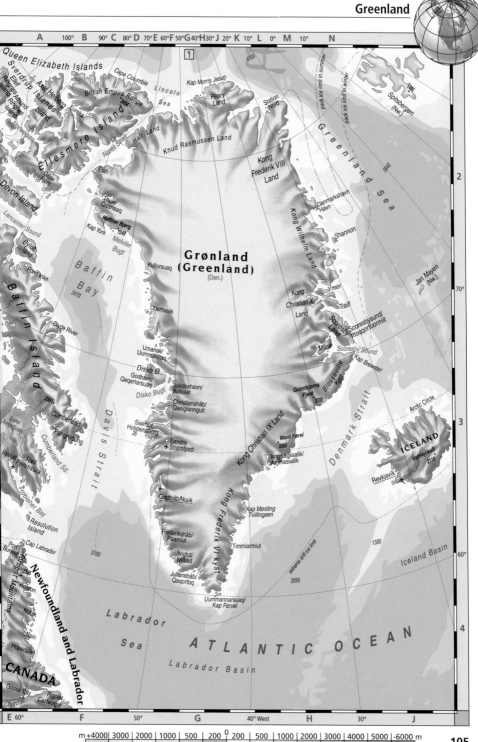

A 100° B 90° C 80° D 70° E 60° F 50° G 40° H 30° J 20° K 10° L 0° M 10° N

1

Queen Elizabeth Islands

Sverdrup Islands
Ellef Ringnes Island
Amund Ringnes Island
Axel Heiberg Island
British Empire Range
Eureka
Cape Columbia
Lincoln Sea
Kap Morris Jesup
Peary Land
Station Nord
pack ice limit in summer
pack ice limit in winter
Spitsbergen (Nw.)

Ellesmere Island
Nares Strait
Hall Land
Knud Rasmussen Land
Kong Frederik VIII Land

Norwegian Bay
Grise Fiord
Etah
Thule/ Qaanaaq
Haffner Bjerg 1248
Kap York
Melville Bugt
Kullorsuaq

Danmarkshavn
Havn
Shannon

Greenland Sea

Devon Island
Lancaster Sound
Bylot Island
Pond Inlet

Baffin Bay 2470

Grønland (Greenland) (Den.)

Kong Wilhelm Land

Kong Christian X Land
Ymer
Traill
Scoresby Land
Scoresbysund/ Ittoqqortoormiit
Milne
Scoresby Sound
Kap Brewster

Jan Mayen (Nw.)

70°

Upernavik

Umanak/ Uummannaq

Disko Ø
Godhavn/ Qeqertarsuaq
Disko Bugt
Jakobshavn/ Ilulissat
Christianshåb/ Qasigiannguit

Gunnbjørns Field 3700
Blosseville Kyst

2591
Clyde River

Davis Strait

Cumberland
Pangnirtung
Cumberland Sd.

Sisimiut Holsteinsborg 29
Søndre Strømfjord

Kong Christian IX Land
Mont Forel 3360
Angmagssalik/ Ammassalik

Denmark Strait

Arctic Circle

ICELAND
Vatnajökull 2119

3

Baffin Island
Lake Amadjuak
Hall Peninsula
Iqaluit
Frobisher Bay
Resolution Island

Godthåb/Nuuk

Kong Frederik VI kyst

Kap Møsting
Tvillingøen

Frederikshåb/ Paamiut
Ivigtut/ Ivittuut

Timmiarmiut

Reykjavik

extreme drift ice limit

1300

Iceland Basin

60°

Cap Labrador
Port Burwell
Torngat Mountains
Hebron
3100
Julianehåb/ Qaqortoq

3090

Uummannarsuaq/ Kap Farvel

Newfoundland and Labrador

Nutak
Nain
Hopedale

Labrador Sea

ATLANTIC OCEAN

4

CANADA
Goose Bay
Rigolet
Churchill
Cartwright

Labrador Basin

E 60° F 50° G 40° West H 30° J

m +4000 | 3000 | 2000 | 1000 | 500 | 200 | 0 | 200 | 500 | 1000 | 2000 | 3000 | 4000 | 5000 | -6000 m

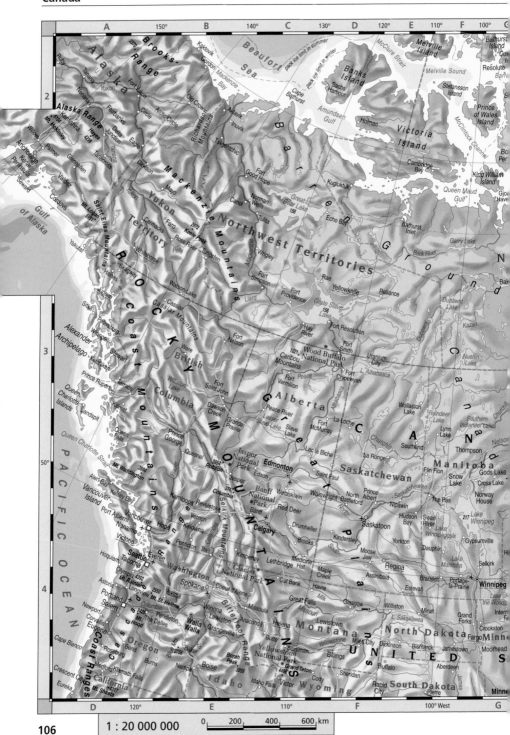

1 : 20 000 000

0   200   400   600 km

United States

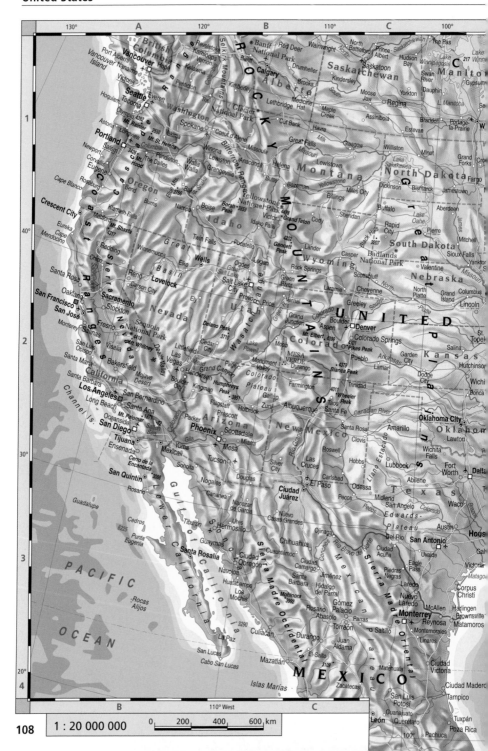

108   1 : 20 000 000   0   200   400   600 km

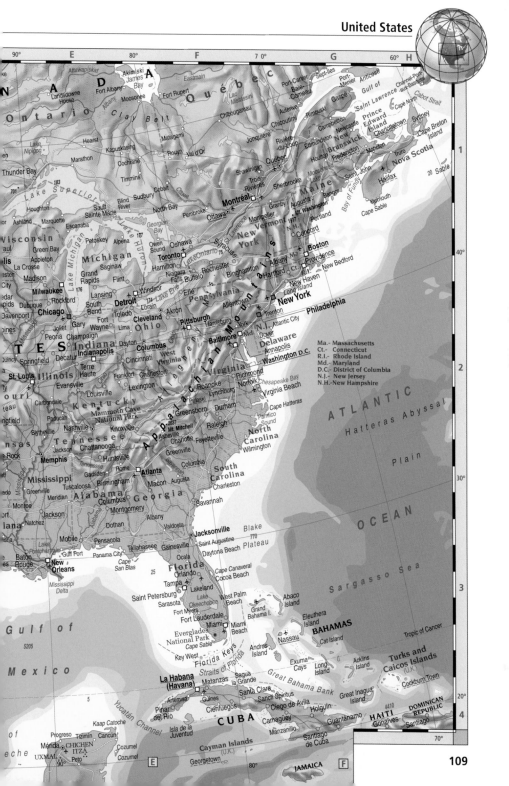

90° E 80° F 7 0° G 60° H

ke
N A D A
Attawapiskat Akimiski Eastmain
Landsdowne James
House Fort Albany Bay Québec Port-Cartier Sept-Îles Gulf of
Albany Moosonee Fort Rupert Baie- Menier Anticosti
Ontario Clay Belt Lac Comeau Port- aux-Basques Channel-Port
Mistassini Auteline Rimouski Gaspé Cape North Cabot Strait
Chibougamau Saint Lawrence
Matagami Jonquière Rivière- Campbellton Newcastle New Prince Sydney
en Hearst du-Loup Moncton Edward Charlottetown
Lake Kapuskasing Rouyn Val-d'Or Québec Edmundston Houlton Fredericton Brunswick Island Cape Breton
Nipigon Marathon Trois- Sherbrooke Saint John Truro Island
Thunder Bay Timmins Rivières Granby Maine Moosehead Halifax Nova Scotia
701 183 Cochrane Shawinigan Montpelier Mt. Washington Bangor Lake Bay of Fundy Cape Sable Yarmouth 20 Sable
Lake Superior Sudbury Cobalt Ottawa Vermont 1917 Portland
Houghton Blind North Bay Montréal N.H. Concord
or Ashland Marquette Sault River Georgian New Albany Ma. Boston
Sainte Marie Bay 117 York Syracuse Providence
Wisconsin Petoskey Alpena Owen Oshawa Rochester Hartford New Bedford
aul Green Bay Michigan Sound Toronto Lake Ontario 75 Binghamton New Haven
lis Appleton Saginaw Hamilton Niagara Rochester Albany Long Island
ester La Crosse Grand Flint Buffalo Pennsylvania New York
City Madison Rapids Lansing Windsor Lake Erie Erie Allentown Philadelphia
edar Milwaukee 176 Lorain Akron Trenton New York
pids Dubuque Rockford South Detroit Cleveland Harrisburg N.J. Atlantic City
Javenport Chicago Bend Toledo Pittsburgh Baltimore Md. Dover
ines Joliet Gary Fort Lima Ohio West Annapolis Delaware
Peoria Champaign Wayne Dayton Columbus Virginia Washington D.C.
T E S Indiana Cincinnati Frankfort Charleston Richmond Chesapeake Bay Ma.- Massachusetts
Quincy Springfield Decatur Indianapolis Terre Lexington Roanoke Norfolk Ct.- Connecticut
St. Louis Illinois Haute Virginia Beach R.I.- Rhode Island
a Evansville Louisville Lynchburg Md.- Maryland
ourri Carbondale Kentucky Pulaski Virginia D.C.- District of Columbia
teau Paducah Mammoth Cave Greensboro Durham Cape Hatteras N.J.- New Jersey
ngfield Blytheville Nashville National Park Knoxville Raleigh Pamlico N.H.-New Hampshire
nsas Jackson Tennessee Mt. Mitchell Charlotte Fayetteville Sound
e Rock Memphis Chattanooga Asheville North ATLANTIC
Huntsville Greenville Carolina Hatteras Abyssal
Mississippi Gadsden Rome Columbia Wilmington
Greenville Tuscaloosa Birmingham South Plain
ado Meridian Alabama Macon Augusta Carolina
Monroe Columbus Georgia Charleston OCEAN
ort Jackson Montgomery Savannah 30°
iana Natchez Dothan Albany
Mississippi Mobile Pensacola Valdosta Jacksonville Blake
Lake Tallahassee Gainesville Saint Augustine 770 Plateau
Baton Pontchartrain Gulf Port Ocala Daytona Beach
es Rouge Panama City Cape Orlando Cape Canaveral Sargasso Sea 3
New San Blas 25 Florida Cocoa Beach
Orleans Tampa Lakeland
Mississippi Saint Petersburg Lake West Palm Abaco
Delta Sarasota Okeechobee Beach Island
Gulf of Fort Myers Grand Eleuthera
5205 Everglades Fort Lauderdale Bahama I. Island BAHAMAS
National Park Miami Miami Andros Nassau Cat Island Tropic of Cancer
Mexico Cape Sable Beach Island
Key West Florida Keys Exuma Acklins Turks and
Straits of Florida Cays Long Island Caicos Islands
5 La Habana Matanzas Sagua Great Bahama Bank Island Cockburn Town (U.K.)
(Havana) la Grande
Artemisa Santa Clara Great Inagua
of Pinar Guines Sancti Spíritus Ciego de Avila Holguín Island 4410 DOMINICAN
Kaap Catoche del Río Cienfuegos C U B A Camagüey HAITI REPUBLIC
Progreso Tizimín Cancún Isla de la Manzanillo Santiago Guantánamo Gonaïves Santiago
eche Mérida Juventud de Cuba
UXMAL CHICHEN Cozumel Cayman Islands
ITZA Cozumel (U.K.)
of Peto 90° Georgetown 80°
E Isla de JAMAICA F

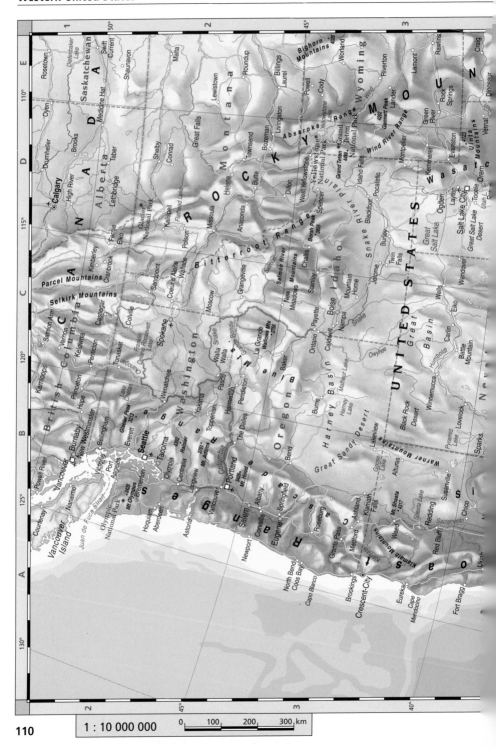

1 : 10 000 000

0   100   200   300 km

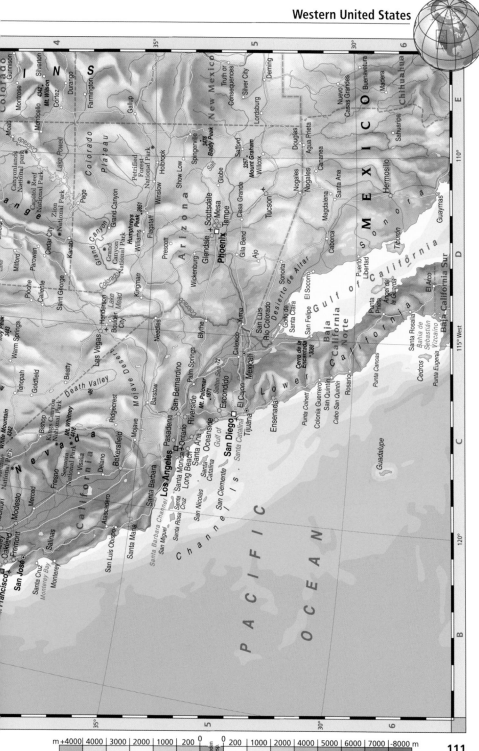

1 : 10 000 000

0 100 200 300 km

m +4000 | 3000 | 2000 | 1000 | 500 | 200 | 0 | 200 | 500 | 1000 | 2000 | 3000 | 4000 | 5000 | -6000 m

113

Central America

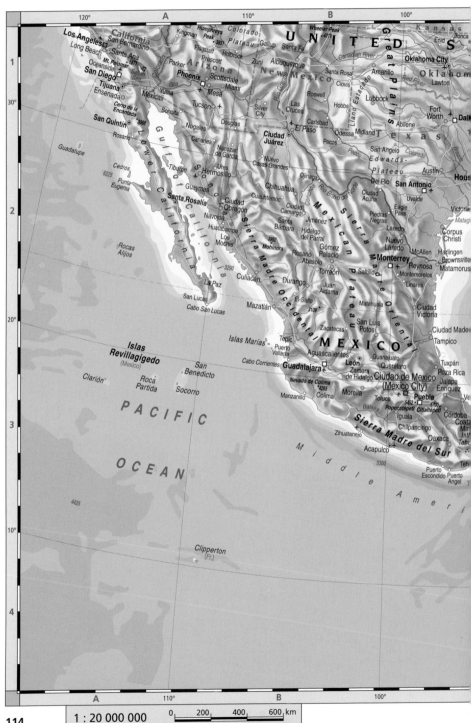

1 : 20 000 000

0 | 200 | 400 | 600 | km

90° D 80° E 70° F

U S

Paducah Kentucky
Blytheville Nashville Knoxville Mt. Mitchell Greensboro Raleigh
Jackson Chattanooga Asheville Charlotte Fayetteville **North Carolina**
Memphis Huntsville Rome Greenville Wilmington
Gadsden Birmingham **Atlanta** Columbia **South Carolina**
Tuscaloosa Macon Augusta
Mississippi Greenville **Alabama** **Georgia** Charleston
Meridian Columbus Montgomery Savannah
Montoe
Jackson Dothan Albany
Natchez Mobile Pensacola Valdosta
Lake Gulf Port Tallahassee Gainesville **Jacksonville** **Blake**
Baton Pontchartrain Panama City Saint Augustine 770
Rouge **New Orleans** Cape Ocala Daytona Beach **Plateau**
San Blas 25 **Florida** Cape Canaveral
Mississippi Orlando Cocoa Beach
Delta Tampa Lakeland
Saint Petersburg Lake West Palm
Gulf of Sarasota Okeechobee Beach
Fort Myers Fort Lauderdale Abaco
Mexico Everglades Miami Island
National Park Miami **Grand**
5205 Cape Sable Beach **Bahama I.**
Key West Nassau **BAHAMAS**
Florida Keys Andros
Island Cat Island
Straits of Florida Great Exuma Tropic of Cancer
Cabo Catoche Cays Long Acklins **Turks and**
Progreso Tizimín Cancún Sagua Santa Clara Island Island **Caicos Islands**
CHICHÉN la Grande Sancti 4410 (U.K.)
Mérida ITZÁ Artemisa Güines Spiritus Grand Inagua Cap- Cockburn Town
Peto Cozumel del Río Cienfuegos Ciego de Avila Island Haïtien **DOMINICAN**
UXMAL Cozumel Pinar **CUBA** Camagüey Holguín Gonaïves Santiago **REPUBLIC**
Campeche Isla de la Manzanillo Guantánamo 3175 Pico Puerto
Yucatán Peninsula Juventud Santiago Windward **HAITI** San Duarte **Santo** Rico
Chetumal Cayman Islands de Cuba Passage Jérémie Port- Juan **Domingo** (U.S.)
ahermosa Corozal (U.K.) 7590 Montego Bay **Kingston** Les Cayes au-Prince
Santanilla Georgetown Spanish 2256 **Antilles**
TIKAL (Honduras) **JAMAICA** Town
Belize City
Flores Belmopan Bajo Nuevo **Netherlands**
YAXCHILÁN **BELIZE** Banco **Antilles**
an Cristobal Islas de la Bahía de Serranilla (NL.)
le las Casas Golfo de Cabo Gracias Willemstad
GUATEMALA Puerto Honduras a Dios Banco Punta Aruba Curaçao
4220 BARRIOS San Pedro 2590 Waspán de Serrana Gallinas
Tajumulco **Guatemala** Sula Coco (Colombia) Guajira
Escuintla **HONDURAS** Puerto Providencia Ríohacha Coro
Santa Ana Cabezas Santa Marta Ciénaga Paraguaná
San Salvador San Vicente Choluteca **Tegucigalpa** Pico **Maracaibo** **Barquisimeto**
EL SALVADOR San Miguel **NICARAGUA** San Andrés Cristóbal Colón **Cabimas**
León Lago de Managua Blufields **Barranquilla** 5775 Lago de 5002
Golfo de Fonseca **Managua** Granada **Cartagena** El Carmen Maracaibo
Lago de Nicaragua San Carlos Gulf of El Banco Mérida
COSTA RICA Limón **Colón** Darién Sincelejo Ocaña Apure
Alajuela Heredia **Panama** Montería Cúcuta **Cordillera**
Nicoya Cartago Golfo de los Turbo Bucaramanga
San José 3329 Mosquitos La Palma New del
Chirripó **PANAMA** Cocuy
David Chitré Gulf of La Palma 5493
Santiago Azuero Panama **COLOMBIA**
Coiba Punta Tunja
Mala **Medellín** **Bogotá**
Cocos Island Tolima
(Costa Rica) 5215
Malpelo Pereira Ibagué
(Colombia) 3901 Palmira
Buenaventura **Cali** Huila Neiva
5750

m +4000 | 4000 | 3000 | 2000 | 1000 | 500 | 200 0 0 200 | 500 | 1000 | 2000 | 3000 | 4000 | 5000 | 6000 | -8000 m

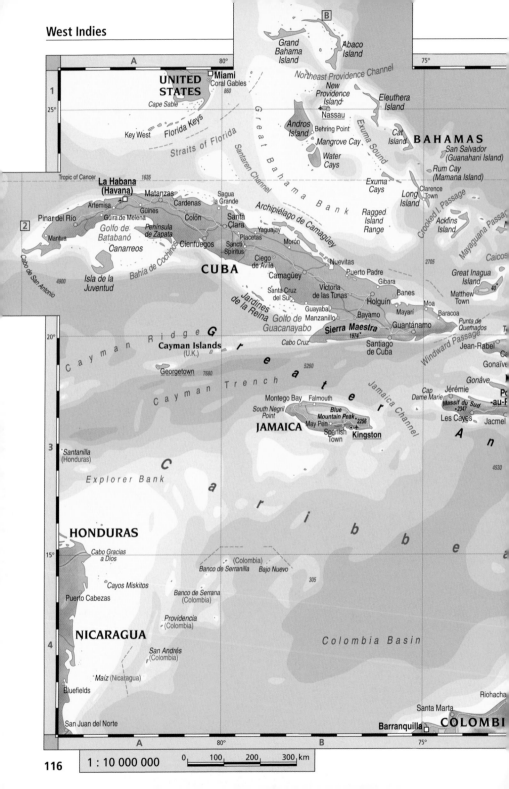

West Indies

Grand
Bahama
Island
Abaco
Island

Northeast Providence Channel

**UNITED
STATES**

Miami
Coral Gables
860

New
Providence
Island
Eleuthera
Island

Cape Sable

Nassau

Key West

Florida Keys

Straits of Florida

Santaren Channel

G
r
e
a
t

B
a
h
a
m
a

B
a
n
k

Andros
Island
Behring Point

Mangrove Cay

Water
Cays

Cat
Island

BAHAMAS

San Salvador
(Guanahani Island)

Rum Cay
(Mamana Island)

Tropic of Cancer

1635

**La Habana
(Havana)**

Matanzas

Sagua
la Grande

Exuma
Sound

Exuma
Cays

Long
Island

Clarence
Town

Pinar del Río

Artemisa

Cardenas

Güira de Melena

Guines

Colón

Santa
Clara

Archipiélago de Camagüey

Ragged
Island
Range

Crooked I. Passage

Ackfins
Island

Mayaguana Passag

Golfo de
Batabanó
Península
de Zapata

Yaguajay

Placetas

Morón

Caicos

Mantua

Cienfuegos

Sancti
Spíritus

Ciego
de Ávila

2705

Canarreos

Bahía de Cochinos

CUBA

Nuevitas

Puerto Padre

Great Inagua
Island

Cabo de San Antonio

4900

Isla de la
Juventud

Camagüey

Santa Cruz
del Sur

Victoria
de las Tunas

Gibara

Banes

Matthew
Town

40

Jardines
de la Reina

Guayabal

Manzanillo

Holguín

Bayamo

Mayarí

Moa

Baracoa

Punta de
Quemados

Golfo de
Guacanayabo

Sierra Maestra
1974

Guantánamo

Windward Passage

Jean-Rabel

Ca

G
r
e
a
t
e
r

Cayman
R i d g e

Cayman Islands
(U.K.)

Cabo Cruz

Santiago
de Cuba

5260

Gonaïve

Georgetown
7680

C a y m a n   T r e n c h

Jamaica Channel

Cap
Dame Marie

Gonâve

Jérémie

Po
au-P

Montego Bay

Falmouth

South Negril
Point

Blue
Mountain Peak
2256

Massif du Sud
2347

Les Cayes

Jacmel

JAMAICA

May Pen

Spanish
Town

Kingston

A
n

Santanilla
(Honduras)

4530

C

E x p l o r e r   B a n k

a

HONDURAS

Cabo Gracias
a Dios

r

(Colombia)
Banco de Serranilla   Bajo Nuevo

i

Cayos Miskitos

Banco de Serrana
(Colombia)

305

b

Puerto Cabezas

Providencia
(Colombia)

b

e

NICARAGUA

San Andrés
(Colombia)

C o l o m b i a   B a s i n

a

Maíz (Nicaragua)

Bluefields

Riohacha

San Juan del Norte

Santa Marta

COLOMBI

Barranquilla

1 : 10 000 000

0   100   200   300 km

70° D 65° E

1

25°

A T L A N T I C

2

O C E A N

**Turks and
Caicos Islands**
(U.K.)
Cockburn Town
Islands
ir Passage
uchoir Bank   Silver Bank

20°

Puerto Rico Trench

a n i o l a
Puerto Plata
ntiago   Nagua
Duarte   Sánchez   Cabo San Rafael
175
La Vega
DOMINICAN   9200
llera Central
llo   Azua
Santo   El Macao
Domingo San La Romana
arahona   Pedro   Saona
REPUBLIC

**Virgin
Islands**
(U.S.-U.K.)
Tortola
Road Town Anegada
Arecibo San Juan   *St. Thomas* (U.K.)
Bayamón   *Anegada Passage*
1338   Caguas   Charlotte   Anguilla (U.K.)
San German   Amalie
Ponce   Vieques   *St. Maarten* St. Barthélémy (Fr.)
Puerto Rico   St. Croix   (Fr. / NL.)   Barbuda
(U.S.)   (U.S.)   Saba (NL.)   **ANTIGUA**
Basseterre **AND BARBUDA**
SAINT KITTS
AND NEVIS   St. John's
Montserrat   *Guadeloupe Passage*
(U.K.)   **Guadeloupe**
Soufrière   (Fr.)
1467   Pointe-à-Pitre
Basse-Terre   Marie-Galante
Dominica Pas.   (Fr.)
1450
DOMINICA Roseau

vieio
o Beata

l l e s

Venezuela

Aves
(Venezuela)

3

L e e w a r d   I s l a n d s

15°

Mona Passage
Mona

S   e   a

5650

B a s i n

360

**Netherlands
Antilles**
(NL.)
as   Aruba
Oranjestad
Curaçao
Willemstad
Punto Fijo
ulf of
ezuela   Coro

Martinique Passage
Mont *1397*
Pelée
Fort-de-France   **Martinique**
(Fr.)

Saint Lucia Channel
Castries
SAINT LUCIA
BARBADOS
St. Vincent Passage
Kingstown
Bridgetown
**SAINT VINCENT AND
THE GRENADINES**
Carriacou
St. George's **GRENADA**

A v e s   R i d g e

L e s s e r

Bonaire
Orchila   *Blanquilla*

W i n d w a r d   I s l a n d s
(Venezuela)
Los Roques
Margarita

70° West

10°

Puerto
Cabello   La Guaira
Valencia   **Caracas**
Maracay

Tortuga
Cumaná   Carúpano
Barcelona Puerto la Cruz
Turimiquire
2596

A n t i l l e s

Dragon's Mouths Tobago
Scarborough

**TRINIDAD
AND TOBAGO**
Port of Spain
Trinidad
San Fernando

4

10°

D **V E N E Z U E L A** E

South America: Physical

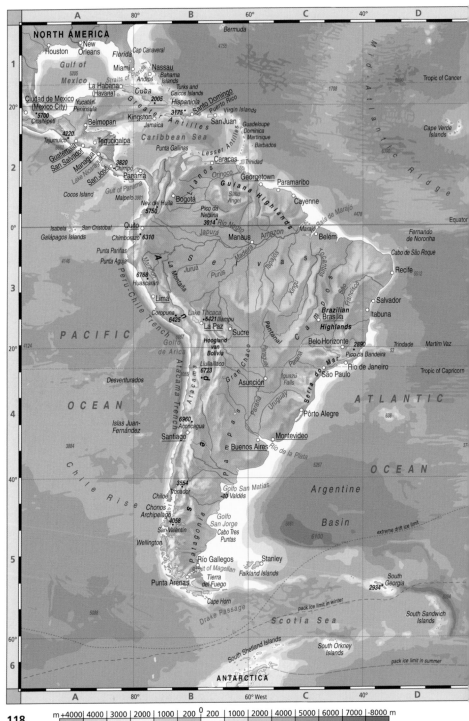

m +4000| 4000 | 3000 | 2000 | 1000 | 200 0 200 | 1000 | 2000 | 4000 | 5000 | 6000 | 7000 |-8000 m

San Antonio
VERENIGDE STATEN
New Orleans
Houston
Jacksonville
Orlando
Tampa
Matamoros
Gulf of Mexico
Miami
MEXICO
Ciudad de Mexico (Mexico City)
Mérida
Yucatán Peninsula
La Habana (Havana)
Santiago de Cuba
CUBA
Cayman Islands (U.K.)
BAHAMAS
Turks and Caicos Islands (U.K.)
DOMINICAN REPUBLIC
Santo Domingo
Puerto Rico (U.S.)
Virgin Islands (U.S./U.K.)
Anguilla (U.K.)
Puebla Veracruz
Tuxtla Gutiérrez
Chetumal
BELIZE Belmopan
HONDURAS
GUATEMALA
Guatemala
Tegucigalpa
Kingston
JAMAICA
HAITI
Port-au-Prince
San Juan
SAINT KITTS AND NEVIS
Martinique (Fr.)
ANTIGUA AND BARBUDA
Guadeloupe (Fr.)
DOMINICA
ST. LUCIA
SAINT VINCENT AND THE GRENADINES
Caribbean Sea
San Salvador
EL SALVADOR
Managua
NICARAGUA
COSTA RICA
San José
PANAMA
Panamá
Cocos Island (Costa Rica)
Malpelo (Col.)
Barranquilla
Maracaibo
S. Cristóbal
Valencia
Caracas
VENEZUELA
BARBADOS
GRENADA
TRINIDAD AND TOBAGO
Ciudad Guayana
Georgetown
SURINAME
Paramaribo
Netherlands Antilles (NL.)
Medellín
Bogotá
COLOMBIA
Cali
Quito
Pasto
ECUADOR
Guayaquil
Cuenca
Piura
Chiclayo
Trujillo
PERU
Lima
Huancayo
Cuzco
Arequipa
Iquitos
Leticia
Tefé
Cruzeiro do Sul
Rio Branco
Pôrto Velho
Riberalta
BOLIVIA
La Paz
Santa Cruz
Sucre
Potosí
Arica
Iquique
Antofagasta
Orinoco
GUYANA
Lethem
French Guiana (Fr.)
Cayenne
Macapá
Içana
Rio Negro
Manaus
Amazon
Santarém
Belém
São Luís
Fortaleza
Imperatriz
Teresina
Natal
Carolina
Paulistana
Campina Grande
Recife
Maceió
Aracaju
Salvador
B R A Z I L
Cuiabá
Brasília
Goiânia
Diamantina
Corumbá
Uberaba
Belo Horizonte
Vitória
Campo Grande
Ribeirão Prêto
Niterói
PARAGUAY
Salta
Asunción
Corrientes
São Paulo
Rio de Janeiro
Nova Iguaçu
Santos
Curitiba
Florianópolis
S. Miguel de Tucumán
Santa Fe
Córdoba
Salto
Uruguay
Paraná
Pôrto Alegre
Pelotas
La Serena
Valparaíso
Santiago
Mendoza
Rosario
URUGUAY
Montevideo
CHILE
Buenos Aires
La Plata
ARGENTINA
Concepción
Temuco
San Carlos de Bariloche
Mar del Plata
Bahía Blanca
Puerto Montt
Chiloé
Viedma
Chonos Archipelago
Wellington
Comodoro Rivadavia
Patagonia
Río Gallegos
Punta Arenas
Falkland Islands (U.K.)
Stanley
Tierra del Fuego
Ushuaia
Cape Horn
Strait of Magellan
Drake Passage
South Shetland Islands
South Orkney Islands
ANTARCTICA

Galápagos Islands (Ecuador)
Desventurados (Chile)
Islas Juan-Fernández (Chile)

P A C I F I C
O C E A N

A T L A N T I C
O C E A N

Bermuda (U.K.)
Tropic of Cancer
CAPE VERDE
Equator
Fernando de Noronha (Brazil)
Trindade
Martim Vaz (Brazil)
Tropic of Capricorn
South Georgia (U.K.)
South Sandwich Islands (U.K.)

1 : 70 000 000   0   700   1400   2100 km

Caribbe

70

4245 Netherla
Punta Antille
Gallinas Aruba (NL.)
Guajira Paraguar

GUATEMALA Guatemala
Esquintla
Santa Ana
San Salvador
EL SALVADOR
San Vicente San Miguel Cord. Isabella
HONDURAS Tegucigalpa
Choluteca
León Lago de Managua
NICARAGUA
Granada Lago de Bluefields
Nicaragua
Managua
San Carlos

Providencia
San Andrés

Banco
de Serrana
(Colombia)

Colombia

Gulf of
Venezuela

Santa Marta Riohacha
Ciénaga 5775 **Maracaibo**
Barranquilla Pico Cristóbal Cabimas
Colón 3750 Barquisi
Cartagena Lago de
Maracaibo
El Carmen Valera
El Banco Mérida 5002
Ocaña Pico Bolívar

COSTA RICA
Alajuela Heredia Limón
San José Cartago 3820
Nicoya Chirripó

Colón Gulf of
Panamá Darién Montería
La Palma Turbo Cúcuta
Bucaramanga San Cristóbal
PANAMA Barrancabermeja Arauca
David Chitré Gulf of Puerto
Santiago Azuero Panama **Medellín** Berrío
Coiba Punta Quibdó Nevado 5493
Mala del Cocuy

Nevado
d. Tolima Tunja Yopal
Manizales 5215 **Bogotá**
Pereira Armenia Ibagué Villavicencio
Buenaventura Tuluá 4560 Orocué
Palmira **COLOMBIA**
Cali 5750 Neiva
Nevado San José
Popayán del Huila Florencia del Guaviare
Tumaco Mocoa Miraflores Mitú
Pasto Puerto Asís
Esmeraldas San Lorenzo Ipiales
Punta Galera Ibarra Lérida
5790 Araracuara Apaporis
Quito Cayambe
5897 Nuevo Caquetá
Manta Portoviejo Cotopaxi Rocafuerte Putumayo La Peo
6310 Ambato Pebas
Chimborazo Riobamba
Guayaquil Macas Iquitos Letici
La Puntilla Santa **ECUADOR**
Golfo de Elena Cuenca
Guayaquil Machala Marañón
Tumbes Loja Zamora Borja
Talara Sullana 3034 Yurimaguas Eiru
Punta Chulucanas Jaén **Bagua**
Pariñas Piura Chachapoyas Orellana Cruzeiro
Punta Desierto do Sul
Aguja de Sechura Tarapoto Tarauacá
Chiclayo Cajamarca Pucallpa
Pacasmayo Juanjuí Acr
Puerto **CHAN** Tingo
Chicama **CHAN** María
Trujillo 6768
Huascarán
Chimbote Huaraz
6601 Huarmey Huánuco
Cerro de Pasco
Huacho Huancayo
Callao **MACHU**
Lima Huancavelica **PICCHU** PISAC
Ayacucho
Chincha Alta Salcantay 6271 Cuzco 6384
Pisco Abancay Ausangate
Punta Ica **PERU** Sicuan
Carreta Puquio
Nazca Cofupuna
6425 Chachani Juli
San Juan 6075!
Yauca Arequipa
Puerto
Chala Camaná Mollendo
6865 Ilo
Golfo
de Arica
Tac

PACIFIC
OCEAN

Cocos Ridge

Cocos Island
(Costa Rica)

Malpelo
(Colombia)

3901

1790

Carnegie Ridge

San Salvador
San Cristóbal
Isabela
Santa Cruz
Galápagos Islands
(Ecuador)

4146

Peru-Chile Trench

Panama Canal
Isthmus
of Panama
Gulf of
Panama

Golfo de los
Mosquitos

Colombia
Basin

Coco
Central
Cordillera Occidental
Cordillera Central
Cordillera Oriental
Sierra de Perijá
Sierra de la Macarena
La Montaña
Cord. de la Costa
Cord. Occidental
Cord. Central
Marañón
Huallaga
Ucayali
Napo
Negro

90° 80°

10°

0°

10°

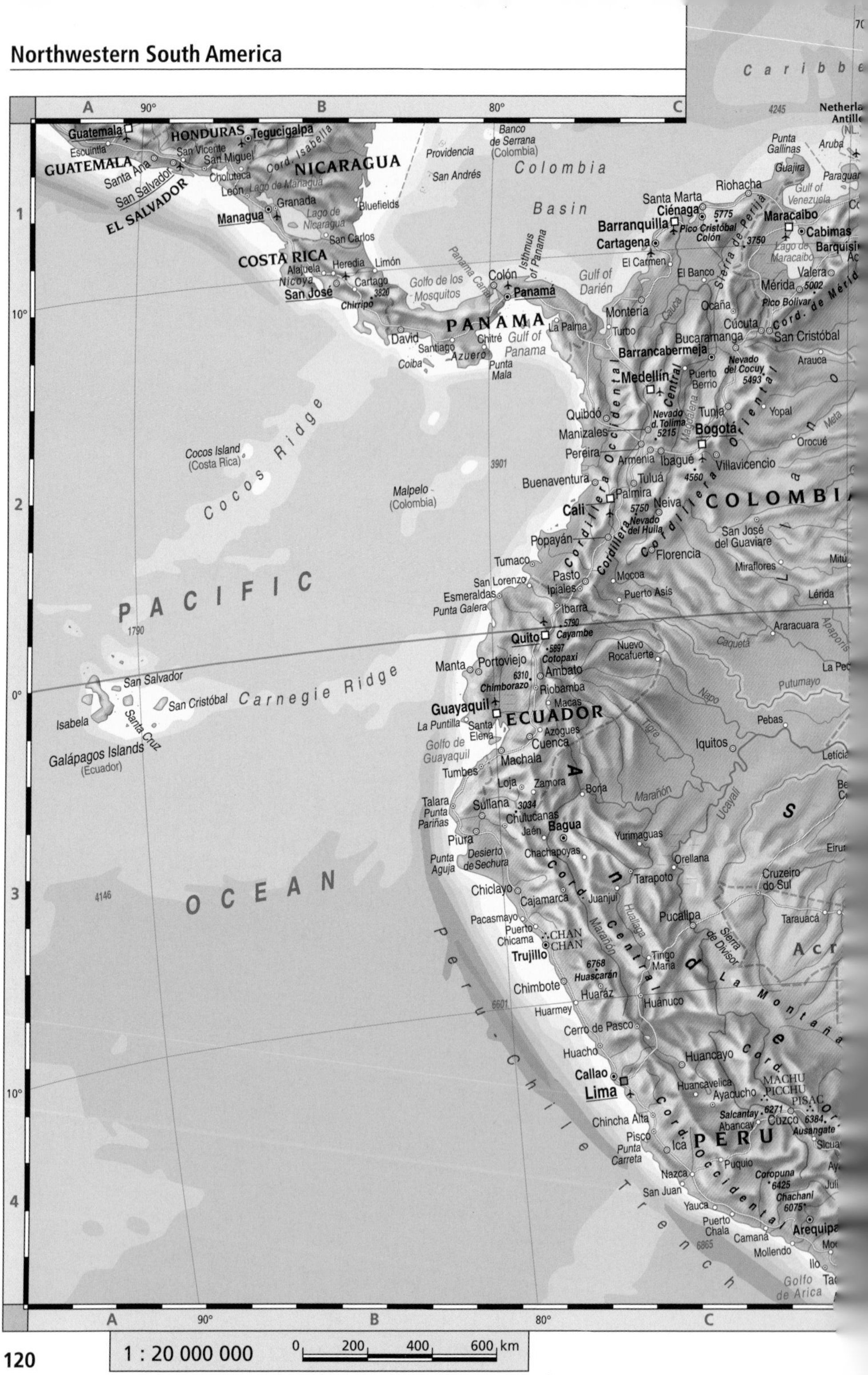

1 : 20 000 000

0 200 400 600 km

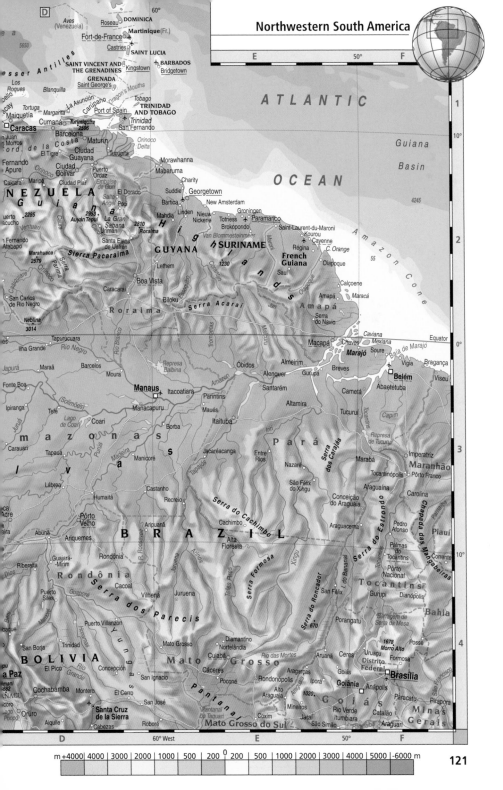

ATLANTIC

OCEAN

Guiana
Basin

4245

VENEZUELA

Aves
(Venezuela)
Roseau
DOMINICA
Fort-de-France
Martinique(Fr.)
Castries
SAINT LUCIA
**SAINT VINCENT AND
THE GRENADINES**
Kingstown
GRENADA
Saint George's
BARBADOS
Bridgetown

Los
Roques
Blanquilla
La Asunción
Tobago
**TRINIDAD
AND TOBAGO**
Margarita
Port of Spain
Trinidad
San Fernando

Maiquetía
Tortuga
Carúpano
Dragon's Mouths
Caracas
Cumaná
Turimiquire
2596
Barcelona
Maturín

El Tigre
Ciudad
Guayana
Orinoco
Delta
Tucupita

Ciudad
Bolívar
Puerto
Ordaz
Mabaruma
Morawhanna

Ciudad Piar
Embalse
de Guri
Charity

Caicara
Marisa
El Dorado
Suddie
Georgetown

Salto
Angel
Pao
Bártica
New Amsterdam
2285
2953
Auyán Tepui
La Gran
Sabana
2810
Roraima
Mahdia
Linden
Groningen
Nickerie
Totness
Paramaribo
Brokopondo

Santa Elena
de Uairén
Uirman
GUYANA
Van Blommesteinmeer
Saint-Laurent-du-Maroni

Marahuaca
2579
Sierra Pacaraima
Santa Elena
de Uairén
SURINAME
1230
Régina
Kourou
Cayenne
C. Orange

San Carlos
de Río Negro
Lethem
Saül
**French
Guiana**
Olapoque
55

Neblina
3014
Caracaraí
Biloku
Serra Acaraí
Amapá
Maracá

Tapurucuara
Iha Grande
Río Negro
Óbidos
Almeirim
Caviana
Mexiana
Equator
0°

Maraã
Barcelos
Moura
Represa
Balbina
Alenquer
Gurupá
Breves
Belém
Braganca
Viseu

Fonte Boa
Manaus
Itacoatiara
Parintins
Santarém
Cametá
Abaetetuba

Tefé
(Solimões)
Manacapuru
Maués
Altamira
Tucuruí
Capim

Coari
Borba
Itaituba
Imperatriz
Carauari
Tapauá
Maniçoré
Jacaréacanga
Entre
Rios
Pará
Serra
dos Carajás
Marabá
Maranhão
Pôrto
Franco

Lábrea
Castanho
Nazaré
São Félix
do Xingu
Tocantinópolis
Carolina

Humaitá
Recreio
Cachimbo
Conceição
do Araguaia
Araguaína
Piauí

Pôrto
Velho
Aripuanã
Alta
Floresta
Araguacema
Pedro
Afonso
Chapada das Mangabeiras

Abunã
Ariquemes
BRAZIL
Palmas
do
Tocantins
Corrente
10°

Riberalta
Guajará-
Mirim
Rondônia
Serra Formosa
Pôrto
Nacional
Tocantins

Puerto
Siles
Cacoal
Vilhena
Juruena
San Félix
Gurupi
Dianópolis
Bahía

Puerto Villanzon
Serra dos Parecis
670
Porangatu
Barragem de
Serra da Mesa

San Borja
Trinidad
Mato Grosso
Diamantino
Nortelândia
Aruanã
Ceres
1678
Morro Alto
Uruaçu
Posse

BOLIVIA
El Pico
Concepción
Mato Grosso
Cuiabá
Rio das Mortes
Aragarças
Goiás
**Distrito
Federal**
Formosa
São Francisco

a Paz
San Ignacio
Poconé
Rondonópolis
Iporá
Alto
Araguaia
1020
Goiânia
Brasília
Anápolis
Paracatu
Pirapora

Cochabamba
Montero
El Cerro
San José
Minéiros
Rio Verde
Jataí
Itumbiara
Catalão
Goiás
**Minas
Gerais**

Oruro
Aiquile
Roboré
Coxim
São Simão
Araguari

**Santa Cruz
de la Sierra**
Cabezas
Pantanal
da Taquari
Mato Grosso do Sul

60°
60° West
50°

m +4000 | 4000 | 3000 | 2000 | 1000 | 500 | 200 | 0 | 200 | 500 | 1000 | 2000 | 3000 | 4000 | 5000 | -6000 m

121

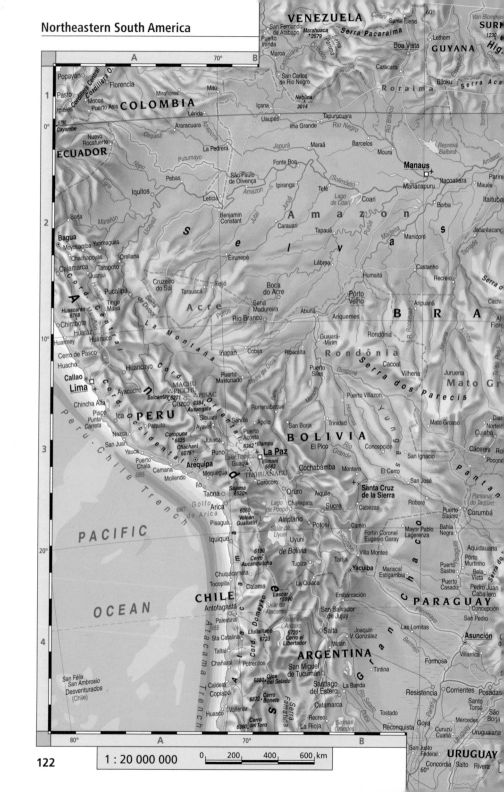

PACIFIC

OCEAN

122

1 : 20 000 000   0 200 400 600 km

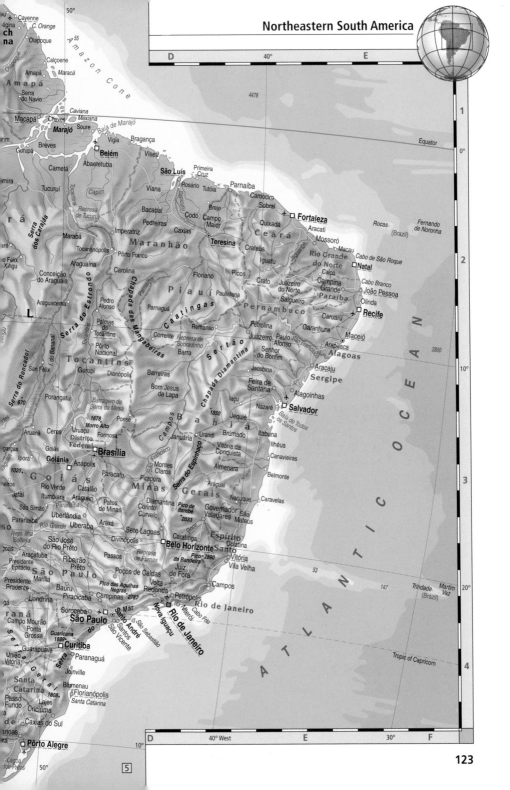

D 40° E

50°
u
égina C. Orange
ch na
Olapoque
Cayenne
55
Calçoene
A m a z o n Cone
Amapá Maracá
A m a p á
Serra
do Navio
Caviana
4478
Macapá Chaves Mexiana
Soure
Marajó
Bala de Marajó
rim Vigia Bragança
Gurupá Breves
Viseu
Belém
Cametá Abaetetuba
mira Tucuruí
São Luís
Primeira
Cruz
Viana Rosário Tutóia
Parnaíba
Capim
Camocim
Sobral
Bacabal
Brejo
Codó Campo
Pedreiras Maior
Caxias
Represa
de Tucuruí
Serra
dos Carajás
Marabá Imperatriz
Tocantinópolis
M a r a n h ã o
Teresina
Pôrto Franco
Araguaína
Carolina
Conceição
do Araguaia
Pedro
Afonso
Araguacema
L
Palmas
do
Tocantins
Pôrto
Nacional
San Félix
Gurupi
Serra do Roncador
670
Porangatu
1678
Morro Alto
Posse
Aruanã Ceres Uruaçu
garças Iporá Goiás
Distrito
Federal
Brasília
1020.
G o i á s
Golânia Anápolis
neiros Rio Verde Catalão
Jataí Itumbiara Araguari
São Simão Paracatu
Paranaíba Uberlândia Patos
de Minas
Repr. Ilha
Solteira Rio Grande Uberaba Araxá
oas São José
Araçatuba do Rio Prêto
Presidente
Epitácio
Presidente Marília
Prudente
S ã o P a u l o
Londrina Bauru
gá Piracicaba
raná Sorocaba
Campo Mourão
Ponta
Grossa
União
Vitória
Santa
Catarina
1808.
Passo
Fundo
a
d e
Caxias do Sul
anoas
ra
Pôrto Alegre
50°
Lagoa
dos Patos

Quixadá
Crateús
Iguatu
Floriano
Picos
Crato
P i a u í
Paulistana
Parnaguá
C a a t i n g a s
Corrente
Barra
Represa de
Sobradinho
Barreiras
Bom Jesus
da Lapa
Barragem de
Serra da Mesa
Dianópolis
Formosa
Januária
Montes
Claros
Pirapora
Diamantina Pico de
Corinto Itambé
Curvelo 2033
Sete Lagoas
Divinópolis
Belo Horizonte
Passos Pico 2890
da Bandeira
Poços de Caldas
Pico das Agulhas
Negras. Volta
Campinas 2787 Redonda
Santo André
Santos
São Vicente
Joinville
Blumenau
Florianópolis
Santa Catarina
Lajes
Criciúma

São Roque
Rio Grande
do Norte
Natal
Cabo Branco
João Pessoa
Olinda
Recife

P e r n a m b u c o
Salgueiro
Petrolina
Juàzeiro Paulo
Afonso
Senhor
do Bonfim
Jacobina
Feira de
Santana
Iaçu
1850
Jequié
Brúmado
Itabuna
Ilhéus
Canavieiras
Belmonte
Caravelas

Garanhuns
Caruaru
Maceió
Arapiaca
A l a g o a s
Aracaju
S e r g i p e
Alagoinhas
Nazaré
Salvador
Bala de Todos
os Santos

Fortaleza
Aracati
Mossoró
Macau
Cabo de São Roque
Caicó
Campina
Grande
Paraíba
Rocas.
(Brazil)
Fernando
de Noronha

4478

Equator 0°

1

2

2800

10°

3

Pico de
Itambé
Pico das
Agulhas
Negras

147
53
Trindade
(Brazil)
Martim
Vaz
20°

Tropic of Capricorn

A T L A N T I C O C E A N

D 40° West E 30° F

5

123

Cabo de São Roque

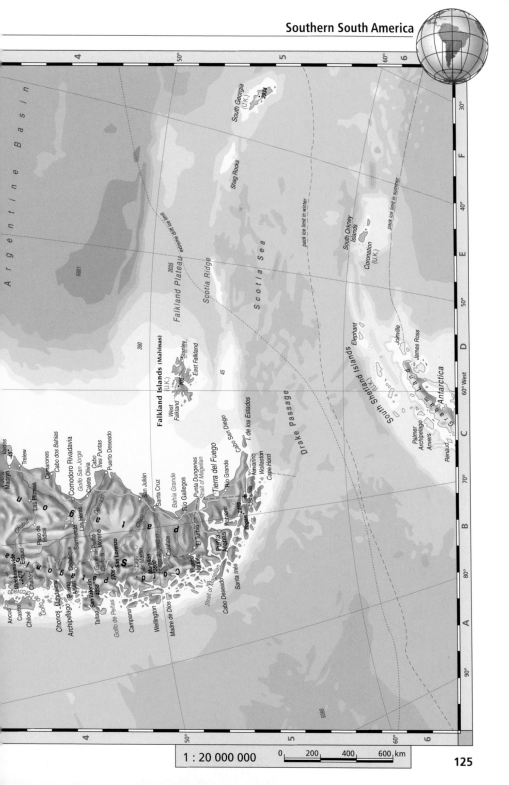

4   50°   5   60°   6

30°   F   40°   E   50°   D   60° West   C   70°   B   80°   A   90°

A r g e n t i n e   B a s i n

South Georgia (U.K.)
2934

Shag Rocks

S c o t i a   S e a

pack ice limit in winter

pack ice limit in summer

South Orkney Islands

Coronation (U.K.)

Falkland Plateau

6681

2025

Scotia Ridge

390

Falkland Islands (Malvinas) (U.K.)

West Falkland

Stanley

East Falkland

45

Elephant

Joinville

James Ross

South Shetland Islands (U.K.)

Antarctica

Palmer Archipelago

Anvers

Renaud

I. de los Estados

Cabo San Diego

D r a k e   p a s s a g e

Valdés

Matryn

Trelew

Camarones

Cabo dos Bahías

Comodoro Rivadavia

Golfo San Jorge

Caleta Olivia

Cabo Tres Puntas

Puerto Deseado

Las Plumas

San Julián

Santa Cruz

Bahía Grande

Río Gallegos

Punta Dungenes

Strait of Magellan

Tierra del Fuego

Río Grande

Ushuaia

Navarino

Wollaston

Cabo Horn

Chubut

Las Heras

Sarmiento

Paso de Indios

Esquel

Chaltén

Perito Moreno

Gobernador Gregores

Cobaique

Balmaceda

Coihaique

El Calafate

Lago Argentino

San Martín

Puerto Natales

Punta Arenas

Porvenir

Yaganes

Cabo San Diego

Santa Inés

Cabo Deseado

Strait of Magellan

Madre de Dios

Wellington

Campana

Golfo de Peñas

Chonos Archipelago

San Rafael

3706 San Lorenzo

4058

Murallón

1880

Taitao

San Martín

Golfo Corcovado

Chiloé

Castro

Ancud

Puerto Montt

Melchor

2470

5088

5088

1 : 20 000 000

0   200   400   600 km

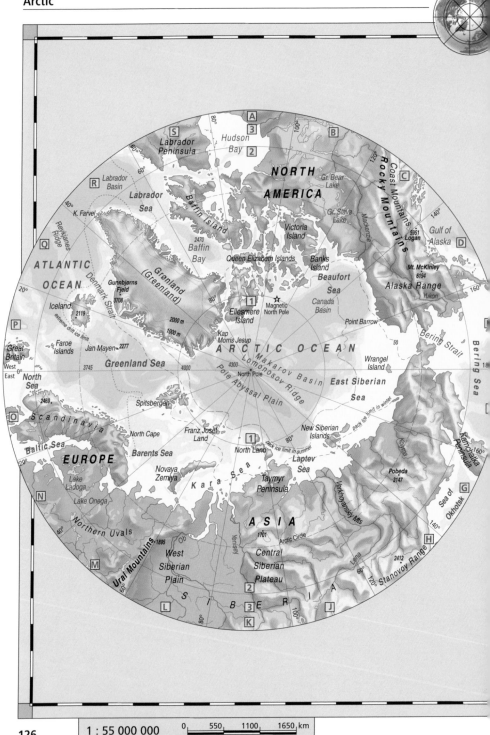

1 : 55 000 000

0 550 1100 1650 km

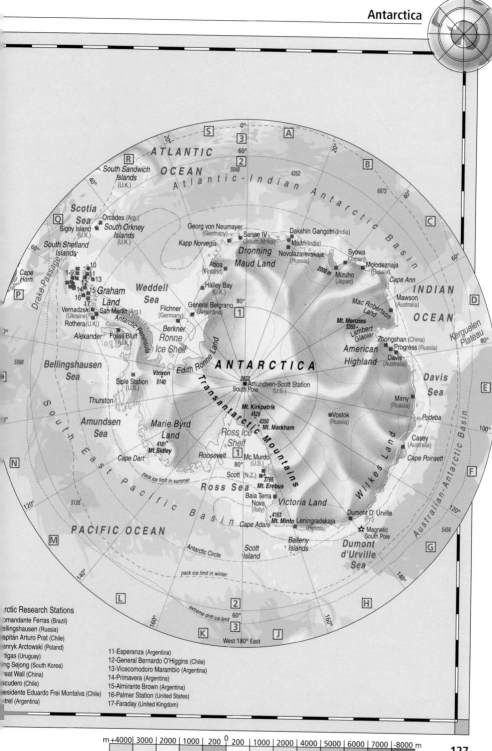

S
3
A
20°
0°
ATLANTIC
60°
20°
OCEAN
5048
2
B
4252
Atlantic-Indian *Antarctic* *Basin*
40°
6972
40°
C
South Sandwich
Islands
(U.K.)
R
Scotia
Sea
Q
Orcades (Arg.)
Signy Island
(U.K.)
South Orkney
Islands
(U.K.)
Georg von Neumayer
(Germany)
Sanae IV
(South Africa)
Dakshin Gangotri (India)
Maitri (India)
60°
South Shetland
Islands
Kapp Norvegia
Dronning
Maud Land
Novolazarevskaja
(Russia)
Syowa
(Japan)
Molodeznaja
(Russia)
INDIAN
Aboa
(Finland)
2000 m
Mizuho
(Japan)
Cape Ann
Cape
Horn
P
10
1-9
11
13
Graham
Land
Weddell
Sea
Halley Bay
(U.K.)
Mac Robertson
Land
Mawson
(Australia)
OCEAN
D
14
15
16
Vernadzskij
(Ukraine)
San Martin (Arg.)
Filchner
(Germany)
General Belgrano
(Argentina)
80°
Mt. Menzies
3355
Lambert
Glacier
Zhongshan (China)
Progress (Russia)
Kerguelen
Plateau
80°
60°
Rothera (U.K.)
Alexander
Fossil Bluff
(U.K.)
Antarctic Pen.
Berkner
Ronne
Ice Shelf
Edith Ronne Land
ANTARCTICA
American
Highland
Davis
(Australia)
Davis
Sea
E
5088
Bellingshausen
Sea
Vinson
5140
Siple Station
(U.S.)
2633
Amundsen-Scott Station
South Pole (U.S.)
Mirny
(Russia)
100°
Thurston
South East Pacific Basin
Amundsen
Sea
Marie Byrd
Land
Mt. Kirkpatrik
4528
4350
Mt. Markham
Vostok
(Russia)
Podeba
Casey
(Australia)
Cape Poinsett
F
N
4181
Mt.Sidley
Cape Dart
Ross Ice
Shelf
Roosevelt
Transantarctic Mountains
Wilkes Land
Australian-Antarctic Basin
5126
pack ice limit in summer
80°
Mc Murdo
(U.S.)
Scott (N.Z.)
3795
Mt. Erebus
120°
120°
PACIFIC OCEAN
M
Ross Sea
Baia Terra
Nova
(Italy)
Victoria Land
4163
Mt. Minto
Dumont D'Urville
(Fr.)
Magnetic
South Pole
5456
G
Leningradskaja
(Russia)
Antarctic Circle
Scott
Island
Balleny
Islands
Dumont
d'Urville
Sea
L
pack ice limit in winter
2
60°
H
140°
extreme drift ice limit
3
140°
160°
160°
K
J
West 180° East

Antarctic Research Stations
omandante Ferras (Brazil)
ellingshausen (Russia)
apitán Arturo Prat (Chile)
enryk Arctowski (Poland)
tigas (Uruguay)
ng Sejong (South Korea)
eat Wall (China)
scudero (Chile)
esidente Eduardo Frei Montalva (Chile)
trel (Argentina)

11-Esperanza (Argentina)
12-General Bernardo O'Higgins (Chile)
13-Vicecomodoro Marambio (Argentina)
14-Primavera (Argentina)
15-Almirante Brown (Argentina)
16-Palmer Station (United States)
17-Faraday (United Kingdom)

m +4000| 3000 | 2000 | 1000 | 200 0 200 | 1000 | 2000 | 4000 | 5000 | 6000 | 7000 |-8000 m

Our planet has experienced countless changes and transformations during its 4.5 billion year history. Natural climate shifts and the powerful forces of plate tectonics have repeatedly altered and continue to shape the topography, vegetation zones, and geology of the Earth.

The first human societies emerged around 10,000 years ago. Humanity has significantly altered the face of our planet in a relatively short period of time through agriculture and industrialization. Recent advances in technology have brought the many cultures of our planet closer together than ever before. Our world is now a global community with an incredible diversity of nations, cultures, religions, and ethnicities.

The World

**Thematic
maps**

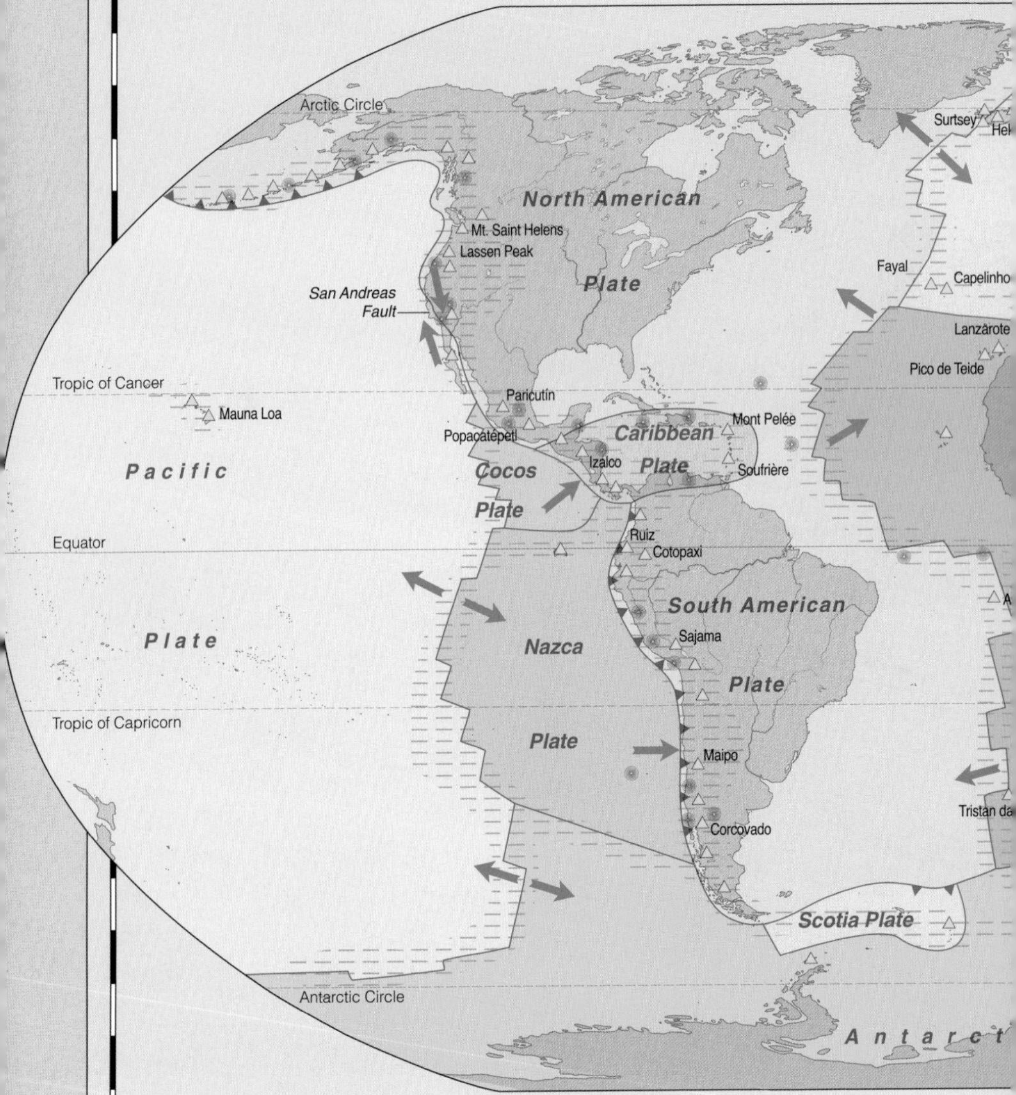

Arctic Circle

Surtsey
Hel

North American

Mt. Saint Helens
Lassen Peak

Plate

Fayal
Capelinho

San Andreas
Fault

Lanzàrote

Tropic of Cancer

Pico de Teide

Mauna Loa

Parícutin

Caribbean

Mont Pelée

Popacatépetl

Cocos

Izalco

Plate

Soufrière

P a c i f i c

Plate

Equator

Ruiz

Cotopaxi

South American

A

Nazca

Sajama

Plate

Plate

Tropic of Capricorn

Plate

Maipo

Tristán da

Corcovado

Scotia Plate

Antarctic Circle

A n t a r c t

VOLCANIC AND SEISMIC ACTIVITY

⌐_ Boundary between tectonic plates

▲▲▲ Ocean trench

1 : 120 000 000   0   1200   2400   3600 km

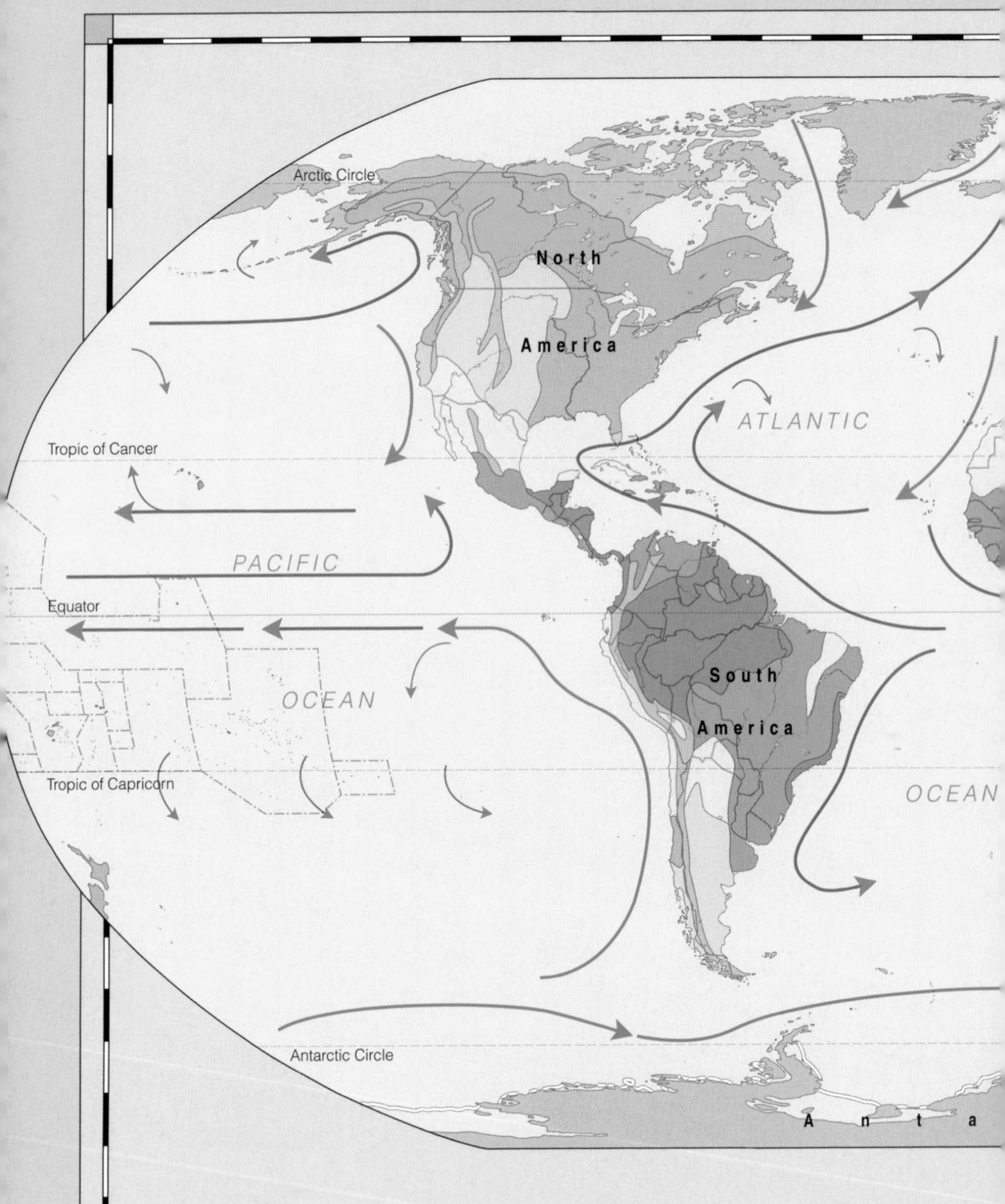

Arctic Circle

North

America

ATLANTIC

Tropic of Cancer

PACIFIC

Equator

OCEAN

South

America

Tropic of Capricorn

OCEAN

Antarctic Circle

A n t a

CLIMATE REGIONS

Polar regions, tundra and
cold mountainous areas

Semi-arid temperate re
(steppes, prairies)

Taiga, sub-arctic regions

Temperate regions
(deciduous and mixed f

1 : 120 000 000

0   1200   2400   3600 km

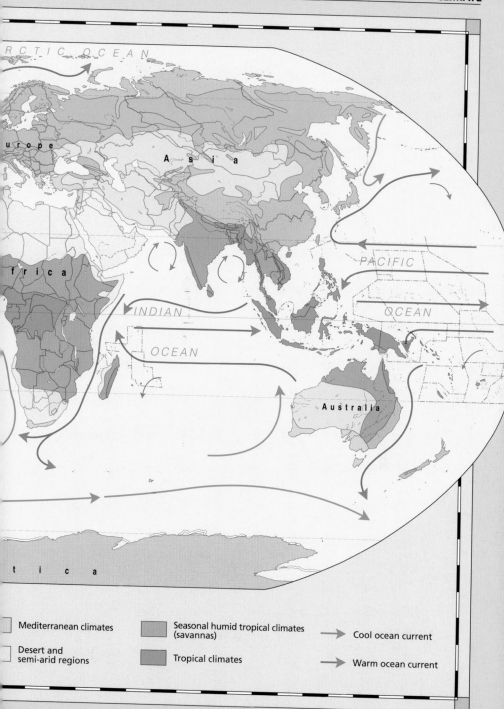

ARCTIC OCEAN

Europe

Asia

Africa

PACIFIC

INDIAN

OCEAN

OCEAN

Australia

Antarctica

| | Mediterranean climates | | Seasonal humid tropical climates (savannas) | → | Cool ocean current |
| | Desert and semi-arid regions | | Tropical climates | → | Warm ocean current |

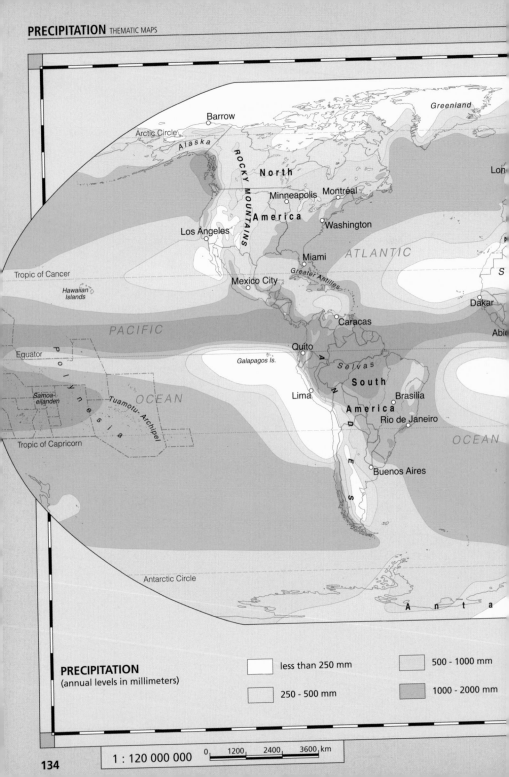

Barrow

Greenland

Arctic Circle

Alaska

ROCKY MOUNTAINS

North

Minneapolis Montréal

America

Washington

Los Angeles

Lon

ATLANTIC

Miami

Tropic of Cancer

Greater Antilles

Mexico City

S

*Hawaiian
Islands*

Dakar

PACIFIC

Caracas

Abi

Quito

Galapagos Is.

Selvas

Equator

P
o
l
y
n
e
s
i
a

A
N
D

South

Lima

America

Brasilia

OCEAN

Samoa-
eilanden

Tuamotu-Archipel

Rio de Janeiro

OCEAN

E
S

Tropic of Capricorn

Buenos Aires

Antarctic Circle

A   n   t   a

PRECIPITATION
(annual levels in millimeters)

less than 250 mm	500 - 1000 mm
250 - 500 mm	1000 - 2000 mm

1 : 120 000 000

0   1200   2400   3600 km

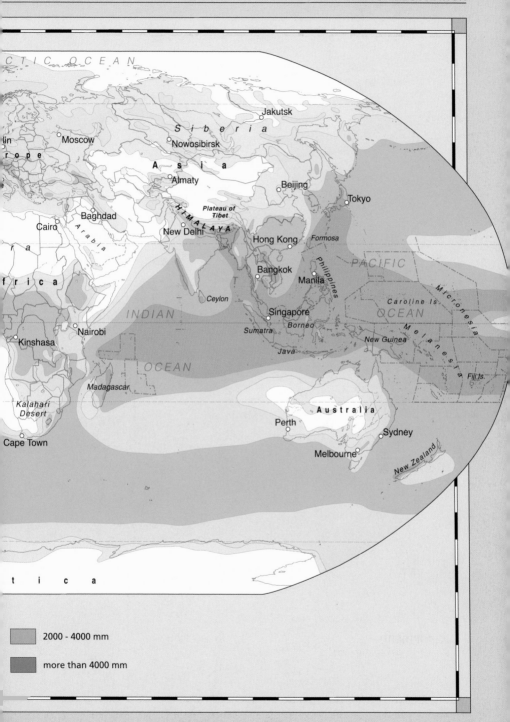

2000 - 4000 mm

more than 4000 mm

Arctic Circle

North

America

ATLANTIC

Tropic of Cancer

PACIFIC

Equator

OCEAN

South

America

Tropic of Capricorn

OCEAN

Antarctic Circle

A n t a

Legend:

	Polar regions		Sub-arctic forests (taiga)		Glasslands (prairies, steppe
	Tundra		Mixed forests		Desert
	Forested tundra		Deciduous forests		Mediterranean vegetation

1 : 120 000 000   0   1200   2400   3600 km

Subtropical forests

Tropical deserts

Humid savannah

Arid savannah

Tropical rainforests

Arctic Circle

North

America

ATLANTIC

Tropic of Cancer

PACIFIC

Equator

OCEAN

South

America

Tropic of Capricorn

OCEAN

Antarctic Circle

A n t a

INHABITANTS PER KM²

uninhabited

less than 1

1 - 10

10 - 50

1 : 120 000 000   0 1200 2400 3600 , km

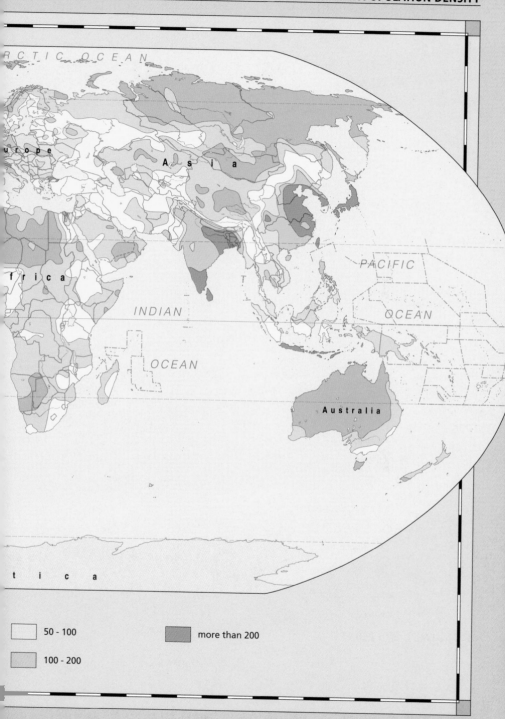

ARCTIC OCEAN

Europe

Asia

Africa

INDIAN

OCEAN

PACIFIC

OCEAN

Australia

tica

50 - 100	more than 200
100 - 200	

Arctic Circle

North

America

ATLANTIC

Tropic of Cancer

PACIFIC

Equator

OCEAN

South

America

OCEAN

Tropic of Capricorn

Antarctic Circle

A   n   t   a

	less than 45 years		50 - 60 yea
	45 - 50 years		60 - 70 yea

1 : 120 000 000   0   1200   2400   3600   km

C T I C   O C E A N

r o p e

A   s   i   a

PACIFIC

r i c a

INDIAN

OCEAN

OCEAN

Australia

t   i   c   a

70 - 75 years

more than 75 years

Arctic Circle

North

America

ATLANTIC

Tropic of Cancer

PACIFIC

Equator

OCEAN

South

America

OCEAN

Tropic of Capricorn

Antarctic Circle

A n t a

GDP per capita
(Purchasing Power Parity)
in US dollars

less than 500$

1,000 - 2,500$

500 - 1,000$

2,500 - 5,000$

1 : 120 000 000

0 1200 2400 3600 km

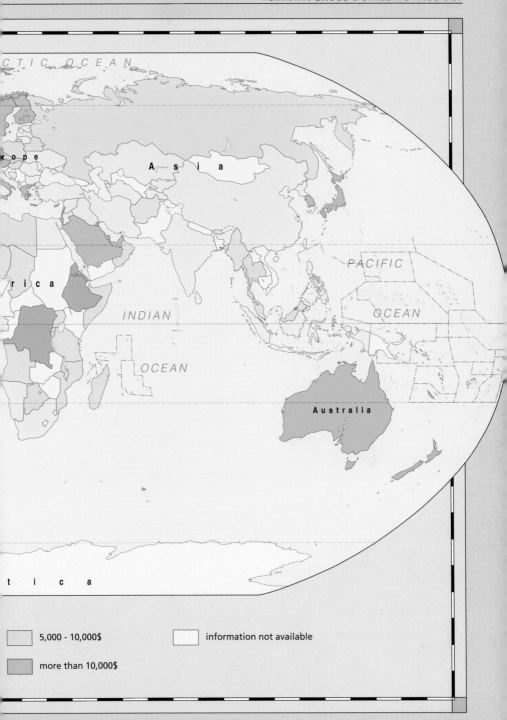

CTIC OCEAN

rope

A s i a

PACIFIC

rica

OCEAN

INDIAN

OCEAN

Australia

t i c a

| | 5,000 - 10,000$ | | | information not available |

more than 10,000$

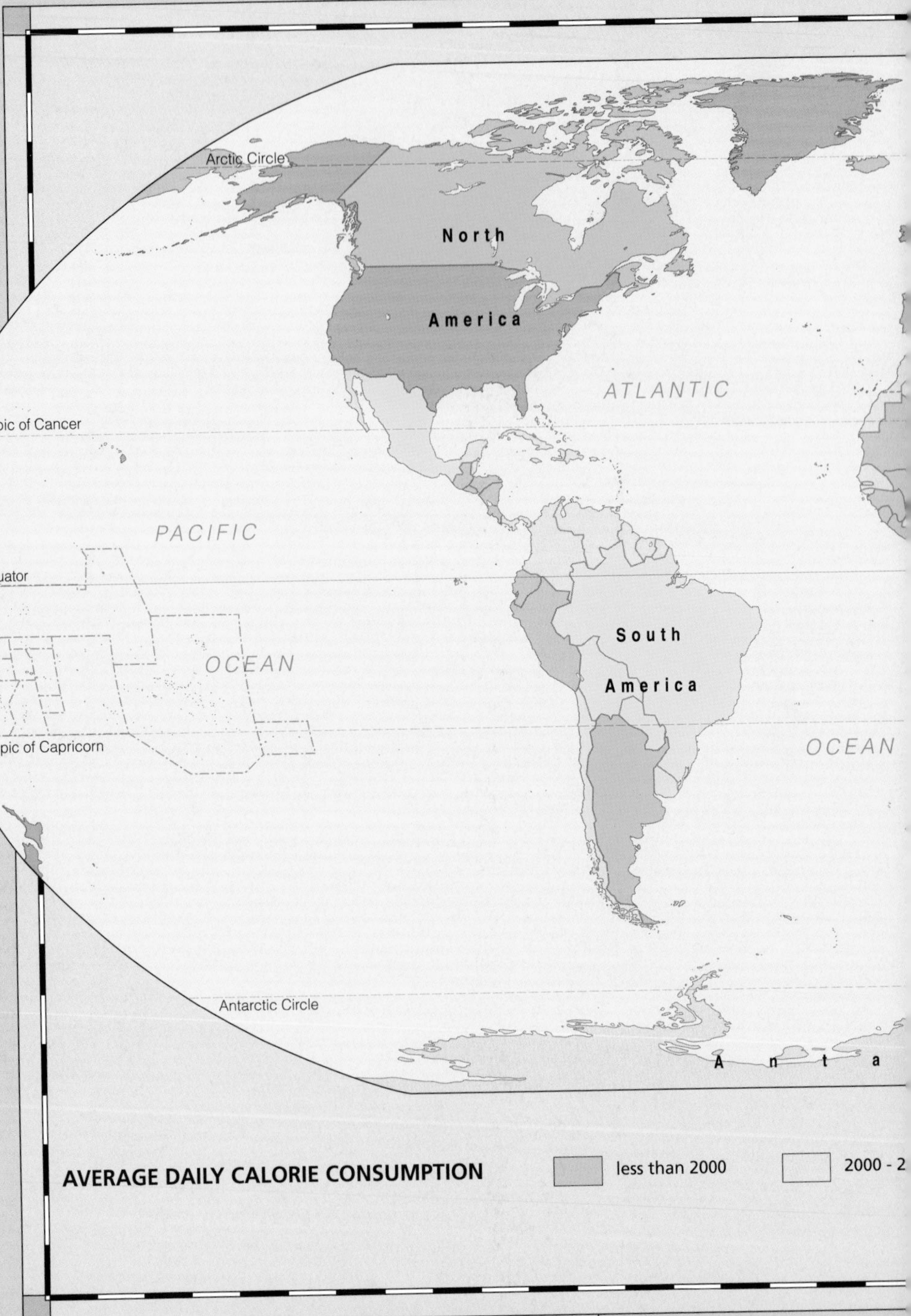

Arctic Circle

North

America

ATLANTIC

Tropic of Cancer

PACIFIC

Equator

OCEAN

South

America

OCEAN

Tropic of Capricorn

Antarctic Circle

A   n   t   a

AVERAGE DAILY CALORIE CONSUMPTION

less than 2000

2000 - 2

1 : 120 000 000   0   1200   2400   3600 km

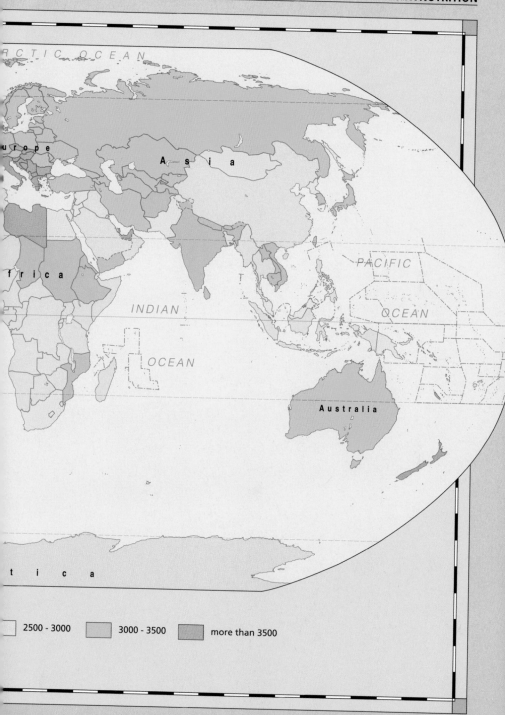

ARCTIC OCEAN

Europe

Asia

Africa

INDIAN

OCEAN

PACIFIC

OCEAN

Australia

t   i   c   a

| | 2500 - 3000 | | 3000 - 3500 | | more than 3500 |

Arctic Circle

E s k i m o

Aleut

French

E n g l i s h

ATLANTIC

Tropic of Cancer

S p a n i s h

Mayan

S p a n i s h

Port

Man

PACIFIC

Dutch

French

Equator

Quechua

Tupi

OCEAN

Spanish

Quechua

Portuguese

Guarani

Tropic of Capricorn

OCEAN

S p a n i s h

Araucanian

Antarctic Circle

	Sino-Tibetan		Austronesian		Amerindi
	Altaic-Uralic		Afro-Asiatic		Isolated language
	Niger-Congo		Dravidian		Uninhabit regions

1 : 120 000 000

0   1200   2400   3600   km

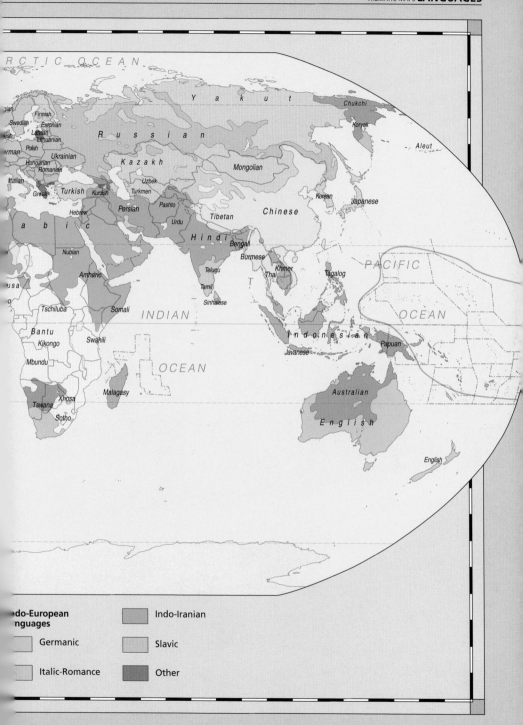

ARCTIC OCEAN

Yakut

Chukchi

Koryak

Aleut

Finnish
Swedish Estonian
Latvian
Lithuanian
Polish
Ukrainian
Hungarian
Romanian

Russian

Kazakh

Mongolian

Italian

Greek Turkish Kurdish
Uzbek
Turkmen
Hebrew Persian Pashto
Urdu

Korean Japanese

Chinese

Tibetan

arabic

Nubian

Hindi
Bengali
Burmese

PACIFIC

Amharic

Telugu
Tamil

Khmer
Thai

Tagalog

usa

OCEAN

Tschiluba

Sinhalese

INDIAN

Bantu
Kikongo

Swahili

Indonesian

Papuan

Somali

Mbundu

OCEAN

Javanese

Malagasy

Xhosa
Tswana
Sotho

Australian

English

English

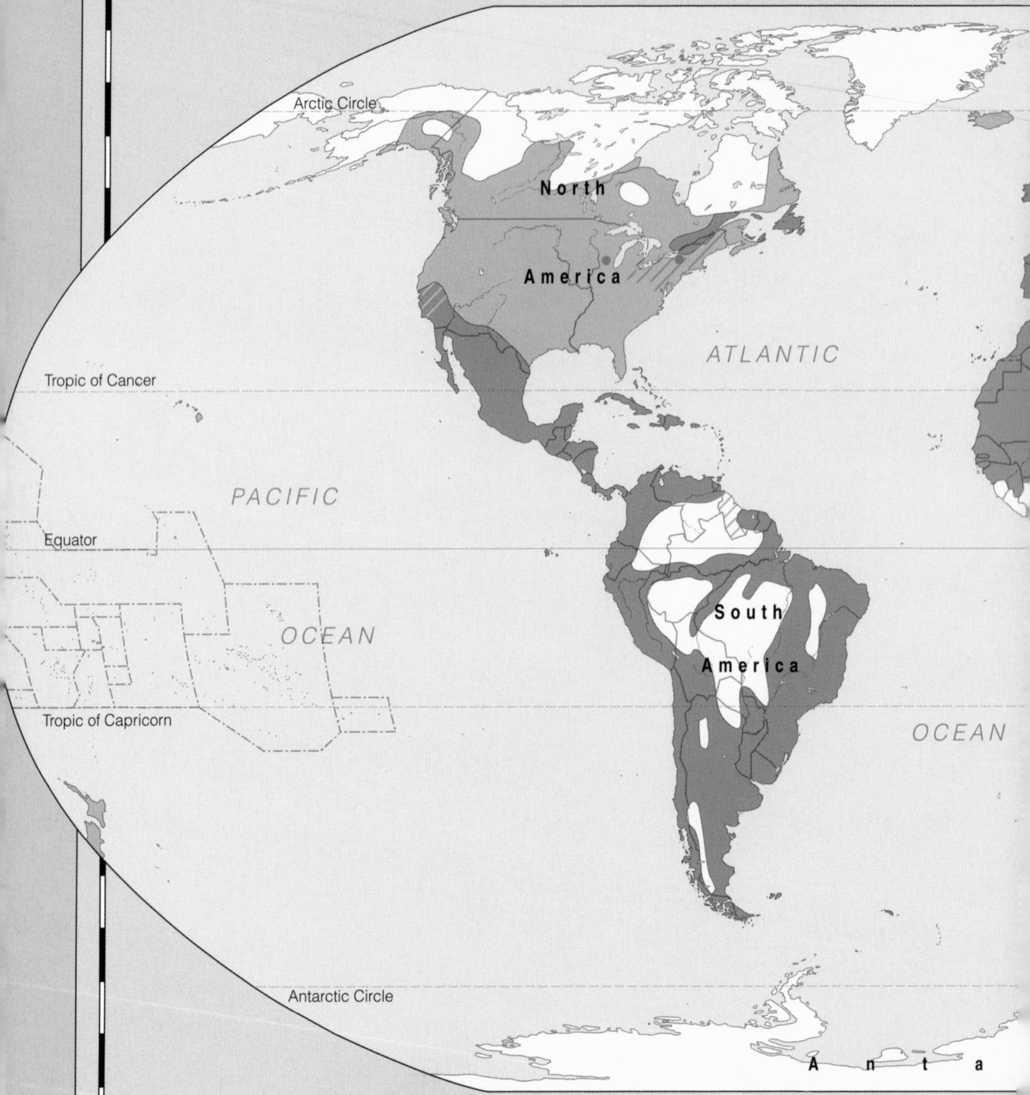

Arctic Circle

North

America

ATLANTIC

Tropic of Cancer

PACIFIC

Equator

OCEAN

OCEAN

South

America

Tropic of Capricorn

Antarctic Circle

A   n   t   a

Christianity

▇ Roman Catholic		▇ Orthodox		
▇ Protestant		▇ Coptic		

Islam

▇ Sunni

▇ Shiite

1 : 120 000 000

0   1200   2400   3600 km

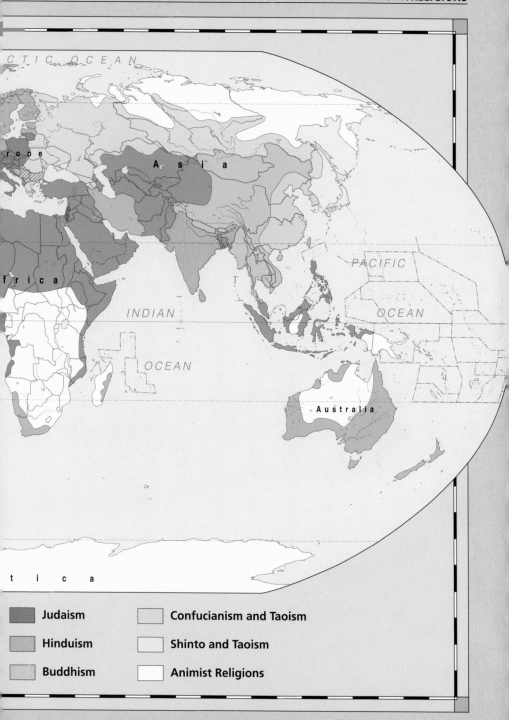

Judaism		Confucianism and Taoism	
Hinduism		Shinto and Taoism	
Buddhism		Animist Religions	

Barrow
Mackenzie
Delta
Arctic Circle
Yukon
Uranium City Ⓤ
Alberta
Montana
Michigan Ⓤ
Nova
Scotia
California
Utah Ⓤ
Appalachian Mountains
Arizona Ⓤ
Texas
Gulf of
Mexico
ATLANTIC
Tampico
Poza Rica
Tabasco
Maracaibo
Maturín
Colombia
Orito
Carmen
Potiguar
Lobitos
Corrientes
Xaréu
Nova Olinda
Perù
Salvador
Santa Cruz
Pocos
de Caldas Ⓤ
Rio Grande
Campo
Durán
Tibagi
Pargo
Neuquen Ⓤ
Commodoro
Rivadavia
Tierra del Fuego
Antarctic Circle

PACIFIC

OCEAN

OCEAN

Tropic of Cancer

Equator

Tropic of Capricorn

Ⓤ

Wa

Ⓤ

Bo

In

ENERGY INDUSTRY

Anthracite

Petroleum

Natural gas

Ⓤ Uranium

1 : 120 000 000

0   1200   2400   3600 km

RCTIC OCEAN

Timan'-
-Pecora
Taymyr

Central
Siberia

Anadyr

Moscow
Basin

Third
Baku

Surgut

Zyryanka

Poland

Kamchatka
Peninsula

Silesia
Krivyj Rih
Donbass
Dzhetygara

Kuzbass

Jakutsk

Irkutsk

Sakhalin

Ruhr

Bucharest
Kerč
Krasnodar
Emba

Ürümqi

Bureya

Italy
Yumurtalik
Baku

Anda

Albania

Al-Mawsil
Fergana
Valley

Yumen

Tianjin

Niigata

Tunisia

Kirkuk
Satlik

Shanxi

Iraq
Bozorgan

Makarwal

Sichuan

Kuwait
Ras
Ghanb
Ghawar
Qeshm

Guizhou

Shanghai

Edjeleh

Sui

Hunan

Arlit

Asab
Oman

Balaghat
Bangladesh
Bose

Lake Chad

Yemen

Bombay

Godavari
Chauk

PACIFIC

ger
lta

Abu Gabra
Bakouma

Gulf of
Thailand
Labuan

OCEAN

Gabon

Brunei

INDIAN

Emeraude
Kalemie

Minas
Jambi

Samarinda
Sorong

Papua
New Guinea

unza

Zambia

Sulawesi

Maamba
Pande

Java

Timor

OCEAN

Rum
Jungle

sing

Molepolole

Madagascar

Rankin

Mary Kathleen
Blair athol

Kimberley

Palm Valley

Brisbane

South Africa

Moonie

Gingin

Broken Hill

Gippsland
Shelf

Satlik · Surgut · Dzhetygara · Kuzbass · Irkutsk

■ Hydropower plants

Arctic Circle

Kimberley

Labrador

Sudbury

Arizona

Tropic of Cancer

Mulberry

ATLANTIC

Guanajuato

Jamaica

Cerro Bolívar

PACIFIC

Nimba Ra

Equator

Gu

OCEAN

Cerro
de Pasco

Itabira

Oruro,
Potosí

OCEAN

Tropic of Capricorn

Antarctic Circle

MINERAL RESOURCES

(Al) Bauxite	(K) Potassium	(Pt) Platinum
(PZ) Lead, Zinc	(Cu) Copper	(Ag) Silver
(Cr) Chromium	(Mn) Manganese	(W) Tungsten
(Fe) Iron	(Ni) Nickel	(Sn) Tin
(Au) Gold	(P) Phosphate	⬡ Diamond

1 : 120 000 000   0   1200   2400   3600 km

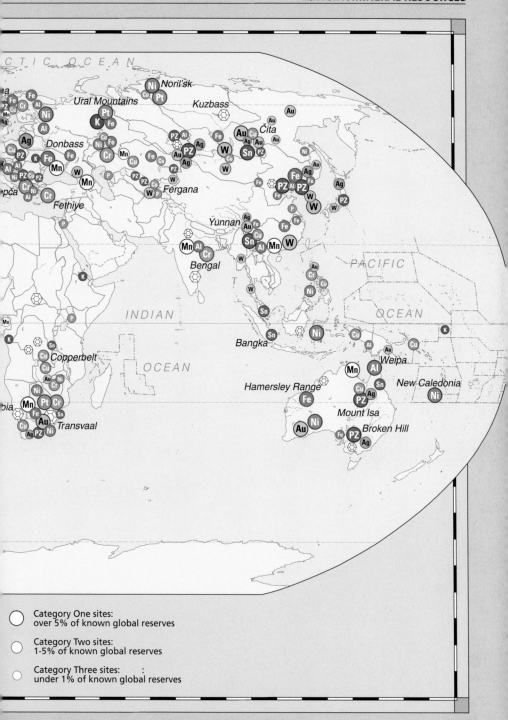

Category One sites:
over 5% of known global reserves

Category Two sites:
1-5% of known global reserves

Category Three sites: :
under 1% of known global reserves

Arctic Circle

North

America

ATLANTIC

Tropic of Cancer

PACIFIC

Equator

OCEAN

South

America

Tropic of Capricorn

OCEAN

Antarctic Circle

A   n   t   a

LAND USE

Semi-nomadic land use. Hunting and fishing

Nomadic livestock herding

Subsistence farming and livestock herding

Advanced large scale farmi and livestock herding

1 : 120 000 000   0   1200   2400   3600 km

ARCTIC OCEAN

Europe

Asia

Africa

PACIFIC

INDIAN

OCEAN

OCEAN

Australia

tica

Subsistence farming

Plantation farming

Uninhabited regions

Large scale farming and livestock herding

Forestry

Arctic Circle

Edmonton

Vancouver
Winnipeg
Montréal

Seattle

Chicago

San Francisco

New York

Los Angeles

Dallas

Atlanta

Casablar

New Orleans

ATLANTIC

Tropic of Cancer

Dakar

Mexico City

Caracas

PACIFIC

Bogotá

Equator

Lima

OCEAN

Belo Horizonte

Rio de Janeiro

São Paulo

OCEAN

Tropic of Capricorn

Santiago

Montevideo

Buenos Aires

Antarctic Circle

IMPORTANT TRADE ROUTES

Significant industrial areas

Important routes
industrial goods

1 : 120 000 000   0 1200 2400 3600 km

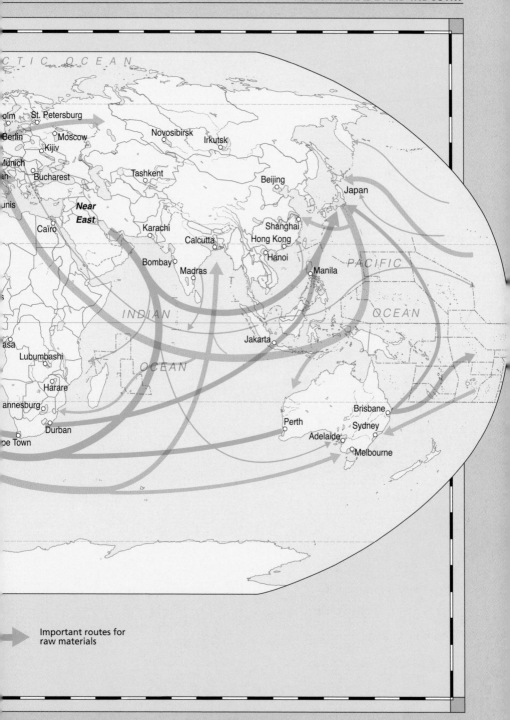

Important routes for
raw materials

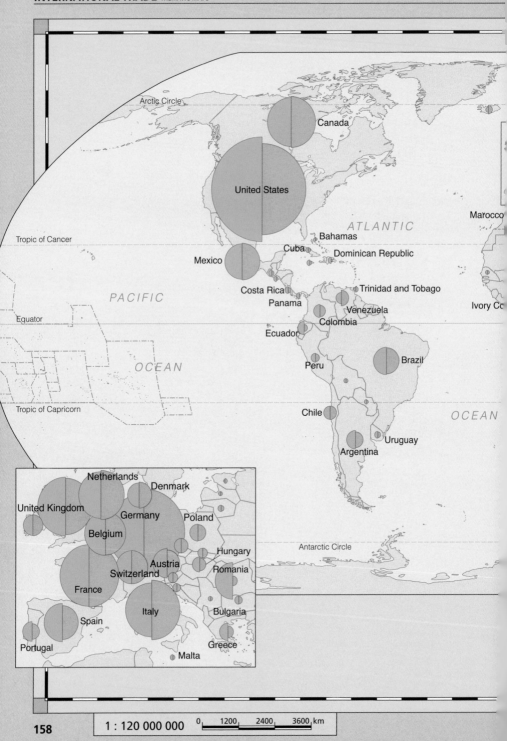

Arctic Circle

Canada

United States

Marocco

ATLANTIC

Tropic of Cancer

Bahamas

Cuba

Dominican Republic

Mexico

Costa Rica

Trinidad and Tobago

PACIFIC

Panama

Venezuela

Ivory Co

Colombia

Equator

Ecuador

OCEAN

Peru

Brazil

Tropic of Capricorn

Chile

OCEAN

Uruguay

Argentina

Netherlands

Denmark

United Kingdom

Germany

Poland

Belgium

Hungary

Antarctic Circle

Austria

Romania

Switzerland

France

Italy

Bulgaria

Spain

Portugal

Greece

Malta

1 : 120 000 000

0   1200   2400   3600 km

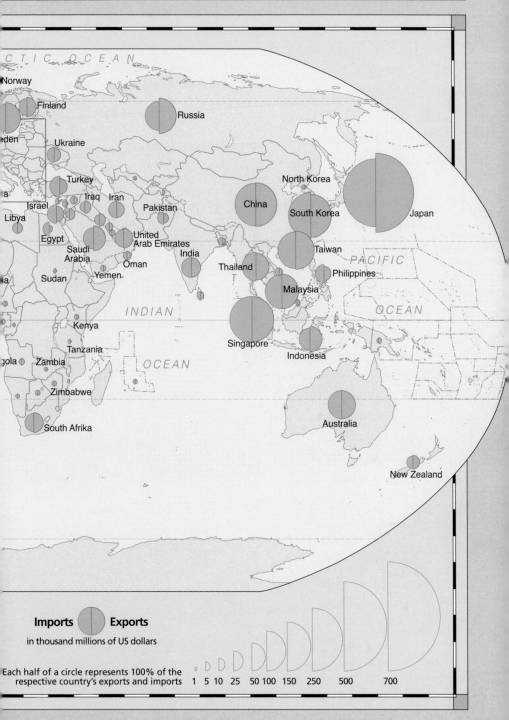

Imports ⬤ Exports
in thousand millions of US dollars

Each half of a circle represents 100% of the
respective country's exports and imports   1 5 10 25 50 100 150 250   500   700

There were 194 sovereign nations on six continents at the start of the 21st century. During the 20th century, the political makeup of our planet changed frequently and the borders of many nations were redrawn. Two world wars, the end of European colonialism, and the decline of communism lead to the creation and collapse of numerous nations and political entities.

Although most of Africa was under the control of European powers at the start of the 20th century, it is now the continent with the most states; 54. Asia is only slightly behind Africa with 47 states and is followed by Europe (44), North America (23), Australia/Oceania (14), and South America (12). Inhospitable Antarctica is the only "stateless" continent.

Nations of
the world

Facts and figures

Andorra
Andorra

Location: Southwestern Europe
Area: 467.7 sq km
Highest Point: Coma Pedrosa (2,946 m)
Capital: Andorra la Vella
Government: Parliamentary princedom
Administrative Divisions: 7 parishes
Population: 69,900
Ethnic Groups: Spaniards (50%),
Catalonians (29%), French (8%),
Portuguese (7%) Britons (2%)
Languages: Catalan (official), Spanish,
French
Religion: Catholics (94%)
Literacy Rate: 99%
GDP per capita: 19,000 US$
Currency: 1 euro = 100 cents

Belarus
Belarus

Location: Eastern Europe
Area: 207,600 sq km
Important Rivers: Dnjepr, Pripjat
Capital: Minsk
Government: Republic
Administrative Divisions: 6 regions and
1 special municipality (Minsk)
Population: 10.3 million
Ethnic Groups: Belarusians (78%),
Russians (13%), Poles (4%),
Ukrainians (3%)
Languages: Belarusian (official),Russian
Religion: Russian-Orthodox (60%),
Catholics (8%)
Literacy Rate: 98%
GDP per capita: 6,000 US$
Currency: 1 belarusian ruble =
100 kopecks

België/Belgique
Belgium

Location: Western Europe
Area: 30,528 sq km
Important Rivers: Schelde, Maas
Capital: Brussels
Government: Parliamentary monarchy
Administrative Divisions: 3 regions and
10 provinces
Population: 10.3 million
Ethnic Groups: Flemish (58%),
Wallonian (32%)
Languages: French, Dutch, German
Religion: Catholic (88%)
Literacy Rate: 99%
GDP per capita: 29,000 US$
Currency: 1 euro = 100 cents

Bosna i Hercegovina
Bosnia and Herzegovina

Location: Southeastern Europe
Area: 52,129 sq km
Capital: Sarajevo
Government: Republic
Population: 4 million
Languages: Bosnian, Serbian, Croatian
Religion: Muslims (44%),
Serbian-Orthodox (31%), Catholics (17%)
Literacy Rate: 86%
GDP per capita: 6,100 US$
Currency: 1 marka

Bŭlgarija
Bulgaria

Location: Southeastern Europe
Area: 110,910 sq km
Highest Point: Musala (2,925 m)
Important Rivers: Danube, Iskar, Marica
Capital: Sofia
Government: Republic
Administrative Divisions: 8 regions,
1 district
Population: 7.5 million
Ethnic Groups: Bulgarians (85%),
Turks (9%), Roma (3%), Macedonians (3%)
Language: Bulgarian
Religion: Orthodox (87%), Muslims (13%)
Literacy Rate: 95%
GDP per capita: 7,600 US$
Currency: 1 lev = 100 stotinki

Ceská Republika
Czech Republic

Location: Central Europe
Area: 78,866 sq km
Important River: Elbe
Capital: Prague
Government: Republic
Administrative Divisions: 72 districts
Population: 10.2 million
Ethnic Groups: Czechs (94%),
Slovaks (4%)
Languages: Czech, Slovak
Religion: Catholics (39%), Protestants (3%),
Non-Denominational (40%)
Literacy: 99%
GDP per capita: 15,700 US$
Currency: 1 Czech koruna =
100 haleru

Città del Vaticano
Vatican City (Holy See)

Location: Rome, Italy (Southern Europe)
Area: 0.44 sq km

Capital: Vatican City
Government: Elected monarchy
Population: 920
Languages: Latin, Italian
Religion: Catholic (100%)
Currency: 1 euro = 100 cents

Danmark
Denmark

Location: Northern Europe
Area: 43,094 sq km;
Greenland 2.1 million sq km
Capital: Copenhagen
Government: Parliamentary monarchy
Administrative Divisions: 14 districts
External Territories: Faeroes, Greenland
Population: 5.4 million
Language: Danish
Religion: Lutherans (89%)
Literacy Rate: 99%
GDP per capita: 31,200 US$
Currency: 1 Danish krone = 100 Øre

Deutschland
Germany

Location: Central Europe
Area: 357,021 sq km
Highest Point: Zugspitze (2,962 m)
Important Rivers: Müritz, Elbe, Oder,
Rhine, Danube
Capital: Berlin
Government: Federal republic
Administrative Divisions: 16 federal
states
Population: 83.2 million
Ethnic Groups: Germans (91%),
Turks (2%), Yugoslavians (1%)
Language: German
Religion: Catholics (43%),
Protestants (33%), Muslims (2%)
Literacy Rate: 99%
GDP per capita: 27,600 US$
Currency: 1 euro = 100 cents

Eesti
Estonia

Location: Northeastern Europe
Area: 45,226 sq km
Capital: Tallinn
Government: Parliamentary republic
Administrative Divisions: 15 regions,
6 districts
Population: 1.3 million
Ethnic Groups: Estonians (65%),
Russians (28%), Ukrainians (2%),
Belarusians (1%), Finns (1%)
Languages: Estonian (official), Russian

Religion: Lutherans (60%),
Russian-Orthodox (5%)
Literacy Rate: 99%
GDP per capita: 12,300 US$
Currency: 1 Estonian krona = 100 senti

Eire/Ireland
Ireland

Location: Western Europe
Area: 70,280 sq km
Important River: Shannon
Capital: Dublin
Government: Parliamentary republic
Administrative Divisions: 26 counties
Population: 4 million
Languages: English, Gaellic
Religion: Catholics (88%),
Anglicans (3%)
Literacy: 99%
GDP per capita: 29,800 US$
Currency: 1 euro = 100 cents

Ellás (Hellás)
Greece

Location: Southeastern Europe
Area: 131,940 sq km
Highest Point: Mt. Olympia (2,917 m)
Capital: Athens
Government: Parliamentary republic
Administrative Divisions: 10 regions
Population: 10.6 million
Ethnic Groups: Greeks (96%),
Macedonians (4%)
Language: Modern Greek
Religion: Greek-Orthodox (97%),
Muslims (1%)
Literacy Rate: 94 %
GDP per capita: 19,900 US$
Currency: 1 euro = 100 cents

España
Spain

Location: Southwestern Europe
Area: 504,782 sq km
Highest Point: Mulhacén (3,478 m)
Important Rivers: Guadiana, Ebro,
Guadalquivir
Capital: Madrid
Government: Parliamentary monarchy
Administrative Divisions: 17 regions,
52 provinces
Population: 40.3 million
Ethnic Groups: Spanish (73%),
Catalonian (18%), Galician (6%),
Basques (2%)
Languages: Spanish (Castilian), Catalonian,
Basque, Galician

Religion: Catholics (96%)
Literacy Rate: 97%
GDP per capita: 22,000 US$
Currency: 1 euro = 100 cents

France
France

Location: Western Europe
Area: 547,030 sq km
Highest Point: Mont Blanc (4,807 m)
Important Rivers: Loire, Rhône, Seine,
Garonne
Capital: Paris
Government: Parliamentary republic
Administrative Divisions: 22 regions,
96 departments, 9 territories
External Territories: French Guiana,
Guadeloupe, Martinique, Réunion,
Mayotte, Saint Pierre and Miquelon,
French Polynesia, New Caledonia,
Wallis and Futuna
Population: 60.4 million
Ethnic Groups: French (94%),
Algerian (1%), Portuguese (1%),
Moroccan (1%)
Language: French
Religion: Catholics (80%),
Protestants (2%), Muslims (5%)
Literacy Rate: 99%
GDP per capita: 27,500 US$
Currency: 1 euro = 100 cents

Hrvatska
Croatia

Location: Southeastern Europe
Area: 56,542 sq km
Capital: Zagreb
Government: Republic
Administrative Divisions: 20 regions,
2 districts
Population: 4.5 million
Language: Croatian
Religion: Catholics (77%),
Orthodox (11%), Protestants (1%),
Muslims (1%)
Literacy Rates: 97%
GDP per capita: 10,700 US$
Currency: 1 kuna = 100 lipa

Ísland
Iceland

Location: Northern Europe
Area: 103,000 sq km
Highest Point: Oraefajökull (2,119 m)
Important Body of Water: Lake Myvatn
Capital: Reykjavik
Government: Republic

Administrative Divisions: 8 regions
Population: 294,000
Ethnic Groups: Icelandic (94%),
Danish (1%)
Language: Icelandic
Religion: Protestants (94%),
Catholics (1%)
Literacy Rate: 99%
GDP per capita: 30,900 US$
Currency: 1 Icelandic krone = 100 aurar

Italia
Italy

Location: Southern Europe
Area: 301,230 sq km
Highest Point: Monte Rosa (4,637 m)
Important Rivers/Bodies of Water: Po,
Arno, Tiber, Lago di Garda, Lago di Como
Capital: Rome
Government: Republic
Administrative Divisions: 20 regions,
95 provinces
Population: 58 million
Ethnic Groups: Italians (94%),
Sardinians (3%),
Language: Italian
Religion: Catholics (85%)
Literacy Rate: 97%
GDP per capita: 26,800 US$
Currency: 1 euro = 100 cents

Kypros/Kibris
Cyprus

Location: Southeastern Europe
Area: 9,250 sq km
Highest Point: Troodos (1,953 m)
Capital: Nicosia
Government: Republic
Administrative Divisions: 6 districts
Population: 776,000
Ethnic Groups: Greeks (85%),
Turks (13%)
Languages: Greek, Turkish, English
Religion: Orthodox (80%), Muslims (19%)
Literacy Rate: 97%
GDP per capita: 16,000 US$ (In the south)
Currency: 1 Cypriot pound = 100 cents

Latvija
Latvia

Location: Northeastern Europe
Area: 64,589 sq km
Capital: Riga
Government: Republic
Administrative Divisions: 33 districts
Population: 2.3 million
Ethnic Groups: Latvians (58%),

Russians (30%),Belarussians (4%)
Poles (2.5%), Lithuanians (1.5%)
Languages: Latvian, Russian
Religion: Lutherans (55%), Catholics
(24%), Russian Orthodox (10%)
Literacy Rate: 98 %
GDP per capita: 10,100 US$
Currency: 1 lats = 100 santims

Liechtenstein
Liechtenstein

Location: Central Europe
Area: 160 sq km
Highest Point: Grauspitze (2,599 m)
Capital: Vaduz
Government: Parliamentary monarchy
Administrative Divisions:
11 municipalities
Population: 33,400
Ethnic Groups: Liechtensteiner (63%),
Swiss (16%), Austrian (8%),
German (4%)
Language: German
Religion: Catholics (83%),
Protestants (7%)
Literacy Rate: 99%
GDP per capita: 25,000 US$
Currency: 1 Swiss franc = 100 rappen

Lietuva
Lithuania

Location: Northeastern Europe
Area: 65,200 sq km
Capital: Vilnius
Government: Parliamentary republic
Administrative Divisions: 10 districts
Population: 3.6 million
Ethnic Groups: Lithuanian (80%),
Russian (9%), Polish (7%)
Belarussians (2%), Ukrainians (1%)
Languages: Lithuanian, Russian
Religion: Catholics (80%)
Literacy Rate: 98%
GDP per capita: 11,200 US$
Currency: 1 litas = 100 centas

Luxembourg/Lëtzebuerg
Luxembourg

Location: Central Europe
Area: 2,586 sq km
Highest Point: Eisling (562 m)
Important Rivers: Sauer, Mosel
Capital: Luxembourg
Government: Constitutional monarchy
Administrative Divisions: 12 cantons
Population: 462,700
Ethnic Groups: Luxembourger (73%),

Portugese (9%), Italians (5%),
Languages: Letzebuergisch, French,
German
Religion: Catholics (95%),
Protestants (1%)
Literacy Rate: 99%
GDP per capita: 55,100 US$
Currency: 1 euro = 100 cents

Magyarország
Hungary

Location: Central Europe
Area: 93,030 sq km
Important River/Body of Water: Danube,
Lake Balaton
Capital: Budapest
Government: Parliamentary republic
Administrative Divisions: 20 districts
Population: 10 million
Ethnic Groups: Hungarians (97%),
Germans (2%), Slovaks (1%)
Language: Hungarian
Religion: Catholics (64%),
Protestants (24%), Orthodox (3%)
Literacy Rate: 99%
GDP per capita: 13,900 US$
Currency: 1 forint = 100 filler

Makedonija
Macedonia

Location: Southeastern Europe
Area: 25,333 sq km
Capital: Skopje
Government: Republic
Administrative Divisions: 38 districts
Population: 2 million
Ethnic Groups: Macedonian (67%),
Albanian (20%), Turks (5%)
Serbians (3%), Roma (2%)
Languages: Macedonian, Albanian, Turkish,
Serbian
Religion: Macedonian-Orthodox (>50%),
Muslim (<20%)
Literacy Rate: 90%
GDP Per capita: 6,700 US$
Currency: 1 Macedonian denar =
100 deni

Malta
Malta

Location: Southeastern Europe
Area: 316 sq km
Capital: Valletta
Government: Republic
Administrative Divisions: 6 districts
Population: 397,000
Ethnic Groups: Maltese (96%),

British (2%)
Languages: Maltese (Arabian Creole),
English, Italian
Religion: Catholics (95%),
Anglicans (11%)
Literacy Rate: 91%
GDP per capita: 17,700 US$
Currency: 1 lira = 100 cents

Moldova
Moldova

Location: Southeastern Europe
Area: 33,700 sq km
Capital: Chisinau
Government: Republic
Administrative Divisions: 40 districts,
10 urban districts
Population: 4.4 million
Ethnic Groups: Moldavian (65%),
Ukrainian (14%), Russian (13%)
Gagausian (4%), Bulgarians (2%)
Languages: Moldavian, Russian
Religion: Orthodox (60%),
Jewish (1.5%)
Literacy Rate: 98%
GDP per capita: 1,800 US$
Currency: 1 leu = 100 bani

Monaco
Monaco

Location: Western Europe
Area: 1.95 sq km
Capital: Monaco-Ville
Government: Principality
Population: 32,300
Ethnic Groups: Monegasque (19%),
French (47%), Italian (17%),
Britons (4%), Germans (2%)
Languages: French, Monegasque, Italian
Religion: Catholics (90%),
Protestants (6%), Jewish (1%)
Literacy Rate: 99%
GDP per capita: 27,000 US$
Currency: 1 euro = 100 cents

Nederland
The Netherlands (Holland)

Location: Western Europe
Area: 41,526 sq km
Important River/Lake: Rhine, Ijsselmeer
Capital: Amsterdam (official),
The Hague (de facto)
Government: Parliamentary monarchy
Administrative Divisions: 12 provinces,
2 external territories
Population: 16.3 million
Ethnic Groups: Dutch (96%), Turkish (1%)

anguages: Dutch, Frisian
eligion: Catholics (34%),
rotestants (25%), Muslims (3%)
iteracy Rate: 99%
DP per capita: 28,600 US$
urrency: 1 euro = 100 cents

lorge
lorway

ocation: Northern Europe
rea: 324,220 sq km
ighest Point: Galdhoppigen (2,470 m)
apital: Oslo
overnment: Parliamentary monarchy
dministrative Divisions: 19 provinces
xternal Territories: Svalbard, Jan Mayen,
ouvet Island, Peter L. Island
opulation: 4.6 million
thnic Groups: Norwegians (97%)
ami/Lapps (1%)
anguages: Norwegian, Sami
eligion: Lutheran (88%)
iteracy Rate: 99%
DP per capita: 37,700 US$
urrency: 1 Norwegian krona =
00 Øre

sterreich
ustria

ocation: Central Europe
rea: 83,870 sq km
ighest Point: Großglockner (3,797 m)
mportant River/Body of Water: Danube,
ake Neusiedler
apital: Vienna
overnment: Federal republic
dministrative Divisions: 9 federal
ates
opulation: 8,2 million
anguage: German
eligion: Catholics (85%), Protestants (6%)
iteracy: 99%
DP per capita: 30,000 US$
urrency: 1 euro = 100 cents

olska
oland

ocation: Central Europe
rea: 312,685 sq km
mportant River: Oder
apital: Warsaw
overnment: Republic
dministrative Divisions: 49 provinces
opulation: 38.6 million
anguage: Polish
eligion: Catholics (94%),
rthodox (2%)

Literacy: 99%
GDP per capita: 11,000 US$
Currency: 1 zloty = 100 groszy

Portugal
Portugal

Location: Southwestern Europe
Area: 92,391 sq km
Highest Point: Serra da Estrela (1,991 m)
Important Rivers/Body of Water: Tejo,
Douro, Guadiana
Capital: Lisbon
Government: Republic
Administrative Divisions: 18 districts,
2 autonomous regions
Population: 10.5 million
Language: Portuguese
Religion: Catholics (95%),
Protestants (1%)
Literacy Rate: 90%
GDP per capita: 18,000 US$
Currency: 1 euro = 100 cents

România
Romania

Location: Southeastern Europe
Area: 237,500 sq km
Highest Point: Moldoveanu (2,543 m)
Important River: Danube
Capital: Bucharest
Government: Republic
Administrative Divisions: 41 districts
Population: 22.4 million
Ethnic Groups: Romanians (78%),
Hungarians (11%), Roma (10%)
Languages: Romanian, Hungarian, German
Religion: Romanian Orthodox (70%),
Griechisch-Orthodoxe (10 %),
Muslime (1 %)
Literacy Rate: 97%
GDP per capita: 6,900 US$
Currency: 1 leu = 100 bani

Rossija
Russia

Location: Eastern Europe/Northern Asia
Area: 17,075,200 sq km
Highest Point: Elbrus (5,642 m)
Important Rivers/Bodies of Water:
Volga, Lena, Yenisey, Caspian Sea, Baikal
Capital: Moscow
Government: Presidential federation
Administrative Divisions: 7 districts,
89 territories
Population: 143.7 million
Ethnic Groups: Russians (82%), Tatars
(4%), Ukrainians (3%)

Languages: Russian, Minority Languages
Religion: Russian Orthodox, Catholics,
Protestants, Armenian Orthodox,
Muslims
Literacy Rate: 99%
GDP per capita: 8,900 US$
Currency: 1 rouble = 100 kopecks

San Marino
San Marino

Location: Southern Europe
Area: 61.2 sq km
Highest Point: Monte Titano (743 m)
Capital: San Marino Città
Government: Republic
Administrative Divisions: 6 castelli
Population: 28,500
Ethnic Groups: Sanmarinese (80%),
Italian (18%)
Language: Italian
Religion: Catholic (95%)
Literacy Rate: 98%
GDP per capita: 34,600 US$
Currency: 1 euro = 100 cents

Shqipëria
Albania

Location: Southeastern Europe
Area: 28,748 sq km
Highest Point: Korab (2,753 m)
Capital: Tirana
Government: Republic
Administrative Divisions: 27 districts
Population: 3.5 milllion
Ethnic Groups: Albanians (98%),
Greeks (2%)
Language: Albanian
Religion: Muslims (65%),
Orthodox Christians (22%), Catholic (13%)
Literacy Rate: 85%
GDP per capita: 4,500 US$
Currency: 1 lek = 100 quindarka

Slovenija
Slovenia

Location: Central Europe
Area: 20,273 sq km
Capital: Ljubljana
Government: Republic
Population: 2 million
Ethnic Groups: Slovenians (90%),
Croatians (3%),Serbians (2%)
Language: Slovenian
Religion: Catholics (90%), Muslims (1%)
Literacy Rates: 99%
GDP per capita: 18,300 US$
Currency: 1 tolar = 100 stotin

Slovenská Republika
Slovakia

Location: Central Europe
Area: 48,845 sq km
Highest Point: Gerlach (2,655 m)
Capital: Bratislava
Government: Republic
Population: 5.4 million
Ethnic Groups: Slovaks (87%),
Hungarians (11%), Czechs (1%)
Languages: Slovakian (official),
Hungarian, Czech
Religion: Roman Catholics (64%),
Protestants (8%)
Literacy Rates: 99%
GDP per capita: 13,300 US$
Currency: 1 Slovakian koruna =
100 hellers

Srbija i Crna Gora
Serbia and Montenegro

Location: Southeastern Europe
Area: 102,350 sq km
Highest Point: Daravica (2,656 m)
Capital: Belgrade
Government: Federal republic
Population: 10.8 million
Ethnic Groups: Serbians (73%),
Albanians (13%), Montenegrins (5%),
Hungarians (4%), Bosnians (3%)
Languages: Serbian, Albanian,
Hungarian
Religion: Orthodox (44%), Catholic (31%),
Muslim (12%)
GDP per capita: 2,300 US$
Currency: 1 new dinar = 100 para

Suisse/Schweiz/Svizzera
Switzerland

Location: Central Europe
Area: 41,290 sq km
Highest Point: Monte Rosa (4,637 m)
Important Rivers: Rhine, Rhone
Capital: Bern
Government: Parliementary confederation
Administrative Divisions: 26 cantons
Population: 7.3 million
Ethnic Groups: Swiss (84%), Italians (6%),
Spaniards (2%) Germans (2%)
Languages: German, French, Italian,
Romansch
Religion: Catholics (47%),
Protestants (43%), Muslims (1%)
Literacy Rate: 99%
GDP per capita: 32,800 US$
Currency: 1 Swiss franc =
100 centimes

Suomi/Finland
Finland

Location: Northern Europe
Area: 337,031 sq km
Capital: Helsinki
Government: Republic
Administrative Divisions: 5 provinces,
1 autonomous region
Population: 5.2 million
Ethnic Groups: Finns (93%), Swedes (6%),
Sami
Languages: Finnish, Swedish, Russian,
Lappish
Religion: Lutheran (98%), Orthodox (1%)
Literacy Rate: 99%
GDP per capita: 27,300 US$
Currency: 1 euro = 100 cents

Sverige
Sweden

Location: Northern Europe
Area: 449,964 sq km
Highest Point: Kebnekaise (2,111 m)
Important Lakes: Vänern, Vättern
Capital: Stockholm
Government: Constitutional monarchy
Administrative Division: 24 districts
Population: 9 million
Ethnic Groups: Swedes, (91%), Finns (3%),
Sami/Lapps (2%)
Languages: Swedish, Finnish, Sami
Religion: Lutheran Church of
Sweden (89%)
Literacy Rate: 99%
GDP per capita: 26,800 US$
Currency: 1 Swedish krona =
100 Ore

Türkiye
Turkey

Location: Middle East
Area:780,580 sq km
Highest Point: Ararat (5,156 m)
Capital: Ankara
Government: Republic
Administrative Divisions: 74 provinces
Population: 68.9 million
Ethnic Groups: Turks (70%),
Kurdish (20%), Arabs (2%)
Languages: Turkish, Kurdish
Religion: Sunnis (70%),
Alevites (15%), Shiites (14%),
Christians and Jews (0.2%)
Literacy Rate: 82%
GDP per capita: 6,700 US$
Currency: 1 Turkish lira =
100 kurus

Ukrajina
Ukraine

Location: Eastern Europe
Area: 603,700 sq km
Important River: Dnepr
Capital: Kiev
Government: Republic
Administrative Divisions: 25 regions,
autonomous region Crimea
Population: 47.7 million
Ethnic Groups: Ukrainians (72%),
Russians (22%)
Languages: Ukrainian, Russian
Religion: Orthodox, Catholics (10%)
Literacy Rate: 95%
GDP per capita: 5,300 US$
Currency: 1 hryvnia = 100 kopiyka

United Kingdom
United Kingdom (Britain)

Location: Western Europe
Area: 244,820 sq km
Highest Point: Ben Nevis (1,343 m)
Important Rivers: Thames, Severn
Capital: London
Government: Constitutional monarchy
Administrative Divisions: 76 boroughs,
36 counties, royal boroughs, cities
and districts
External Territories: Channel Islands,
Isle of Man, Anguilla, Bermuda, British Virgin
Islands, Falkland Islands, Gibraltar, Cayman
Islands, Montserrat, Pitcairn, St. Helena, Turks
and Caicos, South Georgia and Sandwich
Islands
Population: 60.3 million
Ethnic Groups: English (80%),
Scots (10%), Irish (3%), Welsh (2%),
South Asians (2%),
Black African descent (1.5%)
Languages: English, Welsh, Scottish
Religion: Anglican (57%), Catholic (13%),
Presbyterians (7%)
Literacy Rate: 99%
GDP per capita: 27,700 US$
Currency: 1 Pound Sterling = 100 Pence

ASIA

Afghānistān
Afghanistan

Location: Western Asia
Area: 647,500 sq km
Highest Point: Tirich Mir (7,699 m)
Capital: Kabul
Government: Islamic republic

Administrative Divisions: 31 provinces
Population: 28.5 million
Ethnic Groups: Pashtun (40%),
Tajiks (25%), Hazara (15%),
Uzbeks (5%)
Languages: Pashtu, Dari
Religion: Sunnis (84%), Shiites (15%)
Literacy Rate: 31%
GDP per capita: 700 US$
Currency: 1 afghani = 100 puls

Al-Bahrain
Bahrain

Location: Middle East
Area: 665 sq km
Capital: Al-Manama
Government: Emirate
Population: 677,800
Ethnic Groups: Bahraini (64%),
Other Arabs (27%), Indians (6%),
Pakistani (2%), Westerners (1%)
Language: Arabic
Religion: Sunnis (59%), Shiites (31%)
Literacy Rate: 85%
GDP per capita: 17,100 US$
Currency: 1 dinar = 100 fils

Al-Kuwait
Kuwait

Location: Middle East
Area: 17,820 sq km
Capital: Kuwait City
Government: Emirate
Administrative Divisions: 5 provinces
Population: 2.3 million
Ethnic Groups: Kuwaiti (38%), Foreigners
including Indians and Egyptians (62%)
Language: Arabic
Religion: Sunnis (66%), Shiites (29%)
Literacy: 79%
GDP per capita: 18,100 US$
Currency: 1 dinar = 100 dirham =
1,000 fils

Al-Lubnān
Lebanon

Location: Middle East
Area: 10,452 sq km
Highest Point: Lebanon
Capital: Beirut
Government: Republic
Administrative Divisions: 5 provinces
Population: 3.8 million
Ethnic Groups: Lebanese (90%),
Palestinians (10%)
Languages: Arabic, French
Religion: Muslims (60%), Christians (40%)

Literacy Rate: 92%
GDP per capita: 4,800 US$
Currency: 1 Lebanese pound = 100 piaster

Al-Mamlaka al-'Arabiya as-Sa'ūdiya
Saudi Arabia

Location: Middle East
Area: 1,960,582 sq km
Highest Point: Asir (3,133 m)
Capital: Riyadh
Government: Islamic monarchy
Administrative Divisions: 13 regions
Population: 25.8 million
Ethnic Groups: Saudis, Foreigners;
mostly guest workers (27%)
Language: Arabic
Religion: Muslims (98%)
Literacy Rate: 63%
GDP per capita: 11,800 US$
Currency: 1 Saudi riyal = 20 quirshes

Al-Yaman
Yemen

Location: Middle East
Area: 527,970 sq km
Highest Point: Nabi Shuai (3,760 m)
Capital: Sanaa
Government: Republic
Administrative Divisions: 17 provinces
Population: 20 million
Languages: Arabic, English
Religion: Muslims (99%)
Literacy: 38%
GDP per capita: 800 US$
Currency: 1 Yemeni-real = 100 fils

Armenija (Hayastan)
Armenia

Location: Western Asia
Area: 29,800 sq km
Capital: Yerevan
Government: Republic
Administrative Divisions: 37 districts
Population: 3 million
Ethnic Groups: Armenians (93%),
Azerbaijanis (3%), Russians (2%)
Languages: Armenian, Russian
Religion: Armenian Apostolic (95%)
Literacy Rate: 99%
GDP per capita: 3,900 US$
Currency: 1 dram = 100 luma

Azerbajdzan
Azerbaijan

Location: Middle East

Area: 86,600 sq km
Capital: Baku/Baki
Government: Republic
Administrative Divisions: 54 districts,
9 cities, 2 autonomous regions
Population: 7.9 million
Ethnic Groups: Azerbaijanis (85%),
Russians (4%), Armenians (2%)
Languages: Azeri, Turkish, Russian
Religion: Sunnis (59%), Shiites (31%)
Literacy Rate: 95%
GDP per capita: 3,400 US$
Currency: 1 manat = 100 gepik

Bangladesh
Bangladesh

Location: Southeast Asia
Area: 144,000 sq km
Important Rivers: Ganges, Brahmaputra
Capital: Dhaka
Government: Republic
Administrative Divisions: 4 provinces
Population: 141.3 million
Ethnic Groups: Bengalis (95%),
Bihari (1%)
Languages: Bengali, Urdu, Hindi
Religion: Muslims (87%), Hindus (12%)
Literacy Rate: 38%
GDP per capita: 1,900 US$
Currency: 1 taka = 100 poisha

Bhutan
Bhutan

Location: South Asia
Area: 47,000 sq km
Highest Point: Jomo Lhari (7,314 m)
Capital: Thimphu
Government: Constitutional monarchy
Administrative Divisions: 18 districts
Population: 2.2 million
Ethnic Groups: Bhutanese (72%),
Nepalese and other South Asians
Languages: Dzongkha, Tibetan dialects
Religion: Buddhist (72%), Hindus,
Muslims
Literacy Rates: 42%
GDP per capita: 1,300 US$
Currency: 1 ngultrum = 100 chetrum

Brunei
Brunei

Location: Southeast Asia
Area: 5,765 sq km
Capital: Bandar Seri Begawan
Government: Sultanate
Administrative Divisions: 4 districts
Population: 365,000

Ethnic Groups: Malays (67%),
Chinese (16%), Proto-Malays
Languages: Malay, English
Religion: Muslims (67%), Buddhist (12%),
Christian (10%)
Literacy Rate: 88%
GDP per capita: 18,600 US$
Currency: 1 Bruneian dollar = 100 cents

Choson
Democratic Republic of
Korea (North)

Location: East Asia
Area: 120,538 sq km
Capital: Pyongyang
Government: Authoritarian
socialism
Administrative Divisions: 9 provinces,
4 special cities
Population: 22.7 million
Language: Korean
Religion: Atheists (68%), Buddhist and
Confucianist minoritites
Literacy Rate: 95%
GDP per capita: 1,000 US$
Currency: 1 won = 100 chon

Daulat al-Imārāt
al-'Arabiya Al-Muttahida
United Arab Emirates

Location: Middle East
Area: 82,880 sq km
Highest Point: Jabal-Sham (3,017 m)
Capital: Abu Dhabi
Government: Confederation of
emirates
Administrative Divisions: 7 emirates
Population: 2.5 million
Ethnic Groups: Arabs (70%), foreign guest
workers
Language: Arabic
Religion: Sunni (81%), Shiite (15%),
Literacy Rate: 79 %
GDP per capita: 23,200 US$
Currency: 1 dirham = 100 fils

Gruzija (Sakartvelo)
Georgia

Location: Western Asia
Area: 69,700 sq km
Highest Point: Mt'a Shkhara (5,201 sq km)
Capital: Tbilisi
Government: Republic
Administrative Divisions: 79 districts and
cities, 3 autonomous regions
Population: 4.7 million
Ethnic Groups: Georgians (71%),

Armenians (8%), Azerbaijanis (5%),
Russians (5%)
Languages: Georgian, Russian,
Armenian
Religion: Orthodox (65%),
Muslims (11%)
GDP per capita: 2,500 US$
Currency: 1 lari = 100 tetri

India (Bhārat)
India

Location: South Asia
Area: 3,287,263 sq km
Highest Point: Nanda Devi (7,817 m)
Important Rivers: Indus, Ganges
Capital: New Delhi
Government: Republic
Administrative Divisions: 25 states,
7 territories
Population: 1.065 billion
Languages: Hindi, English
Religion: Hindus (80%),
Muslims (11%)
Literacy Rate: 51 %
GDP per capita: 2,900 US$
Currency: 1 rupee = 100 paisa

Indonesia
Indonesia

Location: Southeast Asia
Area: 1,919,440 sq km
Capital: Jakarta
Government: Republic
Administrative Divisions: 27 provinces,
3 special regions
Population: 238.4 million
Ethnic Groups: Javanese (40%),
Sundanese (15%), Madurese (7%),
Others (>25%)
Languages: Indonesian, Javanese
Religion: Muslims (87%), Christians (10%),
Hindus (2%), Buddhists (1%)
Literacy Rate: 84%
GDP per capita: 3,200 US$
Currency: 1 rupiah = 100 dinar

Īrân
Iran

Location: Middle East
Area: 1,648,000 sq km
Highest Point: Damavand (5,671 m)
Capital: Tehran
Government: Islamic republic
Administrative Divisions: 25 provinces
Population: 69 million
Ethnic Groups: Persians (50%),
Azerbaijanis (20%), Kurds (8%), Lur (10%)

Arabs (2%), Turkmen (2%)
Languages: Persian, Lur, Kurdish
Religion: Shiites (90%), Sunnis (8%)
Literacy Rate: 68 %
GDP per capita: 7,000 US$
Currency: 1 rial = 100 dinar

'Īrāq
Iraq

Location: Middle East
Area: 437,072 sq km
Important Rivers: Euphrates, Tigris
Capital: Baghdad
Government: Transitional government
Administrative Divisions: 18 provinces
Population: 25.3 million
Ethnic Groups: Arabs (80%), Kurds (15%),
Turkmen, Armenians
Language: Arabic
Religion: Sunnis (63%), Shiites (32%)
Literacy Rate: 57%
GDP per capita: 1,600 US$
Currency: 1 Iraqi dinar = 1,000 fils

Kâmpŭchéa
Cambodia

Location: Southeast Asia
Area: 181,035 sq km
Capital: Phnom Penh
Government: Constitutional monarchy
Administrative Divisions: 21 provinces
Population: 13.4 million
Ethnic Groups: Khmer (92%),
Vietnamese (5%), Chinese (2%), Thai (1%)
Languages: Khmer, Vietnamese
Religion: Buddhist (89%), Muslim (2%)
Literacy Rate: 35%
GDP per capita: 1,700 US$
Currency: 1 riel = 10 kak

Kazahstan
Kazakhstan

Location: Central Asia
Area: 2,717,300 sq km
Important Body of Water: Aral Sea
Capital: Astana
Government: Republic
Administrative Divisions: 19 regions,
2 cities
Population: 15.1 million
Ethnic Groups: Kazakhs (44%),
Russians (36%), Ukrainians (4%),
Germans (4%)
Languages: Kazakh, Russian
Religion: Muslim (50%), Christian (50%)
Literacy Rate: 7,000 US$
Currency: 1 tenge = 100 tiin

Kyrgyzstan
Kyrgyzstan

Location: Central Asia
Area: 198,500 sq km
Highest Point: Jengish Chokusu/Pik Pobedy (7,439 m)
Capital: Bishkek
Government: Presidential republic
Administrative Divisions: 6 regions, 1 district
Population: 5 million
Ethnic Groups: Kyrgyz (57%), Russians (19%), Uzbeks (13%), Ukrainians (2%)
Languages: Kyrgyz, Russian
Religion: Primarily Muslim, Christians
Literacy Rate: 97%
GDP per capita: 1,600 US$
Currency: 1 som = 100 tyin

Lao
Laos

Location: Southeast Asia
Area: 236,800 sq km
Capital: Vientiane
Government: Socialist republic
Administrative Divisions: 16 provinces, 1 prefecture
Population: 6 million
Ethnic Groups: circa 70 Ethnic Groups incl. Lao-Lum, Lao-Theung, Lao Soung
Language: Lao
Religions: Buddhists (58%), Indigenous Religions (34%)
Literacy Rate: 56%
GDP per capita: 1,700 US$
Currency: 1 kip

Malaysia
Malaysia

Location: Southeast Asia
Area: 329,758 sq km
Capital: Kuala Lumpur
Government: Constitutional monarchy
Administrative Divisions: 13 states, 2 territories
Population: 23.5 million
Ethnic Groups: Malays (53%), Chinese (27%), Indians and Pakistanis (8%)
Languages: Bahasa Melayu, Chinese dialects, Tamil, English
Religion: Muslim (53%), Buddhist (17%), Native religions (12%), Hindus (7%)
Literacy Rate: 83%
GDP per capita: 9,000 US$
Currency: 1 Malaysian ringgit = 100 sen

Maldives (Divehi Rajje)
Maldives

Location: South Asia
Area: 298 sq km
Capital: Male
Government: Republic
Administrative Divisions: 20 districts
Population: 339,300
Ethnic Groups: Maldivian (100%)
Languages: Divehi, English
Religion: Sunni Muslims (99%)
Literacy Rate: 93%
GDP per capita: 3,900 US$
Currency: 1 rufiyaa = 100 laari

Mongol Ard Uls
Mongolia

Location: Central Asia
Area: 1,565,000 sq km
Highest Point: Huyten Orgil (4,374 m)
Capital: Ulan Bator
Government: Republic
Administrative Divisions: 21 provinces, 1 district
Population: 2.8 million
Ethnic Groups: Mongolians (88%), Turkic (7%), Others
Languages: Mongolian, Kazakh, Russian
Religion: Buddhist Lamaism (90%), Native Religions
Literacy Rate: 82%
GDP per capita: 1,800 US$
Currency: 1 tugrik = 100 mongo

Muang Thai
Thailand

Location: Southeast Asia
Area: 513,115 sq km
Capital: Bangkok
Government: Constitutional monarchy
Administrative Divisions: 73 provinces
Population: 64.8 million
Ethnic Groups: Thais (80%), Chinese (12%), Malays (4%), Khmer (3%)
Languages: Thai, English, Chinese
Religion: Buddhist (95%), Muslim (4%)
Literacy Rate: 94%
GDP per capita: 7,400 US$
Currency: 1 baht = 100 stangs

Myanmar
Myanmar (Burma)

Location: Southeast Asia

Area: 678,500 sq km
Capital: Rangoon
Government: Military regime
Administrative Divisions: 7 states, 7 districts
Population: 42.7 million
Ethnic Groups: Burmese (69%), Shan (9%), Karen (6%) Rakhine (4%)
Languages: Burmese, other Indigenous Languages
Religion: Buddhists (89%), Christians (5%), Muslims (4%), Indigenous Religions (3%)
Literacy Rate: 83%
GDP per capita: 1,900 US$
Currency: 1 kyat = 100 pyas

Nepal
Nepal

Location: South Asia
Area: 140,800 sq km
Highest Point: Mt. Everest (8,861 m)
Capital: Kathmandu
Government: Constitutional monarchy
Administrative Divisions: 14 regions
Population: 27 million
Ethnic Groups: Nepalese majority including Bhaman, Chetri, etc.
Languages: Nepalese, Minority Languages
Religion: Hindus (86%), Buddhists (6%), Muslims (3%)
Literacy: 27%
GDP per capita: 1,400 US$
Currency: 1 Nepalese rupee = 100 paisa

Nippon/Nihon
Japan

Location: Pacific Island Chain/East Asia
Area: 377,801 sq km
Highest Point: Mt Fuji (3,776 m)
Important Rivers: Honshu, Tone, Kitakami
Capital: Tokyo
Government: Constitutional monarchy
Administrative Divisions: 47 prefectures
Population: 127.3 million
Ethnic Groups: Japanese (99%), Ainu, Koreans
Language: Japanese
Religion: Shinto (88%), Buddhism (78%), Christian (4%)
Literacy Rate: 99%
GDP per capita: 28,000 US$
Currency: 1 yen = 100 sen

Pākistān
Pakistan

Location: South Asia
Area: 803,940 sq km

Important Rivers: Indus and tributaries
Capital: Islamabad
Government: Islamic republic
Administrative Divisions: 4 provinces, 1 district, 2 regions
Population: 159.2 million
Ethnic Groups: Punjabi (50%), Sindhi (15%), Pashtun (15%)
Languages: Urdu, English, Punjabi, Sindhi
Religion: Muslim (97%)
Literacy Rate: 38%
GDP per capita: 2,100 US$
Currency: 1 Pakistani rupee = 100 paisa

Pilipinas
Philippines

Location: Southeast Asia
Area: 300,000 sq km
Highest Point: Mt. Apo (2,954 m)
Capital: Manila
Government: Republic
Administrative Divisions: 13 regions, 73 provinces
Population: 86.2 million
Ethnic Groups: Christian and Muslim Malays (95%), Chinese (1.5%)
Languages: Tagalog, English, Spanish
Religion: Catholic (84%), other Christians (10%), Muslims (5%)
Literacy Rate: 95%
GDP per capita: 4,600 US$
Currency: 1 Philippine peso = 100 centavos

Qatar
Qatar

Location: Middle East
Area: 11,437 sq km
Capital: Doha
Government: Emirate
Administrative Divisions: 9 districts
Population: 840,000
Ethnic Groups: Arab (45%), South Asians (34%), Iranian (16%)
Language: Arabic
Religion: Muslim (93%), Christians (6%), Hindus (1%)
Literacy Rate: 79%
GDP per capita: 21,500 US$
Currency: 1 Quatar-riyal = 100 dirham

Saltanat 'Umān
Oman

Location: Middle East

Area: 212,457 sq km
Highest Point: Jabal-Sham (3,017 m)
Capital: Muscat
Government: Sultanate
Administrative Divisions: 59 Provinces
Population: 2.9 million
Ethnic Groups: Arabs (88%), Persians (3%), South Asians (3%), Africans (2%)
Languages: Arabic, Persian, Urdu
Religion: Muslims (85%), Hindus (14%)
Literacy Rates: 35%
GDP per capita: 13,400 US$
Currency: 1 Omani rial = 100 baizas

Singapore
Singapore

Location: Southeast Asia
Area: 692.7 sq km
Capital: Singapore
Government: Republic
Administrative Divisions: 5 districts
Population: 4.4 million
Ethnic Groups: Chinese (78%), Malays (14%), South Asians (7%)
Languages: Malay, English, Chinese, Tamil
Religion: Buddhist and Taoist (54%), Muslims (15%), Hindus (4%)
Literacy Rate: 91%
GDP per capita: 23,700 US$
Currency: 1 Singapore dollar = 100 cents

Srī Laṅkā
Sri Lanka

Location: South Asia
Area: 65,610 sq km
Highest Point: Pidurutalagala (2,524 m)
Capital: Colombo
Government: Socialist republic
Administrative Divisions: 9 provinces, 25 districts
Population: 19.9 million
Ethnic Groups: Sinhalese (74%), Tamil (18%)
Languages: Sinhala, Tamil
Religion: Buddhism (70%), Hindus (16%), Muslims (8%), Catholics (7%)
Literacy Rates: 90%
GDP per capita: 3,700 US$
Currency: 1 Sri Lankan rupee = 100 cents

Suriya
Syria

Location: Middle East
Area: 185,180 sq km

Important Rivers: Euphrates
Capital: Damascus
Government: Military governed republic
Administrative Divisions: 13 provinces, 1 district
Population: 18 million
Ethnic Groups: Arabs (89%), Kurds (6%), Armenian (2%)
Languages: Arabic, Kurdish, Armenian
Religion: Sunni Muslims (80%), Alawite (7%), Christians (9%), Other Muslims (3%)
Literacy: 70%
GDP per capita: 3,300 US$
Currency: 1 Syrian pound = 100 piasta

Tadžikistan
Tajikistan

Location: Central Asia
Area: 143,100 sq km
Highest Point: Somoni (7,495 m)
Capital: Dushanbe
Government: Republic
Administrative Divisions: 2 regions, 1 district, 1 Autonomous region
Population: 7 million
Ethnic Groups: Tajikistanis (63%), Uzbeks (24%), Russians (7%)
Languages: Tajik, Russian
Religion: Primarily Islam and Russian Orthodoxy
Literacy Rate: 97%
GDP per capita: 1,000 US$
Currency: 1 Tajik rouble = 100 kopeks

Taehan-Min'guk
Republic of Korea (South)

Location: East Asia
Area: 98,480 sq km
Capital: Seoul
Government: Republic
Administrative Divisions: 15 provinces
Population: 48.6 million
Language: Korean
Religion: Christians (32%), Buddhists (23 %), Confucians (22%)
GDP per capita: 17,700 US$
Currency: 1 won = 100 chon

Taiwan
Taiwan

Location: East Asia
Area: 35,980 sq km
Capital: Taipei
Government: Republic
Administrative Divisions: 16 counties, 5 municipalities, 2 special municipalities

Population: 22.7 million
Ethnic Groups: Taiwanese (84%). Mainland Chinese (14%), Indigenous 2%
Language: Chinese
Religion: Taoists (34%), Buddhists (43%), Christians (14%), Confucianism
Literacy Rate: 92%
GDP per capita: 23,400 US$
Currency: 1 New Taiwan dollar = 100 cents

Timor-Leste
East Timor

Location: Southeast Asia
Area: 15,007 sq km
Capital: Dili
Government: Republic
Administrative Divisions: 13 districts
Population: 1 million
Languages: Portuguese, Tetum, Indonesian
Religion: Catholics (91.4%), Protestant (2.6%), Muslim (1.7%), Hindu (0.3%)
GDP per capita: Estimated at 500 US$
Currency: 1 US dollar = 100 cents

Turkmenistan
Turkmenistan

Location: Central Asia
Area: 488,100 sq km
Capital: Ashgabat
Government: Republic
Administrative Divisions: 5 regions
Population: 4.9 million
Ethnic Groups: Turkmen (73%), Russians (10%), Uzbeks (9%) Kazaks (2%), Tartars (1%)
Languages: Turkmen, Russian
Religion: Sunni Muslims
Literacy Rate: 98%
GDP per capita: 5,700 US$
Currency: 1 manat = 100 tenge

Urdunn
Jordan

Location: Middle East
Area: 92,300 sq km
Important River: Jordan
Capital: Amman
Government: Constitutional monarchy
Administrative Divisions: 8 provinces
Population: 5.6 million
Ethnic Groups: Arabs (98%)
Language: Arabic
Religion: Sunni Islam (80%)
Literacy Rate: 87%
GDP per capita: 4,300 US$

Currency: 1 Jordanian dinar = 1,000 fils

Uzbekistan
Uzbekistan

Location: Central Asia
Area: 447,400 sq km
Capital: Tashkent
Government: Republic
Administrative Divisions: 12 regions, 1 autonomous republic
Population: 26.4 million
Ethnic Groups: Uzbeks (74%), Russians (6%), Tajikistanis (5%), Kazaks (4%)
Languages: Uzbek, Russians
Religion: Sunni Islam
Literacy Rate: 97%
GDP per capita: 1,700 US$
Currency: 1 Uzbek sum = 100 tijin

Viêt-Nam
Vietnam

Location: Southeast Asia
Area: 329,560 sq km
Important River: Mekong
Capital: Hanoi
Government: Socialist republic
Administrative Divisions: 7 regions, 50 provinces, 3 cities
Population: 82.6 million
Ethnic Groups: Vietnamese (87%), 60 minority groups
Language: Vietnamese
Religion: Buddhists (55%), Catholic (7%)
Literacy: 94%
GDP per capita: 2,500 US$
Currency: 1 dong = 1 hao = 10 xu

Yisra'el
Israel

Location: Middle East
Area: 21,946 sq km
Important Bodies of Water/Rivers: Dead Sea, Jordan
Capital: Jerusalem
Government: Republic
Administrative Divisions: 6 districts
Population: 6.2 million, includes settlers outside of Isreal proper.
Ethnic Groups: Jewish Israelis (81%), Israeli Arabs (18%)
Languages: Modern Hebrew, Arabic, English
Religion: Jewish (81%), Muslims (14%)
Literacy Rate: 95%
GDP per capita: 19,700 US$

Currency: 1 new shekel = 100 agorot

Zhongguo
China

Location: East Asia
Area: 9,596,960 sq km
Highest Point: Muztagh (7,723 m)
Important Rivers: Yellow, Pearl, Yangtse
Capital: Beijing
Government: Socialist republic
Administrative Divisions: 23 provinces, 5 autonomous regions, 3 cities, 147 special municipalities
Population: 1.3 billion
Ethnic Groups: Han Chinese (92%), Tibetans, Miao, Mongol, Manchus
Languages: Chinese, Minority Languages
Religion: Buddhists (9%), Muslims (2%), Christians (1%)
Literacy Rate: 81 %
GDP per capita: 5,000 US$
Currency: 1 yuan = 1,000 fen

AUSTRALIA/OCEANIA

Australia
Australia

Location: Indian/Pacific Ocean
Area: 7,686,850 sq km
Highest Point: Kosciuszko (2,230 m)
Capital: Canberra
Government: Parliamentary democracy
Administrative Divisions: 6 states, 2 territories
External Territories: Christmas Island, Cocos Island, Lord Howe Island, Norfolk Island
Population: 19.9 million
Ethnic Groups: European descent (92%), Aborigines (around 1%), Asians (7%)
Language: English
Religion: Catholics (26%), Anglicans (24%), other Protestants (6%), Orthodox (3%)
Literacy Rate: 99%
GDP per capita: 28,900 US$
Currency: 1 Australian dollar = 100 cents

Fiji
Fiji

Location: South Pacific
Area: 18,270 sq km
Capital: Suva
Government: Republic
Administrative Divisions: 4 districts,

171

14 provinces
Population: 880,874
Ethnic Groups: Fijians (51%),
Indians (44%)
Languages: English, Fijian, Hindi
Religion: Christians (53%), Hindus (38%),
Muslims (8%)
Literacy Rate: 91%
GDP per capita: 5,800 US$
Currency: 1 Fijian dollar = 100 cents

Kiribati
Kiribati

Location: South Pacific
Area: 810.5 sq km
Capital: Bairiki
Government: Republic
Administrative Divisions: 6 districts
Population: 100,800
Ethnic Groups: Micronesians (99%),
Polynesians, Chinese, Caucasians
Languages: Kiribati, English
Religion: Christians (93%), Baha'i (3%)
Literacy Rate: 90 %
GDP per capita: 800 US$
Currency: 1 Australian dollar =
100 cents

Marshall Islands
Marshall Islands

Location: Pacific Ocean
Area: 181 sq km
Capital: Majuro
Government: Republic
Administrative Divisions: 24 districts
Population: 57,700
Ethnic Groups: Micronesians (97%),
Americans
Languages: English, Marshallese
Religion: Christians (98%)
Literacy Rate: 91%
GDP per capita: 1,600 US$
Currency: 1 US dollar = 100 cents

Micronesia
Micronesia

Location: Western Pacific
Area: 702 sq km
Capital: Palikir
Government: Federal republic
Administrative Divisions: 4 states
Population: 108,200
Ethnic Groups: Mostly Micronesians and
Polynesians, expats
Languages: English, 9 Indigenous
Languages
Religion: Christian

Literacy Rate: 80%
GDP per capita: 2,000 US$
Currency: 1 US dollar = 100 cents

Nauru (Naoero)
Nauru

Location: South Pacific
Area: 21.3 sq km
Capital: Yaren District
Government: Republic
Administrative Divisions: 14 districts
Population: 12,800
Ethnic Groups: Nauruan (62%),
other Pacific Islanders (25%), East Asians
Languages: English, Nauruan
Religion: Christians (90%)
Literacy Rate: 99%
GDP per capita: 5,000 US$
Currency: 1 Australian dollar = 100 cents

New Zealand
New Zealand

Location: South Pacific
Area: 268,680 sq km
Highest Point: Mt. Cook (3,764 m)
Capital: Wellington
Government: Parliamentary monarchy
Administrative Divisions: 90 counties,
3 townships
External Territories: Cook Islands,
Niue, Tokelau
Population: 4 million
Ethnic Groups: European descent (74%),
Maori (10%), Pacific Islanders (4%)
Languages: English, Maori
Religion: Anglican (22%), Presbyterian
(16%), Catholics (15%)
Literacy Rates: 99%
GDP per capita: 21,600 US$
Currency: 1 New Zealand dollar = 100 cents

Palau
Palau

Location: Pacific
Area: 458 sq km
Capital: Koror
Government: Republic
Administrative Divisions: 16 states
Population: 20,000
Ethnic Groups: Palau (83%), Filipinos
(10%), other Micronesians (2%),
Chinese (2%)
Languages: English, Palauan
Religion: Christians (65%), Animists (25%)
Literacy Rate: 98%
GDP per capita: 9,000 US$
Currency: 1 US dollar = 100 cents

Papua New-Guinea
Papua New Guinea

Location: Western Pacific
Area: 462,840 sq km
Highest Point: Mt. Wilhelm (4,508 m)
Important River: Sepik
Capital: Port Moresby
Government: Constitutional
monarchy
Administrative Divisions: 19 provinces,
1 district
Population: 5.4 million
Ethnic Groups: Mostly New Guineans and
other Melanesians
Languages: English, New Guinean Pidgin,
Motu
Religion: Christians (92%), Animists
Literacy Rate: 72%
GDP per capita: 2,200 US$
Currency: 1 kina = 100 toea

Samoa
Samoa (Western)

Location: Pacific
Area: 2,944 sq km
Capital: Apia
Government: Constitutional
monarchy
Administrative Divisions: 11 districts
Population: 178,000
Ethnic Groups: Polynesians (90%),
Mixed European-Polynesian (9%)
Languages: Samoan, English
Religion: Protestants (71%),
Catholics (22%)
GDP per capita: 5,600 US$
Currency: 1 tala = 100 sene

Solomon Islands
Solomon Islands

Location: Pacific
Area: 28,450 sq km
Capital: Honiara
Government: Parliamentary
monarchy
Administrative Divisions: 8 provinces,
1 district
Population: 523,600
Ethnic Groups: Melanesians (94%),
Polynesians (4%), Micronesians (1%)
Languages: English, Pidgin
Religion: Christians (97%),
Animists (2%)
Literacy Rate: 62 %
GDP per capita: 1,700 US$
Currency: 1 Solomon Island dollar =
100 cents

Tonga
Tonga

Location: Pacific
Area: 748 sq km
Capital: Nuku'alofa
Government: Constitutional monarchy
Administrative Divisions: 3 island groups
Population: 110,200
Ethnic Groups: Polynesians (99%)
Languages: Tongan, English
Religion: Christians (90%), Baha'i (4%)
Literacy Rate: 95%
GDP per capita: 2,200 US$
Currency: 1 pa'anga = 100 seniti

Tuvalu
Tuvalu

Location: Pacific
Area: 26 sq km
Capital: Vaiaku (Funafuti)
Government: Constitutional monarchy
Administrative Divisions: 9 atolls
Population: 11,500
Ethnic Groups: Polynesians (96%), Melanesians
Languages: Tuvalu, English
Religion: Protestants (97%), Adventists, Baha'i
Literacy Rate: 95%
GDP per capita: 1,100 US$
Currency: 1 Australian dollar = 100 cents

Vanuatu
Vanuatu

Location: Pacific
Area: 12,190 sq km
Capital: Port Vila
Government: Republic
Administrative Divisions: 6 provinces
Population: 203,000
Ethnic Groups: Ni-Vanuatu (91%), Pacific Islanders (3%)
Languages: English, French, Bislama
Religion: Christians (80%), Animists
GDP per Capita: 2,900 US$
Currency: 1 vatu = 100 centimes

AFRICA

Al-Ǧazā'ir/Algérie
Algeria

Location: North Africa
Area: 2,381,741 sq km
Capital: Algiers

Government: Republic
Administrative Divisions: 48 districts
Population: 32.1 million
Ethnic Groups: Arabs (70%), Berbers (30%)
Language: Arabic
Religion: Sunni Islam (99%)
Literacy Rate: 60%
GDP per capita: 5,900 US$
Currency: 1 Algerian dinar = 100 centimes

Al-Maġrib/Maroc
Morocco

Location: North Africa
Area: 446,550 sq km
Highest Point: Tourkal (4,167 m)
Capital: Rabat
Government: Constitutional monarchy
Administrative Divisions: 16 regions
Population: 32.2 million
Ethnic Groups: Arab Moroccans (50%), Berbers (40%)
Languages: Arabic, French, Berber dialects
Religion: Islam (99%)
Literacy Rate: 44%
GDP per capita: 4,000 US$
Currency: 1 dirham = 100 centimes

Al-Miṣr/Egypt
Egypt

Location: North Africa
Area: 1,001,450 sq km
Highest Point: Mt. Sinai (2,637 m)
Important River: Nile
Capital: Cairo
Government: Republic
Administrative Divisions: 26 provinces
Population: 76.1 million
Ethnic Groups: Egyptians: of mixed Arab, Black African and Berber descent (80%), Arabs, Sudanese, Nubians, Palestinians
Languages: Egyptian Arabic
Religion: Sunnis (90%), Coptic Christians (10%)
Literacy Rate: 51%
GDP per capita: 3,900 US$
Currency: 1 Egyptian pound = 100 piaster

Al-Saharaw
Western Sahara

Location: Northwestern Africa
Area: 266,000 sq km
Government: Territory of Morocco, annexed in 1979
Administrative Divisions: 4 provinces
Population: 267,000

Ethnic Group: Arabs, Berbers, Moroccans
Languages: Arabic, Spanish, Hassaniya Arabic
Religion: Sunni Muslims (100%)
Currency: 1 Moroccan dirham = 100 centimes

Angola
Angola

Location: Southwestern Africa
Area: 1,246,700 sq km
Highest Point: Morro de Moco (2,629 m)
Important Rivers: Cuanza, Longa
Capital: Luanda
Government: Republic
Administrative Divisions: 18 provinces
Population: 11 million
Ethnic Groups: Bantu speaking ethnicities (90%)
Languages: Portuguese, Bantu Languages
Religion: Christians (89%), Animists (9%)
Literacy Rate: 43%
GDP per capita: 1,900 US$
Currency: 1 kwanza = 100 lwei

As-Sūdān
Sudan

Location: North Africa
Area: 2,505,813 sq km
Important River: White Nile
Capital: Khartoum
Government: Republic
Administrative Divisions: 26 provinces
Population: 39.1 million
Ethnic Groups: Mixed Black African-Arab decent (50%), Black Africans (30%)
Languages: Arabic, English, Hamitic Languages
Religion: Muslim (74%), Animists (19%), Christians (9%)
Literacy Rate: 46%
GDP per capita: 1,900 US$
Currency: 1 Sudanese pound = 100 piaster

Benin
Benin

Location: West Africa
Area: 112,622 sq km
Highest Point: Mont Sokbaro (658 m)
Important Rivers: Niger
Capital: Porto Novo
Government: Republic
Administrative Divisions: 6 Provinces,

78 districts
Population: 7.2 million
Languages: French, Fon, Yoruba,
Other Indigenous Languages
Religion: Animists (62%), Christians (19%),
Muslims (15%)
Literacy Rate: 37%
GDP per capita: 1,100 US$
Currency: 1 CFA franc = 10 centimes

Botswana
Botswana

Location: Southern Africa
Area: 600,370 sq km
Capital: Gaborone
Government: Republic
Administrative Divisions: 11 districts
Population: 1.6 million
Ethnic Groups: Bantu ethnicities (95%),
San (5%)
Languages: Setswana, English
Religion: Animists (60%),
Christians (30%)
Literacy Rate: 70%
GDP per capita: 8,800 US$
Currency: 1 pula = 100 thebe

Burkina Faso
Burkina Faso

Location: West Africa
Area: 274,200 sq km
Highest Point: Tena Kourou (749 m)
Important River: Black Volta
Capital: Ouagadougou
Government: Republic
Administrative Divisions: 45 provinces
Population: 13.6 million
Ethnic Groups: Volta ethnicities (60%),
Mande (17%), Fulbe (10%)
Languages: French, Fulbe,
Other Indigenous Languages
Religion: Animists (60%), Muslim (30%),
Christians (10%)
Literacy Rate: 19%
GDP per capita: 1,100 US$
Currency: 1 CFA franc = 100 centimes

Burundi
Burundi

Location: East Africa
Area: 27,834 sq km
Important Lake: Lake Tanganyika
Capital: Bujumbura
Government: Presidential republic
Administrative Divisions: 15 provinces
Population: 6.2 million
Ethnic Groups: Hutu (85%),

Tutsi (14 %), Twa (1 %)
Languages: Kirundi, French, Kiswahili
Religion: Christians (70%), Animists (30%),
Muslims (1%)
Literacy Rate: 35%
GDP per capita: 600 US$
Currency: 1 Burundi franc =
100 centimes

Cabo Verde
Cape Verde

Location: Islands off the West African coast
Area: 4,033 sq km
Capital: Praia
Government: Republic
Administrative Divisions: 15 districts
Population: 415,000
Ethnic Groups: Mixed Afro-European
descent (71%), Blacks (28%), Whites (1%)
Languages: Portuguese, Creole
Religion: Christian (98%)
Literacy Rate: 72%
GDP per capita: 1,400 US$
Currency: 1 Cape Verde escudo =
100 centavos

Cameroun/Cameroon
Cameroon

Location: Central Africa
Area: 475,442 sq km
Capital: Yaoundé
Government: Presidential republic
Administrative Divisions: 10 provinces
Population: 16.1 million
Ethnic Groups: Highlanders (31%), Other
Bantu ethnicities (30%), Fulani (10%),
Languages: French, English,
Indigenous Languages
Religion: Christians (52%), Animists (26%),
Muslims (22%)
Literacy Rate: 63%
GDP per capita: 1,800 US$
Currency: 1 CFA franc = 100 centimes

Comores
Comoros

Location: Islands off the East African coast
Area: 2,170 sq km
Capital: Moroni
Government: Islamic republic
Administrative Divisions: 3 island
districts
Population: 652,000
Ethnic Groups: Comoros are primarily of
mixed Arab, Madagascan and Black African
descent
Languages: Comoro, French

Religion: Muslims (99%),
Christians (1%)
Literacy Rate: 57%
GDP per capita: 700 US$
Currency: 1 Comorian franc =
100 centimes

Congo
Republic of Congo

Location: Central Africa
Area: 342,000 sq km
Important River: Congo
Capital: Brazzaville
Government: Republic
Administrative Divisions: 9 regions and
4 urban districts
Population: 3 million
Ethnic Groups: Bantu ethnicities (88%)
Languages: French, Bantu languages
Religion: Catholic (54%),
Animists (19%)
Literacy Rate: 74%
GDP per capita: 700 US$
Currency: 1 CFA franc = 100 centimes

Congo, République
démocratique
Democratic Republic of
Congo (Formerly Zaire)

Location: Central Africa
Area: 2,345,410 sq km
Highest Point: Mt. Stanley (5,109 m)
Capital: Kinshasa
Government: Presidential republic
Administrative Divisions: 10 regions,
1 district
Population: 58.3 million
Ethnic Groups: Bantu ethnicities (80%),
Sudanese ethnicities (17%)
Languages: French, Indigenous Languages
Religion: Catholic (48%), Protestants
(29%), other Christians
Literacy Rate: 76%
GDP per capita: 600 US$
Currency: 1 Congo franc = 100 makutta

Côte d'Ivoire
Côte d'Ivoire/ Ivory Coast

Location: West Africa
Area: 322,462 sq km
Highest Point: Nimba (1,752 m)
Important Rivers: Sassandra, Komoe
Capital: Yamoussoukro
Government: Presidential republic
Administrative Divisions:
49 departments
Population: 17.3 million

Ethnic Groups: Akan (41%), Gur (17%), Mandes (27%), Other African Indigenous
Languages: French, Dioula, and Indigenous Languages
Religion: Animists (50%), Muslims (30%), Christians (20%)
Literacy Rate: 40%
GDP per capita: 1,400 US$
Currency: 1CFA franc = 100 centimes

Djibouti
Djibouti

Location: Northeastern Africa
Area: 23,200 sq km
Capital: Djibouti
Government: Republic
Administrative Divisions: 4 districts
Population: 467,000
Ethnic Groups: Somalis (50%), Afar (40%), Arabs, Ethiopians, Europeans
Languages: French, Arabic, Cushitic Languages
Religion: Muslim (96%), Christians (3%)
Literacy Rate: 46%
GDP per capita: 1,300 US$
Currency: 1 Djibouti franc = 100 centimes

Eritrea
Eritrea

Location: Northeastern Africa
Area: 121,320 sq km
Capital: Asmara
Government: Republic
Administrative Divisions: 10 provinces
Population: 4.5 million
Ethnic Groups: Tigrinya (50%), Afar (8%), Tigre (30%)
Languages: Arabic, Tigrinya
Religion: Muslim (50%), Christians (50%)
Literacy Rates: 25%
GDP per capita: 700 US$
Currency: 1 birr = 100 cents

Gabon
Gabon

Location: Central Africa
Area: 267,667 sq km
Highest Point: Iboundji (1,575 m)
Important River: Ogooué
Capital: Libreville
Government: Presidential republic
Administrative Divisions: 9 provinces
Population: 1.4 million
Ethnic Groups: Fang (32%), Nzebi (8%), Other African ethnicites
Languages: French, Bantu languages

Religion: Catholic (50%), Protestants (20%), Animists
Literacy Rates: 63%
GDP per capita: 5,500 US$
Currency: 1 CFA franc = 100 centimes

Gambia
Gambia

Location: West Africa
Area: 11,295 sq km
Important River: Gambia
Capital: Banjul
Government: Presidential republic
Administrative Division: 6 regions, 35 districts
Population: 1.5 million
Ethnic Groups: Mandingo (44%), Fulbe (18%), Wolof (12%)
Languages: English, Mandingo, Wolof, Other Indigenous Languages
Religion: Muslims (90%), Christians, Animists
Literacy Rate: 37%
GDP per capita: 1,700 US$
Currency: 1 dalasi = 100 butut

Ghana
Ghana

Location: West Africa
Area: 239,460 sq km
Important River: White Volta
Capital: Accra
Government: Presidential republic
Administrative Divisions: 10 regions, 110 districts
Population: 20.8 million
Ethnic Groups: Ashanti (52%), Moshi (16%), Ewe (13%), Ga (8%), other indigenous ethnic groups
Languages: English, more than 70 other languages
Religion: Christians (60%), Muslims (16%), Animists
Literacy Rate: 64%
GDP per capita: 2,200 US$
Currency: 1 cedi = 100 pesewa

Guinea-Bissau
Guinea-Bissau

Location: West Africa
Area: 36,125 sq km
Capital: Bissau
Government: Presidential republic
Administrative Divisions: 3 provinces, 8 regions, 1 municipality
Population: 1.4 million
Ethnic Groups: Balantu (25%),

Fulbe (20%), Mandingo (12%)
Languages: Portuguese, Creole
Religion: Animists (54%), Muslim (38%), Christians (8%)
Literacy Rate: 55%
GDP per capita: 900 US$
Currency: 1 Guinea-peso = 100 centavos

Guinea Ecuatorial
Equatorial Guinea

Location: Central Africa
Area: 28,051 sq km
Capital: Malabo
Government: Presidential republic
Administrative Divisions: 7 provinces
Population: 523,000
Ethnic Groups: Bantu ethnicities (80%), Bubi (10%)
Languages: Spanish, English, Indigenous Languages
Religion: Christians (90%), Animists
Literacy Rate: 78%
GDP per capita: 2,700 US$
Currency: 1 CFA franc = 100 centimes

Guinée
Guinea

Location: West Africa
Area: 245,857 sq km
Highest Point: Tamgué (1,538 m)
Important River: Niger
Capital: Conakry
Government: Republic
Administrative Divisions: 4 main regions, 30 lesser regions, 1 district
Population: 9.2 million
Ethnic Groups: Mandingo (45%), Fulbe (30%), Kissi (7%), Kpelle (5%)
Languages: French, Indigenous Languages
Religion: Muslim (90%), Christians (2%), Animists
Literacy Rate: 36%
GDP per capita: 2,170 US$
Currency: 1 Guinean franc = 100 cauris

Îtyopya
Ethiopia

Location: Northeastern Africa
Area: 1,127,127 sq km
Highest Point: Ras Dejen (4,620 m)
Important Lake/River: Lake Tsana, Blue Nile
Capital: Addis Ababa
Government: Federal republic

Administrative Divisions: 9 regions,
1 district (Addis Ababa)
Population: 67.8 million
Ethnic Groups: Oromo (40%),
Amharan (28%), Tigre (9%),
70 other ethnicities
Languages: Amharic, 70 other indigenous
languages
Religion: Christians (45%), Muslim (45%),
Animists
Literacy Rate: 35%
GDP per capita: 700 US$
Currency: 1 birr = 100 cents

Kenya
Kenya

Location: East Africa
Area: 582,646 sq km
Highest Point: Mt. Kenya (5,200 m)
Important Body of Water: Lake Victoria
Capital: Nairobi
Government: Presidential republic
Administrative Divisions: 7 provinces,
1 district (Nairobi)
Population: 32 million
Ethnic Groups: Bantu ethnicities (60%),
Nilotes (24%) Massai (2%)
Languages: Swahili, English,
Indigenous Languages
Religion: Christian and Animist majority,
Muslims (6%)
Literacy Rate: 77%
GDP per capita: 1,000 US$
Currency: 1 Kenyan shilling =
100 cents

Lesotho
Lesotho

Location: Southern Africa
Area: 30,355 sq km
Highest Point: Ntlenyana (3,482 m)
Capital: Maseru
Government: Constitutional
monarchy
Administrative Divisions: 10 districts
Population: 1.9 million
Ethnic Groups: Sotho (99%)
Languages: Sesotho, English
Religion: Catholics (44%),
Protestants (30%), Animists
Literacy Rate: 71%
GDP per capita: 3,000 US$
Currency: 1 loti = 100 lisente

Liberia
Liberia

Location: West Africa

Area: 111,369 sq km
Highest Point: Wuteve (1,380 m)
Capital: Monrovia
Government: Presidential republic
Administrative Divisions: 11 districts,
4 territories
Population: 3.4 million
Ethnic Groups: African ethnicities including
Kru, Grebo, and Kpelle (95%),
Americo-Liberians; of African American
descent (2.5%)
Languages: English, indigenous languages
Religion: Christians, Animists,
Muslim (10%)
Literacy Rate: 39%
GDP per capita: 1,000 US$
Currency: 1 Liberian dollar =
100 cents

Lîbîyâ
Libya

Location: North Africa
Area: 1,759,540 sq km
Highest Point: Pic Bette (2,285 m)
Capital: Tripoli
Government: Authoritarian Islamic
republic
Administrative Divisions: 13 regions
Population: 5.6 million
Ethnic Groups: Libyans of Arab descent,
Berbers, Black Africans
Languages: Arabic, Berber languages
Religion: Muslims (97%)
Literacy: 74%
GDP per capita: 6,400 US$
Currency: 1 Libyan dollar =
1,000 dirham

Madagasíkara
Madagascar

Location: One main island and smaller
islands off the southeastern coast of Africa
Area: 587,041 sq km
Highest Point: Maromokotro (2,876 m)
Important River: Mangoky
Capital: Antananarivo
Administrative Divisions: 28 regions
Population: 17.5 million
Ethnic Groups: Madagascans, of mixed
Malayan and Black African descent (99%)
Languages: Malagasy, French,
Howa
Religion: Animists (50%), Christians (45%),
Muslims (5%)
Literacy Rate: 80%
GDP per capita: 800 US$
Currency: 1 Madagascan franc =
100 centimes

Malawi
Malawi

Location: Southern Africa
Area: 118,484 sq km
Highest Point: Mulanje (3,000 m)
Important Bodies of Water: Lake Nyasa,
Lake Malombe, Lake Chilwa
Capital: Lilongwe
Government: Presidential republic
Administrative Divisions: 3 regions
divided into 27 districts
Population: 11.9 million
Ethnic Groups: Bantu ethnicities,
including the Chewa, Nyanja, Yao,
etc. (95%)
Religion: Christians (75%), Animists (15%),
Muslims
Literacy Rate: 56%
GDP per capita: 600 US$
Currency: 1 Malawian kwacha =
100 tambala

Mali
Mali

Location: West Africa
Area: 1,240,192 sq km
Important River: Niger
Capital: Bamako
Administrative Divisions: 8 regions,
1 district
Population: 12 million
Ethnic Groups: Bambara (32%),
Fulbe (14%) Soninke (9%), Taureg (7%),
Other Indigenous Groups
Languages: French, Bambara,
Other Mandé Languages
Religion: Muslim (80%), Christians (1%),
Animists
Literacy Rate: 30%
GDP per capita: 900 US$
Currency: 1 CFA franc =
100 centimes

Mauritius
Mauritius

Location: Indian Ocean off Southeastern
Africa
Area: 2,040 sq km
Capital: Port Louis
Government: Republic
Administrative Divisions: 9 districts,
3 dependencies
Population: 1.2 million
Ethnic Groups: Indians (69%), Creoles of
black African descent (27%), Chinese (3%),
Whites (3%)
Languages: English, Creole, Hindi

Religion: Hindus (52%), Christians (30%), Muslims (13%)
Literacy Rate: 83%
GDP per capita: 11,400 US$
Currency: 1 Mauritian rupee = 100 kobo

Mawrītāniyah
Mauritania

Location: West Africa
Area: 1,030,700 sq km
Important River: Senegal
Capital: Nouakchott
Government: Islamic republic
Administrative Divisions: 13 regions
Population: 3 million
Ethnic Groups: Arab-Berber descent (81%), Wolof (7%), other major ethnicities (9%)
Languages: Arabic, Niger-Congo Languages
Religion: Muslim (99%)
Literacy Rate: 36%
GDP per capita: 1,800 US$
Currency: 1 ouguiya = 5 khoums

Moçambique
Mozambique

Location: Southern Africa
Area: 801,590 sq km
Highest Point: Binga (2,436 m)
Important Rivers: Zambezi, Limpopo
Capital: Maputo
Government: Republic
Administrative Division: 10 provinces, 1 district
Population: 18.8 million
Ethnic Groups: Makau (47%), Tsonga (23%), Malawi (12%), Shona (11%)
Languages: Portuguese, Bantu languages
Religion: Animists (50%), Christians, Muslims
Literacy Rate: 40%
GDP per capita: 1,200 US$
Currency: 1 metical = 100 centavos

Namibia
Namibia

Location: Southwestern Africa
Area: 825,418 sq km
Highest Point: Konigstein (2,606 m)
Important Rivers: Orange, Cunene, Okavango
Capital: Windhoek
Government: Republic

Administrative Divisions: 13 regions
Population: 1.9 million
Ethnic Groups: Ovambo (47%), Kavango (9%), Herero (7%), Damara (7%) Whites, primarily of German and Afrikaner descent (6%)
Languages: English, Afrikaans, German
Religion: Lutherans (52%), Catholics (20%), Dutch Reformed Church (6%), Anglicans (5%)
Literacy Rate: 40%
GDP per capita: 7,100 US$
Currency: 1 Namibia dollar = 100 cents

Niger
Niger

Location: West Africa
Area: 1,267,000 sq km
Highest Point: Bagzane (2,022 m)
Important River: Niger
Capital: Niamey
Government: Presidential republic
Administrative Divisions: 8 departments
Population: 11.4 million
Ethnic Groups: Hausa (54%), Djerma (21%), Taureg (9%)
Languages: French, Hausa, Other Indigenous Languages
Religion: Muslim (90%), Animists
Literacy Rate: 13%
GDP per capita: 800 US$
Currency: 1 CFA franc = 100 centimes

Nigeria
Nigeria

Location: West Africa
Area: 923,768 sq km
Highest Point: Chappal Waddi (2,419 m)
Important Rivers/Body of Water: Niger, Benue, Lake Chad
Capital: Abuja
Government: Presidential republic
Administrative Divisions: 36 states, 1 capital district
Population: 137.3 million
Ethnic Groups: Hausa-Fulani (21%), Yoruba (21%), Ibo (18%), Ibibo (6%), 430 other ethnicities
Languages: English, Arabic, Indigenous Languages
Religion: Christians (49%), Muslim (45%), Animists
Literacy Rate: 57%
GDP per capita: 800 US$
Currency: 1 Naira = 100 Kobo

République Centrafricaine
Central African Republic

Location: Central Africa
Area: 622,984 sq km
Highest Point: Ngaoui (1,420 m)
Important River: Ubangi
Capital: Bangui
Government: Presidential republic
Administrative Divisions: 16 prefectures, 1 district
Population: 3.7 million
Ethnic Groups: Banda (30%), Baya (24%), Sara (11%)
Languages: French, Sangho
Religion: Animists (57%), Christians (35%), Muslims (8%)
Literacy Rate: 59%
GDP per capita: 1,200 US$
Currency: 1 CFA franc = 100 centimes

Rwanda
Rwanda

Location: East Africa
Area: 26,338 sq km
Highest Point: Karisimbi (4,519 m)
Important Body of Water: Lake Kivu
Capital: Kigali
Government: Presidential republic
Administrative Divisions: 11 prefectures
Population: 7.9 million
Ethnic Groups: Hutu and related ethnicities (85%), Tutsi (14%), Pygmies (1%)
Languages: Kinya-rwanda, French, Swahili, English, Indigenous Languages
Religion: Catholic (45%), Protestants (10%), Muslims (10%), Animists
Literacy Rate: 60%
GDP per capita: 1,300 US$
Currency: 1 Rwandan franc = 100 centimes

São Tomé e Príncipe
Sao Tome and Principe

Location: West Africa
Area: 1,001 sq km
Highest Point: Pico de Sao Tome (2,024 m)
Capital: Sao Tome
Government: Republic
Administrative Divisions: District of Sao Tome and autonomous island of Principe
Population: 182,000
Ethnic Groups: Black Africans,

177

Mixed Afro-European descent, Portuguese
Languages: Portuguese, Creole
Religion: Catholic (90%), Protestant (5%),
Animists
Literacy Rate: 66%
GDP per capita: 1,200 US$
Currency: 1 dobra = 100 centimes

Sénégal
Senegal

Location: West Africa
Area: 196,722 sq km
Important River: Senegal
Capitol: Dakar
Government: Presidential republic
Administrative Divisions: 10 regions
Population: 10.8 million
Ethnic Groups: Wolof (44%), Serer (15%),
Other major ethnic groups (35%)
Languages: French, Wolof
Religion: Muslims (94%), Christians (5%),
Animists
Literacy Rate: 33%
GDP per capita: 1,600 US$
Currency: 1 CFA franc =
100 centimes

Seychelles
Seychelles

Location: Islands off the East African coast
Area: 454 sq km
Capital: Victoria
Government: Republic
Administrative Divisions: 23 districts
Population: 81,000 (175 sq km)
Ethnic Groups: Creoles (89%),
Indians (5%), Madagascans (3%),
Chinese (2%), Malays, Whites
Languages: English, French, Creole
Religion: Catholic (89%), Anglicans (8%),
Hindus (1%)
Literacy Rate: 89%
GDP per capita: 7,800 US$
Currency: 1 Seychelles rupee = 100 cents

Sierra Leone
Sierra Leone

Location: West Africa
Area: 71,740 sq km
Highest Point: Loma Monsa (1,948 m)
Capital: Freetown
Government: Republic
Administrative Divisions: 4 provinces,
1 District
Population: 5.9 million
Ethnic Groups: Mende (35%), Temne
(32%), Creoles (10%),

Small Arab Minority
Languages: English, Creole
Religion: Animists (53%), Muslims (39%),
Christians (8%)
Literacy Rate: 31%
GDP per capita: 500 US$
Currency: 1 leone = 100 cents

Soomaaliya
Somalia

Location: Northeastern Africa
Area: 637,657 sq km
Highest Point: Shimbiris (2,416 m)
Capital: Mogadishu
Government: Republic
Administrative Divisions: 18 provinces
Population: 8.3 million
Ethnic Groups: Somali ethnicities (95%),
Arab and Bantu speaking minorities
Languages: Somali, Arabic, English,
Italian
Religion: Muslims (99%),
Christians (less than 1%)
Literacy Rate: 24%
GDP per capita: 500 US$
Currency: 1 Somali shilling =
100 centesimi

South Africa/Suid-Afrika
South Africa

Location: Southern Africa
Area: 1,219,912 sq km
Highest Point: Njesuthi (3,808 m)
Important River: Orange, Vaal
Capital: Pretoria
Government: Republic
Administrative Divisions: 9 provinces
Population: 43.6 million
Ethnic Groups: Black Africans, mostly Zulu
and Bantu ethnicities (76%), European
descent (13%), Mixed Afro-European
descent (9%), Asians (3%)
Languages: English, Afrikaans, Zulu,
Bantu Languages
Religion: Christians (78%), Hindus (2%),
Muslims (1%), Animists
Literacy Rate: 82%
GDP per capita: 10,700 US$
Currency: 1 rand = 100 cents

Swaziland (kaNgwane)
Swaziland

Location: Southern Africa
Area: 17,363 sq km
Capital: Mbabane
Government: Constitutional
monarchy

Administrative Divisions: 273 clan
districts
Population: 1.2 million
Ethnic Groups: Swazis (97%), Zulus,
Tsonga
Languages: English, Swazi
Religion: Christians (70%),
Animists (30%)
Literacy Rate: 75%
GDP per capita: 4,900 US$
Currency: 1 lilangeni = 100 cents

Tanzania
Tanzania

Location: East Africa
Area: 945,087 sq km
Highest Point: Kilimanjaro (5,895 m)
Important Bodies of Water: Lake
Victoria, Lake Tanganyika
Capital: Dodoma and Dar es Salaam
Government: Federal presidential republic
Administrative Divisions: 25 regions
Population: 36.6 million
Ethnic Groups: Bantu ethnicities (95%),
Other Black Africans (4.5%) Whites, Arabs,
Asians
Languages: Swahili, English
Religion: Christians (45%), Muslims (33%),
Animists
Literacy Rate: 67%
GDP per capita: 600 US$
Currency: 1 Tanzanian shilling =
100 cents

Tchad
Chad

Location: Central Africa
Area: 1,284,000 sq km
Important Body of Water: Lake Chad
Capital: N'Djamena
Government: Presidential republic
Administrative Divisions: 14 prefectures
Population: 9.5 million
Ethnic Groups: Arabs (15%),
Sara (30%), Mixed Arab-African descent
(38%)
Languages: French, Arabic
Religion: Muslims (45%), Christians (30%),
Animists
Literacy Rate: 48%
GDP per capita: 1,200 US$
Currency: 1 CFA franc =
100 centimes

Togo
Togo

Location: West Africa

Location: West Africa
Area: 56,785 sq km
Capital: Lome
Government: Presidential republic
Administrative Divisions: 5 regions
Population: 5.5 million
Ethnic Groups: Ewe (46%),
Volta ethnicities (43%), Hausa, Fulbe
Languages: French, Ewe, Kabye
Religion: Animists (50%), Christians (35%)
Literacy Rate: 52%
GDP per capita: 1,500 US$
Currency: 1 CFA franc = 100 centimes

Tūnisiyah/Tunisie
Tunisia

Location: North Africa
Area: 163,610 sq km
Highest Point: Tellatlas (1,200 m)
Capital: Tunis
Government: Presidential republic
Administrative Divisions: 23 provinces
Population: 9.9 million
Ethnic Groups: Arab/Arabic Berbers (98%),
Berbers (1%)
Languages: Arabic, French,
Religion: Muslim (99%),
Christian and Jewish minorities
Literacy Rate: 66%
GDP per capita: 6,900 US$
Currency: 1 Tunisian dinar = 1,000 millimes

Uganda
Uganda

Location: East Africa
Area: 236,040 sq km
Highest Point: Mt. Stanley (5,109 m)
Important Bodies of Water: Lake Kyoga,
Lake Albert
Capital: Kampala
Government: Presidential republic
Administrative Divisions: 38 districts
Population: 26.4 million
Ethnic Groups: Bantu ethnicities (50%),
Sudanese ethnicities (5%), Nilotes (13%)
Languages: Swahili, English, Luganda
Religion: Catholics (45%),
Protestants (25%), Muslims (5%),
Animists
Literacy Rate: 62%
GDP per capita: 1,400 US$
Currency: 1 Ugandan shilling =
100 cents

Zambia
Zambia

Location: Southern Africa

Area: 752,614 sq km
Highest Point: Mafinga Hills (2,301 m)
Important Body of Water: Lake Kariba
Important River: Zambezi
Capital: Lusaka
Government: Presidential republic
Administrative Divisions: 9 provinces
Population: 10.4 million
Ethnic Groups: African ethnic groups,
including Luba, Lunda, Nyanja, Tonga,
etc. (98%), Whites (1%)
Languages: English,
Bantu languages
Religion: Christians (72%),
Animists (27%)
Literacy Rate: 78 %
GDP per capita: 800 US$
Currency: 1 kwacha = 100 ngwee

Zimbabwe
Zimbabwe

Location: Southern Africa
Area: 390,580 sq km
Highest Point: Inyangani (2,592 m)
Important Body of Water: Lake Kariba
Important River: Zambezi
Capital: Harare
Government: Presidential republic
Administrative Divisions: 8 provinces
Population: 12.6 million
Ethnic Groups: Shona (80%),
Ndebele (17%), Whites (2%)
Languages: English,
Bantu languages
Religion: Animists (40%),
Protestants (17%), Indigenous Christian
Denominations (14%), Catholics (12%)
Literacy Rate: 85%
GDP per capita: 1,900 US$
Currency: 1 Zimbabwean dollar =
100 cents

NORTH AMERICA AND THE CARRIBEAN

Antigua and Barbuda
Antigua and Barbuda

Location: Caribbean Islands
Area: 442 sq km
Capital: St. John's
Government: Constitutional monarchy
Administrative Divisions: 6 districts,
2 dependencies
Population: 68,300
Ethnic Groups: African descent (95%),
Mixed Afro-European descent (4%),

European descent (2%)
Languages: English, Creole
Religion: Christians (97%),
Rastafarians (<1%)
Literacy Rate: 96%
GDP per capita: 11,000 US$
Currency: 1 East Caribbean dollar =
100 cents

Bahamas
Bahamas

Location: Caribbean/Atlantic Ocean Islands
Area: 13,939 sq km
Capital: Nassau
Government: Parliamentary monarchy
Administrative Divisions: 18 districts
Population: 300,000
Ethnic Groups: African descent (72%),
Mixed Afro-European descent (14%),
European descent (12%)
Language: English
Religion: Baptists (32%),
Anglicans (20%), Catholics (19%),
Other Christians (12%)
Literacy Rate: 98%
GDP per capita: 16,800 US$
Currency: 1 Bahamian dollar =
100 cents

Barbados
Barbados

Location: Caribbean Island
Area: 430 sq km
Highest Point: Mt. Hillaby (340 m)
Capital: Bridgetown
Government: Parliamentary monarchy
Administrative Divisions: 11 districts
Population: 276,000
Ethnic Groups: African descent (92%),
Mixed African-European descent (3%),
Whites (3%)
Languages: English, Bajan (local dialect)
Religion: Anglicans (40%), Other Christian
churches (30%)
Literacy Rate: 98%
GDP per capita: 16,200 US$
Currency: 1 Barbados dollar =
100 cents

Belize
Belize

Location: Central America
Area: 22,965 sq km
Highest Point: Maya Mountains (1,122 m)
Capital: Belmopan
Government: Constitutional monarchy
Administrative Divisions: 6 districts

179

Population: 273,000
Ethnic Groups: Mestizos (44%), Creoles of
Afro-European descent (30%),
Amerindians (11%), Garifuna (7%)
Languages: English, Creole, Spanish
Religion: Catholics (58%),
Protestants (28%)
Literacy Rate: 90%
GDP per capita: 4,900 US$
Currency: 1 Belizean dollar =
100 cents

Canada
Canada

Location: North America
Area: 9,984,670 sq km
Highest Point: Mt. Logan (6,050 m)
Important Rivers: St. Lawrence,
Saskatchewan
Capital: Ottawa
Government: Parliamentary monarchy
Administrative Divisions: 10 provinces,
3 territories
Population: 32.5 million
Ethnic Groups: British/Irish descent (28%),
French descent (23%), Other European
(15%), Mixed descent (26%),
Amerindian/Inuit (2%),
African/Asian/Arab descent (6%)
Languages: English, French
Religion: Catholic (47%),
Protestant (36%), other Christians,
Muslims, Jews
Literacy Rate: 99%
GDP per capita: 29,700 US$
Currency: 1 Canadian dollar =
100 cents

Costa Rica
Costa Rica

Location: Central America
Area: 51,100 sq km
Highest Point: Cerro Chirripo (3,820 m)
Capital: San Jose
Government: Presidential republic
Administrative Divisions: 7 provinces
Population: 3.9 million
Ethnic Groups: European descent;
primarily Spanish ancestry (87%),
Mestizos (7%), African descent (3%),
Asians (2%), Amerindians (1%)
Languages: Spanish, English,
West Indian Creole
Religion: Catholics (89%),
Protestants (8%)
Literacy Rate: 95%
GDP per capita: 9,000 US$
Currency: 1 colon = 100 centavos

Cuba
Cuba

Location: Carribean Island
Area: 110,860 sq km
Highest Point: Sierra Maestra (1,974 m)
Capital: Havana
Government: Socialist republic
Administrative Divisions: 14 provinces,
1 special administrative zone
Population: 11.3 million
Ethnic Groups: Mixed Afro-European
descent (51%), European descent (37%),
African descent (11%), East Asians
Language: Spanish
Religion: Catholics (39%),
Protestants (5%),
Nondenominational Christians, Atheists
Literacy Rate: 96%
GDP per capita: 2,800 US$
Currency: 1 Cuban peso =
100 centavos

Dominica
Dominica

Location: Caribbean Island
Area: 750 sq km
Highest Point: Morne Diablotins (1,447 m)
Capital: Roseau
Government: Republic
Administrative Divisions: 10 districts
Population: 70,000
Ethnic Groups: African descent (91%),
Mixed Afro-European descent (6%),
East Indians (2%)
Languages: English, Patois
Religion: Catholic (78%),
Protestants (16%)
Literacy: 94%
GDP per capita: 5,400 US$
Currency: 1 East Caribbean dollar =
100 cents

El Salvador
El Salvador

Location: Central America
Area: 21,041 sq km
Highest Point: Santa Ana (2,381 m)
Important Body of Water: Ilopango
Capital: San Salvador
Government: Presidential republic
Administrative Divisions: 14
departments
Population: 6.6 million
Ethnic Groups: Mestizos (89%),
Amerindians (10%), European descent (1%)
Languages: Spanish, Indigenous
Languages

Religion: Catholics (83%), Large and fast
growing Evangelical minority
Literacy: 71.5%
GDP per capita: 4,800 US$
Currency: 1 Salvadoran colon =
100 centavos

Grenada
Grenada

Location: Caribbean Island
Area: 344 sq km
Highest Point: Mt. Saint Catherine (840 m)
Capital: St. George's
Government: Constitutional Monarchy
Population: 89,300
Ethnic Groups: African descent (82%),
Mixed Afro-European descent (13%),
East Indians
Languages: English, Patois
Religion: Catholic (55%),
Protestant (35%)
Literacy: 95%
GDP per capita: 5,000 US$
Currency: 1 East Caribbean dollar =
100 cents

Guatemala
Guatemala

Location: Central America
Area: 108,889 sq km
Highest Point: Tajumulco (4,220 m)
Capital: Guatemala City
Government: Presidential republic
Administrative Divisions: 22
departments
Population: 14.3 million
Ethnic Groups: Amerindians; including
Maya (60%), Mestizos (30%)
Languages: Spanish, Indigenous Languages
Religion: Catholics (80%),
Protestants (20%)
GDP per capita: 4,100 US$
Currency: 1 quetzal = 100 centavos

Haïti
Haiti

Location: Caribbean Island
Area: 27,750 sq km
Highest Point: Massif du Sud (2,347 m)
Capital: Port au Prince
Government: Presidential republic
Administrative Divisions: 9 departments
Population: 7.6 million
Ethnic Groups: Black (95%), Whites and
Mixed Afro-European descent (5%)
Languages: French, Haitian Creole
Religion: Catholics (80%), Protestants

(15%), Animism including Voodoo
Literacy Rate: 45%
GDP per capita: 1,600 US$
Currency: 1 gourde = 100 centimes

Honduras
Honduras

Location: Central America
Area: 112,088 sq km
Highest Point: Cerro Las Minas (2,840 m)
Capital: Tegucigalpa
Government: Presidential republic
Administrative Divisions: 18 districts
Population: 6.8 million
Ethnic Groups: Mestizos (90%),
Indians (6%), African descent (2%)
Languages: Spanish, English, Indigenous
Languages
Religion: Catholics (85%),
Protestants (10%)
Literacy Rate: 73%
GDP per capita: 2,600 US$
Currency: 1 lempira = 100 centavos

Jamaica
Jamaica

Location: Caribbean Island
Area: 10,990 sq km
Highest Point: Blue Mountain Peak
(2,256 m)
Capital: Kingston
Government: Parliamentary monarchy
Administrative Divisions: 14 districts
Population: 2.7 million
Ethnic Groups: African descent (76%),
Mixed Afro-European descent (15%), East
Indians, Chinese
Languages: English, Patois
Religion: Protestants (60%),
Catholics (5%), Rastafarians (5%)
Literacy Rate: 85%
GDP per capita: 3,800 US$
Currency: 1 Jamaican dollar = 100 cents

México
Mexico

Location: Central America
Area: 1,972,550 sq km
Highest Point: Citlaltepetl (5,700 m)
Important River: Rio Grande
Capital: Mexico City
Government: Presidential government
Administrative Divisions: 5 regions,
31 states, 1 federal district
Population: 105 million
Ethnic Groups: Mestizos (75%),
Amerindians (14%), Whites(10%)

Languages: Spanish, Indigenous
Languages
Religion: Catholic (90%),
Protestants (5%)
Literacy Rate: 90%
GDP per capita: 9,000 US$
Currency: 1 new Mexican peso =
100 centavos

Nicaragua
Nicaragua

Location: Central America
Area: 129,494 sq km
Highest Point: Cerro Mogoton (2,107 m)
Important Lakes: Lake Nicaragua,
Lake Managua
Capital: Managua
Government: Presidential republic
Administrative Divisions: 16
departments
Population: 5.3 million
Ethnic Groups: Mestizos (69%),
European descent (14%),
African descent (9%), Amerindian (4%),
Mixed Afro-European descent
Languages: Spanish, Chibcha
Religion: Catholic (90%),
Protestants (5%)
Literacy Rate: 66%
GDP per capita: 2,200 US$
Currency: 1 córdoba =
100 centavos

Panamá
Panama

Location: Central America
Area: 78,200 sq km
Highest Point: Chiriqui (3,475 m)
Capital: Panama City
Government: Presidential republic
Administrative Divisions: 9 provinces,
Canal Zone
Population: 3 million
Ethnic Groups: Mestizos (65%),
African descent (13%),Asians (2%)
European descent (10%), Amerindians (8%),
Languages: Spanish, English
Religion: Catholic (95%),
Protestants (5%)
Literacy Rate: 91%
GDP per capita: 6,300 US$
Currency: 1 balboa = 100 centesimo

República Dominicana
Dominican Republic

Location: Caribbean Island
Area: 48,730 sq km

Highest Point: Pico Duarte (3,175 m)
Capital: Santo Domingo
Government: Presidential republic
Administrative Division: 26 provinces,
1 special district
Population: 8.8 million
Ethnic Groups: Mixed Afro-European
descent (60%), European descent (28%),
African descent (12%)
Language: Spanish
Religion: Catholic (90%), Protestants,
Jewish, Bahai
Literacy Rate: 82%
GDP per capita: 6,000 US$
Currency: 1 Dominican peso =
100 centavos

Saint Kitts and Nevis
Saint Kitts and Nevis

Location: Caribbean Island
Area: 261.6 sq km
Highest Point: Mt. Liamuiga (1,156 m)
Capital: Basseterre
Government: Constitutional monarchy
Administrative Divisions: 14 districts
Population: 39,000
Ethnic Groups: African descent (86%),
Mixed Afro-European descent (11%),
European descent (2%)
Language: English
Religion: Anglicans (36%),
Methodists (32%), Catholics (11%)
Literacy Rate: 90%
GDP per capita: 8,800 US$
Currency: 1 East Caribbean dollar =
100 cents

Saint Lucia
Saint Lucia

Location: Caribbean Island
Area: 616.3 km
Highest Point: Mt. Gimie (958 m)
Capital: Castries
Government: Constitutional monarchy
Administrative Divisions: 11
municipalities
Population: 164,000
Ethnic Groups: African descent (91%),
Mixed Afro-European descent (6%),
Asians (3%), European descent (1%)
Languages: English,
Patois (local French Creole)
Religion: Catholics (77%),
Protestants (15%)
Literacy Rate: 82%
GDP per capita: 4,500 US$
Currency: 1 East Caribbean dollar =
100 cents

Saint Vincent and the Grenadines
Saint Vincent and the Grenadines

Location: Caribbean Island
Area: 389 sq km
Highest Point: Soufriere (1,234 m)
Capital: Kingstown
Government: Constitutional monarchy
Administrative Divisions: 6 districts
Population: 117,000
Ethnic Groups: African descent (66%), Mixed Afro-European descent (19%), East Indian (6%), Whites (4%), Zambos of Mixed Afro-Amerindian descent (2%)
Language: English
Religion: Protestant (75%), Catholics (10%)
Literacy Rate: 82%
GDP per capita: 2,900 US$
Currency: 1 East Caribbean dollar = 100 cents

Trinidad and Tobago
Trinidad and Tobago

Location: Caribbean Islands
Area: 5,128 sq km
Capital: Port of Spain
Government: Presidential republic
Administrative Divisions: 8 counties, 3 municipalities, autonomous district of Tobago
Population: 1.1 million
Ethnic Groups: East Indians (40%), African descent (40%), Mixed descent (19%)
Language: English
Religion: Catholic (30%), Hindus (24%), Anglicans (11%), Muslims (6%)
Literacy Rate: 98%
GDP per capita: 9,600 US$
Currency: 1 Trinidad-Tobago dollar = 100 cents

United States of Amerika
United States of America

Location: North America
Area: 9,631,418 sq km
Highest Point: Mt. McKinley (6,193 m)
Important Bodies of Water/Rivers: The Great Lakes, Great Salt Lake, Mississippi/Missouri River, Colorado River, Rio Grande, Arkansas River
Capital: Washington D.C
Government: Federal republic
Administrative Divisions: 50 states,

1 federal district (Washington D.C)
External Territories: Northern Marianas, Puerto Rico, American Virgin Islands, American Samoa, Guam, Midway Island
Population: 293 million
Ethnic Groups: Whites (74%), African-Americans (13%), Latinos (13%), Asians/Pacific Islanders (4%), Amerindians (1%)
Languages: English, Spanish, Amerindian Languages
Religion: Protestant denominations, including Baptists, Methodists, Presbyterians, and Lutherans (50%), Catholics (26%), Jewish (3%), Muslims (2%), Orthodox Christians (2%)
Literacy Rate: 98%
GDP per capita: 37,800 US$
Currency: 1 US dollar = 100 cents

SOUTH AMERICA

Argentina
Argentina

Location: Southern S. America
Area: 2,766,889 sq km
Highest Point: Aconcagua (6,959 m)
Important Rivers: Colorado, Rio Negro/Parana
Capital: Buenos Aires
Government: Federal republic
Administrative Divisions: 22 provinces, 1 federal district, 1 territory
Population: 39.1 million
Ethnic Groups: European descent (90%), Other Latin Americans (6%), Mestizos (5%), Amerindians
Language: Spanish
Religion: Catholic (91%), Protestant (2%), Jewish (1%)
Literacy Rate: 96%
GDP per capita: 11,200 US$
Currency: 1 Argentinean peso = 100 centavos

Bolivia
Bolivia

Location: Central S. America
Area: 1,098,581 sq km
Highest Point: Illimani (6,882 m)
Important Bodies of Water: Lake Titicaca, Lake Poopó
Capital: Sucre
Government: Presidential republic
Administrative Divisions: 9 departments
Population: 8.7 million
Ethnic Groups: Amerindians (42%),

Mestizos (31%), European descent (27%)
Languages: Spanish, Quechua, Aymara
Religion: Catholic (93%), Protestants
Literacy Rate: 83%
GDP per capita: 2,400 US$
Currency: 1 boliviano = 100 centavos

Brasil
Brazil

Location: Eastern S. America
Area: 8,511,996 sq km
Highest Point: Pico de Neblina (3,014 m)
Important Rivers: Amazon, Parana
Capital: Brasilia
Government: Federal republic
Administrative Divisions: 26 states, 1 district
Population: 184 million
Ethnic Groups: European descent (53%), Mixed Afro-European descent (34%), African descent (11%), Mestizos, Japanese, Arabs, Amerindian
Languages: Portuguese, Indigenous Languages
Religion: Catholic, (85%), Protestants (10%), Afro-Brazilian religious practices
Literacy: 83%
GDP per capita: 7,600 US$
Currency: 1 real = 100 centavos

Chile
Chile

Location: Southern S. America
Area: 756,950 sq km
Highest Point: Llullaillaco (6,723 m)
Capital: Santiago de Chile
Government: Presidential Republic
Administrative Divisions: 12 regions and 1 capital district
Population: 15.8 million
Ethnic Groups: Mestizos and European descent (92%), Amerindians (7%), Others (<1%)
Language: Spanish
Religion: Catholics (80%), Protestants (10%)
Literacy Rate: 95%
GDP per capita: 9,900 US$
Currency: 1 Chilean peso = 100 centavos

Colombia
Columbia

Location: Northwestern S.America
Area: 1,138,910 sq km

Highest Point: Nevado del Huila (5,750 m)
Important River: Putumayo
Capital: Bogotá
Government: Republic
Administrative Divisions:
32 departments, 1 capital district
Population: 42.3 million
Ethnic Groups: Mestizos (58%),
European descent (20%),
Mixed Afro-European descent (14%),
African descent and Zambos of mixed
African and Indian descent (>4%)
Amerindians (1%)
Language: Spanish
Religion: Catholic (95%), Protestant (1%)
Literacy Rate: 91%
GDP per capita: 6,300 US$
Currency: 1 Colombian peso =
100 centavos

Ecuador
Ecuador

Location: Northwestern S. America
Area: 283,560 sq km
Highest Point: Chimborazo (6,310 m)
Capital: Quito
Government: Presidential republic
Administrative Divisions: 22 provinces
Population: 13.2 million
Ethnic Groups: Mestizos (35%),
European descent (25%),
Amerindians (20%), Mixed Afro-European
descent (15%), African descent (5%)
Languages: Spanish,
Indigenous Languages
Religion: Catholics (93%)
Literacy Rate: 90%
GDP per capita: 3,300 US$
Currency: 1 sucre = 100 centavos

Guyana
Guyana

Location: Northern S. America
Area: 214,969 sq km
Highest Point: Pico da Neblina (3,014 m)
Important River: Essequibo
Capital: Georgetown
Government: Presidential republic
Administrative Divisions: 10 regions
Population: 706,000
Ethnic Groups: East Indians (51%),
African descent (29%),
Mixed descent (11%), Amerindians (5%)
Languages: English, Hindi, Urdu
Religion: Protestants (34%),
Hindus (33%), Catholics (20%),
Muslims (8%)
Literacy Rate: 98%

GDP per capita: 4,000 US$
Currency: 1 Guyanese dollar =
100 cents

Paraguay
Paraguay

Location: Central S. America
Area: 406,752 sq km
Important River: Paraguay
Capital: Asuncion
Government: Presidential republic
Administrative Divisions:
17 departments
Population: 6.2 million
Ethnic Groups: Amerindians and Mestizos
(95%), European descent (2%)
Languages: Spanish, Guarani
Religion: Catholic (95%), Protestants (1%)
Literacy Rate: 92%
GDP per capita: 4,600 US$
Currency: 1 guarani =100 centimos

Perú
Peru

Location: Western S. America
Area: 1,285,216 sq km
Highest Point: Huascaran (6,768 m)
Important Body of Water: Lake Titicaca
Capital: Lima
Government: Presidential republic
Administrative Divisions: 25 regions
Population: 27.5 million
Ethnic Groups: Amerindians (47%),
Mestizos (33%), European descent (12%),
Afro-Peruvians, East Asians
Languages: Spanish, Quechua, Aymara
Religion: Catholics (90%),
Protestants (3%), Animists
Literacy: 89%
GDP per capita: 5,200 US$
Currency: 1 nuevo sol = 100 centimos

Suriname
Suriname

Location: Northern S. America
Area: 163,265 sq km
Highest Point: Julianatop (1,280 m)
Important Body of Water: Lake Van
Blommestein
Capital: Paramaribo
Government: Presidential republic
Administrative Divisions: 10 districts
Population: 437,000
Ethnic Groups: East Indians (34%), Creoles
of African and European descent (33%),
Javanese (18%), Maroons (9%),
Amerindians (2%)

Languages: Dutch, Hindustani, Javanese,
English
Religion: Hindus (26%), Catholics (23%),
Muslims (20%), Protestants (19%), Animists
Literacy Rate: 93%
GDP per capita: 3,500 US$
Currency: 1 Surinamese guilder =
100 cents

Uruguay
Uruguay

Location: South S. America
Area: 176,215 sq km
Important Rivers: Rio de la Plata,
Uruguay, Rio Negro
Capital: Montevideo
Government: Presidential republic
Administrative Divisions:
19 departments
Population: 3.4 million
Ethnic Groups: European descent (85%),
Mestizos (5%), African descent (3%)
Language: Spanish
Religion: Catholic (75%), Protestants (2%),
Jewish (1%)
Literacy Rate: 97%
GDP per capita: 12,600 US$
Currency: 1 Peso Uruguayo =
100 centesimos

Venezuela
Venezuela

Location: Northern S. America
Area: 912,050 sq km
Highest Point: Pico Bolivar (5,002 m)
Important River: Orinoco
Capital: Caracas
Government: Presidential republic
Administrative Divisions: 22 states,
1 district
Population: 25 million
Ethnic Groups: Mixed descent (69%),
White (20%), African descent (9%),
Amerindians (2%)
Language: Spanish
Religion: Catholic (93%), Protestants (5%)
Literacy Rate: 91%
GDP per capita: 4,800 US$
Currency: 1 bolivar = 100 centimos

During the 3rd century BC, the Byzantine Philon compiled a list of the seven wonders of the world including the Great Pyramids of Giza, the Hanging Gardens of Babylon, the Statue of Zeus at Olympia, the Temple of Atemis, the Halicarnassus Mausoleum, the Colossus of Rhodes, and the lighthouse of Alexandria. Philon chose his wonders, not for their aesthetic beauty, but instead because they were the boldest achievements of engineering and construction that he knew of.

The world has always been fascinated by the largest and grandest achievements of nature and mankind. Tourists travel the globe to stare and be amazed by these superlative structures and the human urge to build ever larger and bolder wonders remains.

The world in records

Man-made and natural highlights

The Universe
Infinite Space

Like many other cultures, the Babylonians were intrigued by the movements of the heavenly bodies in the night sky. The ancient Babylonians produced incredibly accurate maps of the night sky and relied on the movements of the stars to keep pace of time.

More than 13 billion years have passed since the big bang occurred, the moment at which our universe was born. The incredible vastness of our universe is almost as incomprehensible as the notion that the universe has not always existed. In recent years, humanity has been able to view even the most distant galaxies with the use of modern astronomical equipment. The galaxy RD1 is situated around 12.2 billion light years away from our planet. The largest known galaxy, located in the Abell Cluster, has a diameter of 5.6 million light years. In comparison, our galaxy the Milky Way has a diameter of "only" 100,000 light years.
But what is the structure of our gigantic universe and the space surrounding our Earth? The Sun, around which our planet and eight others revolve, is just one of many billions of stars in the universe. There are 40 more stars in the area within 16 light years of the Solar System. Alpha Centauri is located 4.3 light years from the sun and Proxima Centauri is even closer but the dim star is invisible to the naked eye.
Our sun and the surrounding stars are part of a large group of more than 100 million stars – the Milky Way galaxy. Our galaxy is so large that light takes 100,000 years to travel from one end to the next. The Milky Way galaxy has a shape similar to that of an elongated disc and is only a few thousand light years wide at some points. The sun is situated 25,000 light years from the galaxy's centre.
The Milky Way is just one of many galaxies. Together with 30 other galaxies, the Milky Way is part of a galaxy cluster called the Local Group. Even galaxy clusters are often part of larger groups of galaxies – the Local Group is part of the Virgo or Local Supercluster. Even these superclusters, however, are not evenly distributed throughout the galaxy and are surrounded by inconceivably vast voids of relatively empty space that contains few galaxies.

Superlatives in Space

The largest galaxies in the Local Group

Andromeda Galaxy (M 31)
130,000 light years diameter
Milky Way Galaxy (our galaxy)
100,000 light years diameter
Maffei 1
100,000 light years diameter
Triangulum Galaxy
52,000 light years diameter
Large Magellanic Cloud
30,000 light years diameter
Small Magellanic Cloud
16,000 light years diameter
M32
12,000 light years diameter
NGC 205
8,000 light years diameter
NGC 1613
8,000 light years diameter
Fornax
7,000 light years diameter

The largest known star Betelgeuse in the constellation Orion has a diameter of 700 million kilometers.

The heaviest star Eta Carinae in the Eta Carinae Nebula has 150 to 200 times more mass than the sun.

The nearest star Proxima Centauri 4.22 light years (40 billion kilometers)

The Brightest Stars

Sirius -1.46 magnitude
Canopus -0.72 magnitude
Alpha Centauri -0.27 magnitude
Arcutus -0.04 magnitude
Vega 0.03 magnitude
Capella 0.08 magnitude
Rigel 0.12 magnitude
Procyon 0.38 magnitude
Achernar 0.46 magnitude
Hadar 0.61 magnitude
Altair 0.77 magnitude
Aldebaran 0.85 magnitude
The visible brightness of stars as seen from the Earth is measured in magnitude – the lower the value, the brighter the star

Astronomical Measurements

Astronomical Unit (AU) A measurement equal to the mean distance between the Sun and the Earth. One Astronomical Unit is equal to around 150 million kilometers or 93 million miles.

Light year (ly) A measurement equal to the distance that light travels in one year. Light speed equals 300,000 km per second and 1 ly equals 9,460,528,000,000 kilometers.

The Solar System
Planets Orbiting the Sun

The Earth and eight other planets travel in different orbits and at different speeds around our Sun.

Closest to the Sun is the planet Mercury. It needs only 88 days to complete one orbit around the Sun. Following Mercury are the planets Venus and Earth, respectively. Beyond the Earth's orbit are Mars, Jupiter, Saturn, Uranus, and Neptune.
The planet farthest from the Sun is Pluto. This small planet needs 247 years to complete one orbit around the Sun. The immense dimensions of our Solar System can be illustrated by the time that sunlight needs to travel through it and to the different planets. Sunlight reaches the Earth in 8.2 minutes, Pluto after almost 6 hours, and Alpha Centauri A in 4.3 years. Incredible distances when you realize that light can circle the Earth 7.5 times in a second.
In the 16th century Copernicus discovered that the planets orbit around the sun. Johannes Kepler realized in the 17th that the orbits of the planets were not circular but elliptical. In the same century Newton confirmed that the planets were held in their orbits around the sun by the forces of gravitational pull.
Today we know that the planets are a by-product from the development of stars. Our solar system was formed around 4.5 billion years ago from a large cloud of gas and dust. Most of the material in this cloud formed the sun but much of the rest became rotating masses that eventually solidified and formed planets.

The Sun
Maximum Diameter: 1,392,700 sq km
Mass: 332,270 times Earth's Mass – 743 times the combined mass of all other known bodies in the solar system
Core Density: 1.41 g/cm³
Temperature: In the core minimum 15 mil-

lion K, on the visible surface (photosphere) 5,785 K, in the chromosphere 8,000 K, the outermost layer (corona) has temperature between 1 and 3 million K.

The Planets from Largest to Smallest

Jupiter (5th Planet)
Diameter: 142,700 km
Median distance from the sun:
778.3 million km
Revolution around the sun: 4,333 days
Rotation: 9.8 hours
Surface Temperature: -130° C
Satellites: Jupiter has at least 60 satellites, including the largest satellite in the solar systems Ganymede (larger than the planet Mercury), Europa, Io, and Callisto; all of which are larger than our moon. Jupiter is generally considered the planet with the largest number of satellites in our Solar System.

Saturn (6th Planet)
Diameter: 120,800 km
Median distance from the sun:
1,428 million km
Revolution around the sun: 10,756 days
Rotation: 10.2 hours
Surface Temperature: -185° C
Seven ring systems with a total diameter of 270,000 km.
Satellites: Saturn has at least 30 moons. Saturn's moon Titan , also the second largest satellite in the Solar System, is the only known moon with a significant atmosphere.

Uranus (7th Planet)
Diameter: 51,600 km
Median distance from the sun:
2,872 million km
Revolution around the sun: 30,685 days
Rotation: 17.24 hours
Surface Temperature: -215° C
Rings: Ten ring systems
Satellites: Uranus has at least 15 satellites, ten of which were first discovered by the NASA space probe Voyager 2.

Neptune (8th Planet)
Diameter: 48,600 km
Median distance from the sun:
4,498 million km
Revolution around the sun: 60,189 days
Rotation: 19.1 hours
Surface Temperature: -110° to -220° C
Rings: One ring system
Satellites: Neptune has eight satellites, five

of which have diameters less than 100 kilometers. Six of the planet's moons were first discovered in 1989.

Earth (3rd Planet)
Diameter: 12,756 sq km
Median distance from the sun:
149.6 million km
Revolution from the sun: 365.26 days
Rotation: 23.93 hours
Surface Temperature: 15° C
Satellites: One moon

Venus (2nd Planet)
Diameter: 12,100 km
Median distance from the sun:
108.2 million km
Revolution around the sun: 224.7 days
Rotation: 243.2 days
Surface Temperature: circa 460° C, the hottest planet
Rings: Venus like all of the other inner planets has no ring systems.
Satellites: Venus has no moons.

Mars (4th Planet)
Diameter: 6,800 km
Median distance from the sun:
227.9 million km (Mars has a highly elliptical orbit and the planet travels at distances between 206.6 and 249.2 million km away from the sun)
Revolution around the sun: 686 days
Rotation: 24.6 days
Surface Temperature: -50° C
Satellites: Mars has two moons, Phobos with a diameter of 27 km and Deimos with a diameter of 15 km. Scientists predict that Phobos will eventually crash into the planet's atmosphere, while the other moon Deimos appears to be slowly drifting away from its orbit around Mars.

Mercury (1st Planet)
Diameter: 4,900 km
Median distance from the sun:
56.9 million km
Revolution around the sun: 87.9 days
Rotation: 58.6 days
Surface Temperature: 430° during the day and -170° C at night
Satellites: Mercury has no satellites

Pluto (9th Planet)
Diameter: 2,300 km
Median distance from the sun:
5,910 million km
Revolution around the sun: 90,465 days; since the planet's discovery no complete orbit around the sun has been observed.

Rotation: 6.37 days
Surface Temperature: -230° C
Satellites: Charon has a diameter of 1,186 km and is only slightly smaller than Pluto – many astronomers consider the two twin planets or bodies because of their similar sizes and synchronized orbits

The Largest Moons in our Solar System

Ganymede (Jupiter) 5,262 km diameter
Titan (Saturn) 5,150 km diameter
Callisto (Jupiter) 4,800 km diameter
Io (Jupiter) 3,630 km diameter
Moon/Luna (Earth) 3,476 km diameter
Europa (Jupiter) 3,138 km diameter
Triton (Neptune) 2,720 km diameter
Titania (Uranus) 1,610 km diameter
Oberon (Uranus) 1,550 km diameter
Rhea (Saturn) 1,530 km diameter
Iapetus (Saturn) 1,435 km diameter
Charon (Pluto) 1,200 km diameter
Umbriel (Uranus) 1,190 km diameter
Ariel (Uranus) 1,160 km diameter
Dione (Saturn) 1,120 km diameter
Tethys (Saturn) 1,048 km diameter

Earth
The Blue Planet

The Earth was formed around 4 billion years ago from the leftover materials in our solar system. Around the same time the moon was formed and since then has followed the Earth from a distance of 350,000 km.

After the early development of the planet Earth, an atmosphere of carbon dioxide and nitrogen was formed containing little oxygen. 3.6 billion years ago the first primitive forms of life appeared on the Earth. This early life relied on photosynthesis and inorganic substances such as water and carbon dioxide for survival. Our planet is the only planet that we know of to contain liquid water, a key ingredient for the development of organic life, because it was only after algae and other aquatic plants produced sufficient oxygen that more advanced animal life forms could evolve. The moon is the closest heavenly body to the Earth and the gravitational pull between the two bodies is significant. On the Earth the moon's gravitational pull produces tides and floods, and the Earth's gravity creates earthquakes on the moon. The moon today is a geologically inactive body with no active volcanoes. The many craters on the surface of the moon are the result of countless meteor impacts. Unlike Earth, the moon has no significant atmosphere or bodies of liquid water. From the Earth, we can only see one side of the moon and it is only through space exploration that we have able to discover the dark side of the moon in recent decades.

Facts about the Earth

Age: around 4.3 billion years old
Diameter: 12,756 km at the equator
Distance from the sun: Maximum distance 152 million km; minimum distance 152 million km, estimated mean distance 149.6 million km
Rotation: 23.93 hours
Revolution around the sun: 365.26 days
Surface: 510,083 million sq km
Water Coverage: 361,445 million sq km (71 % of surface)
Land Area: 148.628 million sq km (29%)
Mass: $5,973 \cdot 10^{27}$g
Core Density: 5,520 kg/m³
Speed: 11,200 m per second
Layers:
Inner Core 5,100 km
Outer Core 2,900-5,100 km
Lower Mantle 950-5,100 km
Upper Core 40-2,900 km
Crust 0-40 km
Hottest Point: 4,530° C (Inner Core)
Atmosphere: Contents: nitrogen 78.09%, oxygen 20.95%, argon 0.93%, carbon dioxide 0.03%. The troposphere extends up to 11 km, the stratosphere up to 50 km, the mesosphere up to 80 km, the thermosphere up to 400 km, and the exosphere, the outermost layer, extends between 100 and 400 km above the Earth's surface.

The Moon

Diameter: 3,476 km
Median distance from the Earth: 384,403 km
Revolution around the Earth: 29.5 days
Surface: 37.69 million sq km
Mass: $7.35 \cdot 10^{25}$g
Surface Temperature: 117° C to -163° C
Deepest Crater: Newton 7,000-8,500 m
Largest Crater: Mare Orientale, 965 km diameter

The Moon Landings

Apollo 11: July 20, 1969
Armstrong, Collins, Aldrin
Apollo 12: November 11, 1969
Conrad, Gordon, Bean
Apollo 14: February 2, 1971
Shepard, Roose, Mitchell
Apollo 15: July 30, 1971
Scott, Worden, Irwin
Apollo 16: April 4, 1972
Young, Mattingly, Duke
Apollo 17: December 11, 1972
Cernan, Evans, Schmitt

The Continents
The Blue Planet

The modern continents were formed around 245 million years ago as the mega-continent Pangaea broke apart and the continents drifted into their present positions.

As the continents drifted away from one another most of their low-lying edges were submerged but some remained above water to form continental islands such as the British Isles or Newfoundland off the coast of mainland Canada. Most islands are younger and were created through underwater volcanic activities. The planet's tectonic plates continuously collide with one another. For this reason regions near the borders of plates such as the western coast of North America are sites of frequent geological activity. This leads to earthquakes, volcanic eruptions, and the gradual formation of mountain chains.

Continents from Largest to Smallest

Asia
Area: 44,614,000 sq km (without Papua New Guinea)
The largest and most populated continent covers almost a third of Earth's land surface. It is also the continent with the highest mountain chain (Himalayas).

Africa
Area: 30,273,000 sq km
Africa, the birthplace of humanity, is the hottest continent with average temperatures between 25 and 28° C.

**North America
(Including Greenland)**
Area: 24, 219, 000 sq km

South America
Area: 17, 839,000 sq km

Antarctica
Area: 13, 200,000 sq km
Antarctica is the windiest and coldest continent on our planet with an average temperature of -40° C. Antarctica holds almost 90% of the Earth's ice and is with an average elevation of 2,280 m the highest elevated continent.

Europe
Area: 9,839,000 sq km

Australia/Oceania
Area: 8, 937,000 sq km
Australia is the world's flattest and smallest continent.

The Oceans
The Source of all Life

Water covers almost two-thirds of the Earth's surface, approximately 361,445,000 sq km. The seven continents divide this mass of water into four oceans, each with its own independent currents and tides.

The Pacific Ocean, the largest of the four oceans, dominates almost half of the Earth's surface. The water of the oceans differs from the fresh water of most lakes and rivers because of its high salt content. In some regions the salt content of ocean water can exceed 35g per 1,000g of water. The oceans are also the source of all life on our planet because it was there, billions of years ago, that the first primitive life began to evolve.

Oceans from Largest to Smallest

Pacific Ocean
Area: 181,349,000 sq km
Average Depth: 4,000 m

Atlantic Ocean
Area: 106,575,000 sq km
Average Depth: 3,292 m

Indian Ocean
Area: 74,120,000 sq km
Average Depth: 3,800 m

Arctic Ocean
Area: 13,950,000 sq km
Average Depth: 1,328 m

Ocean Depths

Pacific Ocean
Mariana Trench
Challenger Deep 11,033 m
Tonga Trench
9,100 m

Atlantic Ocean
Puerto Rico Trench
Milwaukee Depth 9,219 m
South Sandwich Trench
Meteor Deep 8,264 m
Cayman Trench
7,680 m

Indian Ocean
Sunda Trench
Planet Deep 7,455 m
Southeast Asian Basin
6,857 m
North Australian Basin
6,840 m

Arctic Ocean
Eurasian Basin
5,449 m
Greenland Basin
Sweden Deep 4,846 m

Largest Ocean Animals

Mammal
Blue Whale – this species, the world's largest mammals, can grow to weigh between 100-150 tons and reach lengths between 25-35 meters.

Fish
Great White Shark, 18 meters long

Turtle
Leatherback Turtle, up to 560 kg heavy

Cephalopod
Giant Squid, up to 35 meters long

Jellyfish
Lion's Mane Jellyfish, up to 4 meters long and more than 1,000 tentacles

Crab
Japanese Giant Crab, its legs can grow to almost 2 meters

Mussel
Tridacna Clams, up to 300 kg heavy and 1.5 meters wide

Islands
Oases in the Sea

Scientists distinguish between two types of islands, continental and oceanic. The first group includes islands such as Ireland, Great Britain, and the two main islands of New Zealand. Oceanic islands are created as a result of volcanic activity.

The relatively short history of most oceanic islands is fascinating. These islands go through a rapid cycle of formation and expansion. The birth of an oceanic island begins with the eruption of a large underwater volcano. Hot magma from the Earth's crust released by an eruption forms layer upon layer of stone until this underwater mountain breaches the ocean's surface as a new island. The world's highest volcanoes and highest mountains, when measured from the ocean floor, are the volcanoes of the Hawaiian Islands in the Pacific Ocean. Mauna Kea for example is 10,205 meters tall from its base on the ocean floor to its peak, which is situated 4,205 meters above sea level.

The Largest Islands

Greenland 2,175,600 sq km
New Guinea 771,900 sq km
Borneo 746,950 sq km

Europe
Britain 219,801 sq km
Iceland 103,000 sq km
Ireland 84,426 sq km
Spitsbergen 39,368 sq km
Sicily 25,400 sq km

Asia
Borneo 746,950 sq km
Sumatra 425,979 sq km
Honshu 230,636 sq km
Celebes 174,000 sq km
Java 129,000 sq km

Africa
Madagascar 587,041 sq km
Reunion 2510 sq km
Bioko 2043 sq km

Australia/Oceania
New Guinea 771,900 sq km
New Zealand – South Island 153,947 sq km
New Zealand – North Island 114,729 sq km

The Americas
Greenland 2,175,600 sq km
Baffin Island 517,890 sq km
Victoria Island 217,290 sq km

Coral Reefs and Atolls
Living Islands

Coral reefs cover around 600,000 sq km of the Earth's surface. They are common in many tropical bodies of water.

Coral reefs are living Islands that formed by large amounts of organic coral. Coral grows mostly in mineral and oxygen-rich water with a minimum temperature of 20° C. Atolls are ring-shaped coral reefs that encircle lagoons.

The Largest Coral Reefs

The Great Barrier Reef is located off the north-eastern coast of Australia and with an area of 250,000 sq km and a length of 2024 km is the world's largest reef.

Barrier Reef located near the island Grand Terre in New Caledonia is the world's second longest coral reef with a length of 802 km.

The Belize Barrier Reef (Grande Recife Maya) stretches along the coast of Belize and the Yucatan. The 300 km-long reef is the longest in the western hemisphere.

The Largest Atolls

Kwajalein Atoll in the Marshall Islands has a land area of 16 sq km and encircles the world's largest lagoon.

Kiritimati in Polynesia has the largest land area of any atoll covering 388 sq km.

Coastal Areas
Shaped by the Seas

The world's coasts are the areas where land and bodies of water meet and merge. Coastal areas have always been shaped by the effects of wind and water erosion. Erosion and storms often cause coastlines to rapidly and dramatically change their form.

The Longest Bays

Bay of Bengal 1,850 km
Hudson Bay 1,560 km
Gulf of Mexico 1,330 km

The Largest Tides

Bay of Fundy, Canada: on average between 16 and 18 meters, 21 meter tides have been observed
Shelikof Strait: high tide averages 12.9 meters in the area
Gulf of Alaska: 12 meters
Bay of Bengal: 10.7 meters
Bay of Mezen: 10 meters

Vegetation Zones
Living Landscapes of the Earth

The Earth's land areas can be divided into several distinct vegetation zones. These zones are identified by their different climates, flora, and fauna. It is also significant that similar vegetation zones are usually found along or near the same latitudes.

The polar regions of Antarctica and the Arctic are covered by glaciers and icecaps. In the northern hemisphere this region is bordered by tundra, a zone with extremely cold temperatures in winter and where the frost-covered ground only briefly thaws in summer.
The mild climate of the temperate zones is home to mixed forests and extensive shrubbery growth. Large-scale agriculture is common in these regions. The temperate regions

are located primarily in the northern hemisphere; in Europe and North America but also in New Zealand, southern South America, and parts of Australia. Around and beyond the twentieth latitudes lie the world's subtropical regions. The subtropics are characterized by a diverse variety of ecosystems and landscapes. The Everglades in Florida and the eucalyptus forests of Australia are located in this zone.
The tropical belt of the Earth stretches along and above the equator through the Amazon rain forest, Central Africa, and South Asia. Most tropical regions are bordered by extensive grasslands such as savannah landscapes or semi-arid regions. The Llanos of South America, the Serengeti in East Africa, and large sections of Australia are typical savannahs. The various regions between the 15th and 35th latitudes with less than 250 mm annual precipitation are classified as deserts.

Polar Regions

Around 15 million sq km of the Earth's surface is covered by ice and glaciers, of this amount the vast majority or around 12.7 million sq km is located in Antarctica. The rest of this amount is scattered around the globe including 1.8 sq km of ice coverage in Greenland, 300,000 sq km in the areas surrounding the Arctic Ocean and Antarctica, 120,000 sq km in Asia, 100,000 sq km in North and South America, and 10,000 sq km in Europe. Because of its inhospitable climate and terrain, Antarctica remains the world's only continent without permanent human inhabitants.

The Largest Glaciers
Vatnajokull, 8,540 sq km
Iceland
Malaspina Glacier, 3,900 sq km
Alaska
Siachen Glacier, 1,150 sq km
India
Fedchenko Glacier, 907 sq km
Tajikistan
Nabesna Glacier, 819 sq km
Alaska
Baltoro Glacier, 754 sq km
Pakistan
Biafo Glacier, 620 sq km,
Pakistan
Muldrow Glacier, 516 sq km
Alaska
Jostedalsbreen, 415 sq km
Norway

Polar Wildlife
Largest Land Mammal: Polar Bear
Largest Aquatic Bird: Emperor Penguin
Largest Seals: Southern Elephant Seals

Tundra

Tundra is the name of the regions bordering the Polar Regions and above the tree lines of many mountainous areas. The tundra of Canada and Siberia alone cover nearly 10 percent of the Earth's land area. The climate of the tundra is characterized by cold temperatures and low levels of precipitation. The ground in the tundra is not always covered by ice and hardy plants such as mosses, lichens, and shrubs can thrive in this hostile environment. Reindeer, moose, caribou, and wolves are among the animals that populate tundra regions. On the coast around tundra you might find seals, walruses, and a variety of aquatic birds.

Taiga

Taiga or boreal forests are forest landscapes consisting of coniferous trees that lie south of the polar regions in North America and Eurasia. 70% of the world's taiga regions are located in Russia. These expansive landscapes contain one third of the world's forests. Pines, fir trees, and spruces are all abundant in this type of vegetation zone. The ground of the taiga is usually covered by weeds, moss, and shrubbery.

Northern Wildlife
Largest Bear: Kodiak Brown Bear, Alaska
Largest Feline: Siberian Tiger, Russia

Temperate Forests

The world's temperate broadleaf deciduous forests, or simply temperate forests, are located mostly in the Northern Hemisphere. These regions contain approximately 18% of the world's forests.
In the past, far larger regions of North America and Europe were covered by temperate forests but as the population density of Europe rose and North America opened up to European settlement most of these forests were leveled. Today the most intact temperate forests can be found in eastern North America. The forests there are famous for the color changes their leaves display particularly in autumn.

Forest Wildlife

Largest Predator: Brown Bear
Largest Canine Predator: Wolves
Largest Songbirds: Common Raven
Fastest Birds: Peregrines
Largest Land Mammal (Europe): Bison
Largest Deer Species (Europe): Red Deer
Largest Canine Species (Europe): Lynx
Largest Trees: Giant Sequoia (Redwood)
Oldest Tree Species: Ginkgo

Between Temperate and Tropics

Between the temperate forest and the tropics lie a variety of vegetation zones. There are the humid and warm subtropical regions including areas like Florida and South China. There are also numerous deserts and semi-arid grasslands in the area between the tropics and temperate zone.

Subtropical Wildlife

Largest Felines: Bengal Tiger
Largest Reptile (North America):
American Alligator
Highest Tree Species: Eucalyptus, up to 130 meters
Largest Fern Species: Giant Tree Ferns

Tropical Forests

Tropical forests comprise almost half of the world's forests. The rain forest belt that stretches along the equator covers 6% of the Earth's land area. The largest area of continuous tropical rain forest is located in the vast Amazon River basin of South America and covers an area of approximately 3.6 million sq km.
Other large tropical rain forests are located in Guyana, West and Central Africa, South and Southeast Asia, and Oceania. The most fascinating aspect of the rain forests is their remarkable diversity of plant and animal life. More than half of the world's known plant and animal species inhabit the tropical rain forests.

Tropical Wildlife

Largest Land Mammal: African Elephant
Largest Mammal (South America):
Baird's Tapir
Largest Predator (South America):
Jaguar
Largest Primate: Western Gorilla
Longest Reptile: Anaconda
Largest Insect: Pharnacia serratipes, up to 35 cm in length

Savannas

Between many of the world's tropical forest and deserts you can find extensive grasslands called Savannas. Among the world's major savannas are the Serengeti in Africa, Brazil's Campos, and the arid grasslands on Australia. A distinctive characteristic of the savannas are the distinct dry and wet seasons. Various grasses thrive in the savannas, and oases of trees dot these landscapes. Once the rainy season begins the savannas are transformed into seas of green grass.

Wildlife of the Savanna

Largest Land Mammal: African Elephant
Largest Feline: Lion
Fastest Land Animal: Cheetah
Tallest Land Animal: Giraffe
Largest Bird: African Ostrich

Deserts

Deserts cover 30% of the Earth's surface. Most of these deserts are located between the 15th and 35th latitudes. Deserts are the warmest and driest regions on our planet. Day and nighttime temperatures in deserts can differ by as much as 50° C. Seasons are less distinctive in the deserts than in other regions.

The Largest Deserts

Sahara: 9.7 million sq km; this figure includes the Libyan and Nubian deserts. The Sahara is the world's largest desert and grows 10,000 sq km larger every year. The desert has a maximum length of 5,150 km from east to west and 2,250 km from north to south. Daytime temperatures in the Sahara often exceed 40° C.
Gobi: 1.3 million sq km; this Asian desert lies at an average height of 1,000 m above sea level.
Kalahari: 1 million sq km; the large arid basin in southern Africa lacks outflow waterways.

Africa

Sahara 9.7 million sq km
Kalahari 1 million sq km
Arabian Desert (Egypt and Sudan) 182,000 sq km
Namib 135,000 sq km; this desert along the coast of south-western Africa stretches more than 1,300 km from north to south and has an average width of around 100 kilometers. The Namib is one of the world's driest deserts.

Asia

Gobi (China and Mongolia) 1.3 million sq km
Rub al Khali (Saudi Arabia) 800,000 sq km
Taklamakan (China) 400,000 sq km
Karakum (Turkmenistan) 350,000 sq km
Kyzylkum (Kazakhstan and Uzbekistan) 300,000 sq km
Kevir (Iran) 260,000 sq km
Syrian Desert 260,000 sq km
Thar (India and Pakistan) 250,000 sq km
Negev (Israel) 12,300 sq km

Australia

Great Sand Desert 520,000 sq km
Gibson 330,000 sq km
Great Victoria Desert 274,000 sq km
Simpson 250,000 sq km

Americas

Atacama (northern Chile) 400,000 sq km
Sonora, including the Colorado and Yuma Deserts (USA) 310,000 sq km
Mojave (USA) 38,900 sq km

Europe

The only true deserts in Europe are located in the Russian republic of Kalmykia. These deserts are manmade, the result of overuse of the region's once fertile soils. Today deserts cover at least 80% of Kalmykia's territory.

Climate
Hot and Cold

The word weather describes the atmospheric condition of an area for a specific relatively short period of time. Climate on the other hand is a general description of the dominant atmospheric conditions in a region year-round. Mountains and large bodies of water are important.

Climatic Extremes

Lowest Temperature Recorded

In 1983 at Vostok in Antarctica and at a height of 3,420 meters temperatures -89.2° C/-128° Fahrenheit were recorded. This is the lowest temperature ever measured on the Earth's surface.

Highest Temperature Recorded
In Al' Azziyah, Libya the temperature reached 58° C/ 136° Fahrenheit on September 13,1922.

Hottest Region
During an average year Dallol in Ethiopia is the warmest place on the Earth's surface. The average temperature between 1960 and 1966 at any time of the year was 34° C/94° Fahrenheit.

Coldest Region
The coldest area in Anarctica is located at the coordinates 78° south, 96° east, where the average temperature is -58° C/-72.4° Fahrenheit.

Rainiest Region
On the Hawaiian Island of Kauai it rains an average 350 days in the year.

Sunniest Region
In Yuma, Arizona, the sun is visible during 91% of the daytime hours.

Most Rainfall
The area around Mawsynram in the Indian state of Megalaya receives an average of 11,873 milimeters of rainfall in a year.

Driest Region
The driest place on Earth is located on Chile's pacific coast between Arica and Antofagasta. During an average year less than one millimeter of precipitation falls in this arid region.

Windiest Region
Commonwealth Bay in Australia is the windiest place on Earth. Storms in this bay can produce winds reaching speeds up to 320 km/h.

Natural Disasters:
Wind and Weather

On average one meter of precipitation falls to the Earth's surface during a year. In reality, however, this rain and snowfall is unevenly distributed across the globe.

The greatest levels of precipitation occur in the tropics. Countries such as Bangladesh are often devastated by floods and typhoons.

Every year powerful storms form off the coast of West Africa; many of these storms become immense tropical cyclones capable of crossing the Atlantic Ocean. These storms often reach land in the Caribbean Sea and continental North America. With winds that can reach 300 km/h, tropical cyclones – more commonly known as hurricanes and typhoons – are one of the most destructive forces of nature. Hurricanes and typhoons can devastate entire regions in a matter of hours. The heavy rainfall and severe floods that usually accompany hurricanes add to their destructive power.

Deadly Storms and Floods
Resulting deaths

Yellow River, China: 1887 flood 900,000
Bangladesh: 1970 typhoon 300,000
Bangladesh: 1991 typhoon 150,000
Japan: 1896 tsunami 22,000
Galveston, Texas: 1900 hurricane 6,000
Yangtze River, China: 1998 4,000
Papua New Guinea: 1998 tsunami 3,000
England, The Netherlands: 1953 flood 2,000
Midwestern United States: 1925 Tri-State tornado 689
United States, Canada, Caribbean: 1993 "Storm of the Century" 220

Natural Disasters:
An active planet

Our planet is an active and energetic world. In the subterranean layers of the Earth huge masses of stones and magma are constantly on the move. The massive tectonic plates beneath the Earth's surface move along and collide into one another, often creating earthquakes. These quakes originate from sources between 5 and 30 kilometers under the surface.

Around 500,000 instances of seismic activities occur every year. Of this number only about 100,000 can be felt on the Earth's surface. Unfortunately, there is still no effective method to predict the occurrence of earthquakes. Volcano eruptions are also difficult to pre-

dict but not impossible. In 1991 the population living near Mt. Pinatubo was evacuated before a violent eruption devastated the area. The ash released from this one eruption affected the world's climate long afterwards. At present there are 1,343 active volcanoes around the world.

The Strongest Earthquakes: 20th Century
Magnitude on the Richter Scale

Chile: May 22, 1960 (9.5)
Alaska: March 28, 1964 (9.2)
Alaska: March 3, 1957 (9.1)
Russia: April 11, 1952 (9.1)
Ecuador: Jan. 01, 1906 (8.8)
Japan: Nov. 06, 1958 (8.7)
Alaska: Feb. 02, 1965 (8.7)
India: August 08, 1950 (8.6)
Argentina: Nov. 11, 1922 (8.5)
Indonesia: Jan. 02, 1938 (8.5)

Volcanic Eruptions
Resulting deaths

Tambora, Indonesia: 1815 90,000
Miyi, Indonesia: 1793 53,000
Pelè, Martinique: 1902 40,000
Krakatau, Indonesia: 1883 36,300
Nevado del Ruiz, Columbia: 1985 22,000
Mt. Etna, Italy: 1669 20,000
Laki, Iceland: 1783 20,000
Unzen, Japan: 1792 15,000
Vesuvius, Italy: 75 A.D 10,000
El Chicón, Mexico: 1982 3500

Volcanoes
Smoke and Fire

The world's numerous active volcanoes are the most dramatic reminders of the violent natural processes that occur beneath the surface of our planet. These mountains of fire are often unpredictable. Some active volcanoes like Hawaii's Kilauea constantly release lava, while others are prone to powerful and sudden eruptions.

The regions near the border of tectonic plates are also the regions with the most volcanic activity. One such area is the so-called Ring of Fire along the coasts of the Pacific. Many countries in this region including Japan, Indonesia, and the Phillipines are home to active volcanoes.

The Tallest Active Volcanoes
(worldwide)

Volcan Guallatiri, Chile: 6,060 m
Volcan Láscar, Chile: 5,990 m
Tupungatito, Chile: 5,900 m
Cotopaxi, Ecuador: 5,897 m
Popcatepetl, Mexico: 5,452 m

(Europe)
Mt. Etna 3,350 m
Beerenberg 2,277m
Mt. Hekla 1,491 m

Asia
Kluchevskaya Sopke 4,750 m
Kerinci 3,800 m
Tolbachik 3,682 m

Oceania
Mauna Loa 4,170 m
Mt. Ruapeha 2,797 m

Africa
Mt. Cameroon 4,070 m
Mt. Nyirangongo 3,475 m
Emi Koussi 3,415 m

North America
Popocatépetl 5,452 m
Mt. Rainier 4,392 m
Volcan Colima 3,984 m

South America
Volcan Guallatiri 6,060 m
Volcan Lascar 5,990 m
Cotopaxi 5,897 m

Antartica
Mt. Erebus 3,795 m

Geysers
Erupting Wonders

Geysers are geological wonders that can be found in many regions around the world. These spectacular gushing fountains of water often erupt in regular cycles.

Geysers are formed when extremely hot magma approaches the Earth's surface and warms underground water sources. These eventually reach boiling point and gradually force their way to the surface as an explosive plume. Minerals in the water fall to the ground, gradually forming the stone structure of a geyser. A large number of the world's geysers are concentrated in America's Yellowstone National Park. Yellowstone's largest geyser, Old Faithful, is also the world's most famous geyser. Iceland and New Zealand are also home to a large number of geysers. The largest known geyser was once located in the New Zealand city of Waimangu. Before it became inactive in 1917, the Waimangu Geyser regularly produced a 450-meter-high plume of water.

The Tallest Geysers
(Water Plumes)

United States, Yellowstone National Park
Service Steamboat 60-115 meters
Old Faithful 50 meters

Iceland
Geysir 60 meters
Strokkur 25-30 meters

New Zealand
Pohutu 31 meters
Lady Knox 10-15 meters

Russia
Velican 40 meters

Mountains
Stone Giants

Humanity has always been in awe of the majestic beauty of mountains. Even today many people around the world view mountains as the home of gods and other spirits.

Far into the last century many peaks of the world's most famous mountains, including the Himalayas, remained unconquered. In 1953 Edmund Hillary and Norgay Tenzing became the first men to reach the summit of Mount Everest. The Himalayas like most mountain chains were formed by the convergence of tectonic plates. When tectonic

plates push into one another an enormous amount of pressure is put on the surrounding earth. With no way to go but up, this process eventually leads to the formation of mountain systems. Mountains formed in this way are referred to as folded mountains. Because this process continues today, most of the world's highest mountains continue to expand upwards by an average of one centimeter every year.

Major Mountain Systems
(including highest mountains)

Asia
Himalayas (main range)
Mt. Everest 8,861 m
Karakoram Range
K2 8,610 m
Kunlun Mountains
Kongur Tagh 7,719 m

North America
Alaska Range
Mt. McKinley 6,194 m
St. Ellas Mountains
Mt. Logan 5,951 m
Sierra Madre Oriental
Citlaltepetl 5,700 m

South America
Andes
Aconcagua 6,960 m
Sierra Nevada de Santa Maria
Pico Cristobal 5,800 m

Africa
Mt. Kilimanjaro
Kibo 5,963 m
Mt. Kenya
Batian 5,201 m
Ruwenzori Range
Mount Stanley 5,109 m

Europe
Caucasus Mountains
Mount Elbrus 5,633 m
Alps
Mont Blanc 4,807 m
Sierra Nevada
Cunbre de Mulhacen 3,478 m
Pyrenees
Pico de Aneto 3,404 m

Oceania
Surdiman Range
Puncak Jaya 5,030 m
Southern Alps
Mount Cook 3,764 m

Antarctica
Elisworth Range
Vinson Massif 5,140 m
Queen Alexandra Range
Mount Markham 4,350 m
Executive Committee Range
Mount Sidley 4,181 m

The Highest Mountains

Mount Everest (Nepal) 8,863 m
first successful ascent in 1953
K2 (Pakistan) 8,610 m
first successful ascent in 1954
Kangchenjunga (Nepal) 8,586 m
first successful ascent in 1955
Lhotse (Nepal) 8,511 m
first successful ascent in 1956
Makalu (Nepal) 8,463 m
first successful ascent in 1955
Dhaulagiri (Nepal) 8,167 m
first successful ascent in 1960
Manaslu (Nepal) 8,125 m
first successful ascent in 1956
Cho Oyu (Nepal) 8,153 m
first successful ascent in 1954
Nanga Parbat (Nepal) 8,125 m
first sucessful ascent in 1953
Annapurna I (Nepal) 8,091 m
first successful ascent in 1950
Gasherbrum I (Pakistan) 8,068 m
first sucessful ascent in 1958
Broad Peak (Pakistan) 8,047 m
first successful ascent in 1957
Gasherbrum II 8,035 m
first succesful ascent in 1956
Sishapangma (China) 8,027 m
first sucessful ascent in 1964

Basins and Depressions
Areas Below Sea Level

Depression and basin are the terms used to describe an area of land that is situated at a significant depth below sea level. The world's depressions were formed through tectonic activity or wind erosion.

The Deepest Basins/Depressions
(distance below sea level)

Dead Sea, -400 m below sea level
Israel, Jordan

Assal Depression, -155 m
Djibouti
Turfan Depression, -154 m
China
Qattara Depression, -133 m
Egypt
Mangyshlak Basin, -132 m
Kazakhstan
Lake Asal, -116 m
Ethiopia
Death Valley, -86 m
California, United States
Salton Sink, -85 m
California
Ustyurt Basin, -70 m
Kazakhstan
Caspian Depression, -67 m
Kazakhstan
Al Fayyum Oasis, -50 m
Egypt
Salinas Grande, -40 m
Argentina

The Largest Basins/Depressions

Caspian Depression 394,000 sq km
Kazakhstan
Qattara Depression 20,000 sq km
Egypt

Canyons and Gorges
Wonders of Erosion

Rivers have played a major role in the shaping the world's surface. Canyons are valleys surrounded by stone walls and cliffs. The world's gorges and canyons were created over many centuries by rivers. The powerful eroding effects of rivers cut through the hardest of surfaces over time forming large gashes in the land.

The shape of a canyon or gorge is determined by the flow of the river that forms it and the nature of stone it is carved from. The hardness of the stone determines the direction of the eroding effects that produce a canyon. The upper course of a river is usually the section with the fastest speed and the section with the greatest eroding power. Most of the world's deep canyons were formed on the upper course of a large river.

Because there are so many factors that can influence the formation of a canyon, these natural wonders come in a variety of shapes and sizes. The Colorado River began eroding the ground near what is now the Grand Canyon around 26 million years ago. After numerous centuries the canyon began to emerge out of the hard stone in the region. The 24-kilometer-wide Grand Canyon is now one of world's most visited and famous natural attractions.

The Deepest Canyons
(maximum depth in meters)

North America
Grand Canyon 1,800 m – the world's largest canyon
USA
Hell's Canyon 1,700 m
USA
Barranca del Cobre 1,400 m
Mexico
Black Canyon 700 m
USA
Bryce Canyon 600 m
USA

Africa
Fish River Canyon 600 m
Namibia
Dades Gorge 400 m
Morocco
Wadi Kantara 400 m
Algeria

Asia
Wu Gorge 900 m
China
Black River Canyon 800 m
Vietnam
Sanmen Gorge 600 m
China

Europe
Vicos Gorge 900 m
Greece
Via Mala 700 m
Switzerland
Neretva Canyons 800 m
Bosnia and Herzegovina
Grand Canyon du Verdon 700 m
France

Oceania
Milford Sound 600 m
New Zealand
Vaihiria 550 m
Tahiti, French Polynesia

South America
Colca Canyon 3,400 m – the world's deepest canyon
Peru

Rivers
The Arteries of our Planet

Rivers bring life to large areas of land; they nurtured ancient civilizations, and have functioned throughout history as the important means of transportation for people around the world. Many of the world's great rivers begin as small creeks before merging with other rivers and flowing into the seas and oceans.

97.5% of the world's water is saltwater. On top of this at least 70% of the world's freshwater is frozen in the polar ice caps and most of the remaining 30% lies in underground sources that are practically inaccessible. Only around 0.007% of the world's water is currently available for human use. The world's rivers contain 42,700 km³ of water. That is more water than the amount contained in Lake Tanganyika, Baikal, and Victoria together.
The world's longest river is the Nile in Africa. Its source was sought by explorers for many centuries before its discovery in the 19th century. The Nile River Valley is a fertile oasis surrounded by barren deserts.
The world's largest river is the Amazon in South America. The Amazon is 200 km shorter than the Nile but contains far more water – the river contains at least one-fifth of the world's river water. In addition to its size the Amazon is noteworthy because it is the foundation of an amazing and important ecosystem, the vast Amazon rain forest.

The Longest Rivers
(Worldwide)

Nile 6,672 km
Amazon 6,437 km
Yangtze 6,300 km
Mississippi/Missouri 6,020 km

North America
Mississippi/Missouri 6,020 km
Mackenzie-Peace River 4,241 km

Yukon 3,185 km
St. Lawrence 3,058 km
Rio Grande 3,034 km
Colorado 2,334 km

Africa
Nile 6,672 km
Zaire (Congo) 4,374 km
Niger 4,184 km
Zambezi 2,736 km
Ubangi-Uele 2,300 km

Asia
Yangtze 6,300 km
Irtysch 5,410 km
Huang He 4,875 km
Mekong 4,500 km
Amur 4,416 km

Europe
Volga 3,351 km
Danube 2,858 km
Ural 2,428 km
Dnieper 2,200 km

Australia
Darling 2,740 km
Murray 2,570 km
Murrumbidgee 2,160 km

South America
Amazon 6,437 km
Parana-La Plata 4,264 km
Madeira 3,240 km
Rio Purus 3,211 km

Waterfall
Rivers in Freefall

Waterfalls are formed when a stream of water flows over an area with a sudden drop in elevation. There are several types of waterfalls and many of the most famous and beautiful are popular natural attractions. Every year, millions of tourists around the world enjoy the awe-inspiring beauty of these natural spectacles

The Largest Waterfalls (width)

Khone Pha Pheng 10,800 m
Laos

Iguacu Falls 4,000 m
Brazil, Argentina
Victoria Falls 1,700 m
Zambia, Zimbabwe
Niagara Falls 1,150 m
United States, Canada

The Highest Waterfalls
(by continent)

North/South America
Angel Falls 948 m – the world's highest waterfalls
Venezuela
Yosemite Falls 739 m
United States
Cuquean Falls 610 m
Guyana, Venezuela
Roraima Falls 457 m
Guyana
Kaieteur Falls 226 m
Guyana

Africa
Tugela 411 m
South Africa
Maletsunyane 192 m
Lesotho
Augrabies 146 m
South Africa
Ruacana 120 m
Namibia, Angola
Victoria Falls 110 m
Zambia, Zimbabwe

Asia
Falls of Gersoppa 253 m
India
Cauvery Falls 101 m
India
Kegon Falls 101 m
Japan
Juizhaigou 78 m
China
Gokaks 52 m
India

Australia/New Zealand
Sutherland Falls 580 m
New Zealand
Wollomombi Falls 335 m
Australia
Wallaman Falls 285 m
Australia
Tully 270 m
Australia
Wentworth Falls 187 m
Australia

195

Europe
Mardalsfossen 517 m
Norway
Gavarnie Falls 422 m
France
Krimmler Falls 380 m
Austria
Giessbach Falls 300 m
Switzerland
Skykkjedalsfoss 300 m
Iceland

Lakes
Inland Seas

Most of the world's large lakes are gla-cial lakes, formed as huge glaciers melted after the last ice age. But the world's oldest lakes including Lake Baikal and Victoria were formed as a re-sult of tectonic activity. Lake Tangayika, the world's longest lake with a length of 655 km, owes its unusual narrow shape and existence to tectonic activity. Endorheic lakes are lakes with no out-flowing waterways. Such lakes, located mostly in deserts, often exhibit rapid changes in shape and depth.

The Largest Lakes
(With area and maximum depth)

Caspian Sea 371,800 sq km – the world's largest lake, salt water lake, maximum depth 1,025 m
Kazakhstan, Russia, Azerbaijan, Turkmeni-stan, Iran
Lake Superior 82,103 sq km, 406 m
USA, Canada
Lake Victoria 69,484 sq km, 406 m
Kenya, Tanzania, Uganda
Lake Huron 59,570 sq km, 229 m
USA, Canada
Lake Michigan 58,140 sq km, 282 m
USA
Lake Tanganyika 34,000 sq km, 1,435 m
Tanzania, Burundi, Zaire, Zambia

North America
Lake Superior 82,103 sq km, 406 m
USA, Canada

Lake Huron 59,570 sq km, 229 m
USA, Canada
Lake Michigan 58,140 sq km, 282 m
USA

Africa
Lake Victoria 69,484 sq km, 406 m
Kenya, Uganda, Tanzania
Lake Tanganyika 34,000 sq km, 1,435 m, the world's longest lake with a maximum length of 655 km
Tanzania, Burundi, Zaire, Zambia
Lake Malawi 30,800 sq km, 706 m
Malawi, Tanzania

Asia
Caspian Sea 371,800 sq km, 1,025 m
Russia, Turkmenistan, Iran, Azerbaijan, Kazakhstan,
Aral Sea 33,640 sq km, 52 m – the lake is rapidly declining is size and has become increasingly saline due to man-made en-vironmental damage
Kazakhstan, Uzbekistan
Lake Baikal 31,500 sq km, 1,620 m
Russia

Australia
Lake Eyre 9,323 sq km, 12 m
Lake MacKay 3,494 sq km, N.A
Lake Amadeus 1,032 sq km, N.A
All three of Australia's largest lakes are dry salt lakes which only periodically contain water and reach maximum depths less than one meter.

Europe
Lake Ladoga 18,180 sq km, 230 m
Russia
Lake Onega 9,950 sq km, 127 m
Russia
Lake Vaenern 5,564 km, 92 m
Sweden

South America
Lake Maracaibo 13,512 sq km, 50 m
Venezuela
Lake Titicaca 8,559 sq km, 281 m – the world's highest elevated lake
Peru, Bolivia
Lake Popoo 2,530 sq km, 3 m
Bolivia

Reservoirs
Man-Made Lakes

Reservoirs are large man-made lakes and are usually created by constructing dams to obstruct rivers. Most reservoirs are used to store drinking water or for flood prevention.

In addition to these benefits, reservoirs also provide recreational opportunities. But the construction of reservoirs often brings dis-advantages for some regions and people. The resettlement of entire communities and the destruction of ecosystems are issues that arise with the creation of reservoirs. The Three Gorges Dam in China has resulted in the resettlement of over one million people.

The Largest Reservoirs

Owens Falls 204,800 million m³
Uganda
Lake Kariba 180,600 million m³
Zambia, Zimbabwe
Bratsk 169,270 million m³
Russia
Lake Nasser 168,900 million m³
Egypt
Lake Volta 148,000 million m³
Uganda
D. Johnson 141,852 million m³
Canada
Tarbela 141,000 million m³
Pakistan
Guri 138,000 million m³
Venezuela
Krasnoyarsk 73,000 million m³
Russia

The Largest Dams
(with names of obstructed rivers)

Rogun Dam 335 meters
Tajikistan, Vakhsh River
Nurek Dam 300 meters
Tajikistan, Vakhsh River
Grand Dixence 284 meters
Switzerland, Dixence River
Inguri Dam 272 meters
Georgia, Inguri River
Chicoasen 264 meters
Mexico, Rio Grijalva
Tehri 261 meters
India, Bhagirathi River
Vaiont 259 meters
Italy, Piave River
Mica Dam 250 meters
Canada, Columbia River
Sayano-Shushkenskaya Dam 245 meters
Russia, Yenisei River
Guavio Dam 240 meters
Columbia, Rio Guavio

Nations
The World's Political Patchwork

At the end of the last century there were 193 independent nations on our planet. Throughout the course of the 20th century the world map changed form on many occasions. Two world wars, decolonization in Africa and Asia, as well as the fall of European communism were the most important factors that contributed to the rise and fall of so many nations.

The nations of the world are separated by large division in wealth and political influence. The richest nations on the planet including the United States, Canada, Japan, the EU member nations, and several other states, are collectively referred to as the developed nations. The developing nations – also known as Third World nations – in Africa, Asia, and Latin America are characterized by widespread poverty, economic weakness and the dominant role of agriculture in their economies. The developing countries are home to the majority of the world's population but their political power remains relatively limited due to their lack of economic influence and financial resources. Measurements of GDP (gross domestic product) per capita are often used to rank and compare the wealth of different nations. Unfortunately these measurements do not take into account the often extreme gaps between rich and poor in individual nations. GDP measurements also ignore other important factors that affect the quality of life in a society, including political stability, social mobility, tolerance, and climate. Around 150 of the world's nations are developing nations. Hunger, high mortality rates, and often explosive population rates are among the many widespread problems these nations must solve.

The Largest Countries

Russia/Russian Federation 17,075,200 sq km
Canada 9,984,670 sq km
United States 9,631,418 sq km
China 9,596,960 sq km
Brazil 8,511,996 sq km

North America
Canada 9,984,670 sq km
United States 9,631,418 sq km
Mexico 1,972,550 sq km

Africa
Sudan 2,505,813 sq km
Algeria 2,318,741 sq km
Democratic Republic of Congo 2,345,410 sq km

Asia, excluding Russia
China 9,596,960 sq km
India 3,287,263 sq km
Kazakhstan 2,717,300 sq km

Europe
Russia 17,075,200 sq km
Ukraine 603,700 sq km
France 547,030 sq km

Oceania
Australia 7,686,850 sq km
Papua New Guinea 462,840 sq km
New Zealand 268,680 sq km

South America
Brasil 8,511,996 sq km
Argentina 2,766,889 sq km
Peru 1,285,216 sq km

Where are the different nations?

Africa 54 countries
Asia 47
Europe 44
North America/Caribbean 23
Oceania 14
South America 12

The Wealthiest Nations
(GDP per capita)

Luxembourg 55,100 US$
United States 37,800 US$
Norway 37,700 US$
San Marino 34,600 US$
Switzerland 32,800 US$
Denmark 31,200 US$
Iceland 30,900 US$
Austria 30,000 US$

The Poorest Nations
(GDP per capita)

Sierra Leone 500 US$
Somalia 500 US$
East Timor 500 US$
Democratic Republic of Congo 600 US$
Tansania 600 US$
Burundi 600 US$
Malawi 600 US$
Ethiopia 700 US$

The Largest Economies
(By purchasing power parity in US dollars)

USA 10.98 trillion US$
China 6.45 trillion US$
Japan 3.56 trillion US$
India 3.02 trillion US$
Germany 2.27 trillion US$
United Kingdom 1.66 trillion US$
France 1.65 trillion US$
Italy 1.55 trillion US$

Population
Explosive Growth

More than six billion people live on our planet. United Nations estimates predict a global population between 7.9 and 11 billion in the year 2050. The vast majority of this growth will take place in the developing nations of Africa and Asia.

Increased productivity in agriculture, improved living conditions, and medical advancements were the primary factors behind the dramatic growth of the world's population in the 20th century. The world's population is, however, unevenly distributed across our planet. Some continents such as Europe are densely populated, while others such as Australia are home to relatively few people. The populations of the different continents are also distributed unevenly with populations often concentrated in certain regions while others remain sparsely populated – most Australians for example, live in a few large coastal cities.

World Population (by continent)

Asia 3596.4 million
Africa 760.4 million
Europe 760.3 million
Central and South America 520 million
North America 309.5 million
Australia/Oceania 30.2 million

Most Populous Nations

Europe
Russia 143.7 million
Germany 83.2 million
United Kingdom 60.3 million

Asia
China 1.3 billion
India 1.06 billion
Indonesia 238.4 million

North America
United States 293 million
Mexico 105 million
Canada 32.5 million

South America
Brazil 184 million
Columbia 42.3 million
Argentina 39.1 million

Africa
Nigeria 137.3 million
Egypt 76.1 million
Ethiopia 67.8 million

Oceania
Australia 19.9 million
Papua New Guinea 5.4 million
New Zealand 4 million

Population Density

Highest population density
Bangladesh 898 inhabitants per sq km

Lowest population density
West Sahara 1 inhabitant per sq km

Cities
Centers of Growth

At the beginning the 19th century, there were only a handful of cities with more than a million inhabitants. In the past 100 years, however, the numbers of large cities on our planet have increased rapidly and the populations of the world's largest cities have also increased substantially.

Dealing with the rapid growth of urban areas in the developing world will be one of the greatest challenges of the 21st century. Few of these cities have been able to expand their infrastructures fast enough to cope with explosive population growth and the already poor environmental conditions in many third world cities continue to deteriorate.

According the UN estimates, most of the world's population will live in cities by 2015. The trend of people in developing nations abandoning rural areas for better economic and social conditions in large cities will continue for many decades. This rapid urbanization of the developing world will only exacerbate existing urban overcrowding problems. The cities of the developing world lack the housing, transportation networks, and jobs to provide most urban migrants with a substantially better standard of living. Most of these cities are surrounded by vast slums and temporary settlements inhabited by the poor. At least 85% of Cairo's area consists of residential areas with mostly substandard housing. Other cities in the developing world are better able to cope with rapid growth due to improving economic conditions. The population of Shanghai, the center of China's impressive economic boom, has expanded by several million in recent years.

The Largest Metropolitan Areas

Tokyo-Yokohama 34.9 million,
Japan
New York City (Tri-State area) 21.65 million,
United States
Seoul 21.1 million,
Republic of (South) Korea
Mexico City 20.7 million,
Mexico
Sao Paolo 20.2 million,
Brazil
Mumbai (Bombay) 18.1 million,
India
Osaka-Kobe 18 million,
Japan
Delhi 17.1 million,
India
Los Angeles 16.8 million,
United States
Jakarta 15.8 million,
Indonesia

Europe
Moscow 8.7 million,
Russia
Istanbul 8.2 million,
Turkey

London 7.6 million in Greater London,
United Kingdom
Paris 2 million (city), 9.3 (metro area)
France
St. Petersburg 5.5 million,
Russia

Asia
Shanghai 13 million,
China
Mumbai (Bombay) 11.9 million,
India
Seoul 10.2 million,
Republic of Korea
Jakarta 8.2 million,
Indonesia
Tokyo 8.1 million (city population),
Japan

Australia
Sydney 3.9 million
Melbourne 3.3 million
Brisbane 1.5 million

Africa
Cairo 14.8 million in metro area,
Egypt
Khartoum 7.3 million in metro area,
Sudan
Lagos 7.2 million in metro area,
Nigeria
Kinshasa 6.1 million in metro area,
Democratic Republic of Congo
Alexandria 4.8 million,
Egypt

North and South America
Sao Paolo 9.7 million,
Brazil
Mexico City - Distrito Federal 8.5 million,
Mexico
New York City 8.2 million,
United States
Lima 7.5 million,
Peru

Skyscrapers
Modern Giants

The world's first skyscraper, completed in 1902, had a height just over 180 meters. Improved engineering and construction techniques were the main factors behind the rapid vertical growth of our planet's cities in the 20th century.

The invention of the elevator made the construction of skyscrapers practical and was another major factor behind the development of highrise buildings. New York City is still home to the largest concentration of skyscrapers. However, most of the world's tallest buildings under construction at the moment are in the booming cities of East Asia. The Taipei Financial Center in Taiwan has a height of 508 meters and replaced Malaysia's Petronas Towers as the world's tallest building in 2004. There are currently plans to construct the world's tallest skyscraper on the site of the former World Trade Center towers, but the project could lose the title before it is completed because there are several other projects competing for the title of world's tallest building. With city populations growing rapidly and skyscrapers remaining symbols of progress and wealth it is unlikely the age of the skyscraper will end in the near future.

The Tallest Buildings

Taipei Financial Center (Taipei 101)
508 m, 101 floors
Taipei, 2004
Petronas Towers 452 m, 88 floors,
Kuala Lampur, 1998
Sears Tower 442 m, 110 floors,
Chicago, 1974
Jin Mao Tower 421 m, 88 floors
Shanghai, 1998
Two International Financial Center
415 m, 88 floors
Hong Kong, 2003
Citic Plaza 391 m, 80 floors
Guangzhou, 1997
Shun Hing Square 384 m, 69 floors
Shenzen, 1996
Empire State Building 381 m, 102 floors
New York City, 1931

Asia
Taipei Financial Center (Taipei 101)
508 m, 101 floors
Taipei, 2004
Petronas Tower 1 452 m, 88 floors,
Kuala Lumpur, 1998
Petronas Tower 2 452 m, 88 floors
Kuala Lumpur, 1998
Jin Mao Tower 421 m, 88 floors
Shanghai, 1998
Two International Finance Centre
415 m, 88 floors
Hong Kong 2003
Citic Plaza 391 m, 80 floors
Guangzhou, 1997

Shun Hung Square 384 m, 69 floors
Shenzhen, 1996
Central Plaza 374 m, 78 floors
Hong Kong, 1992
Bank of China Tower 367 m, 72 floors,
Hong Kong, 1990

The Americas
Sears Towers 374 m, 78 floors,
Chicago, 1992
Empire State Building 381 m, 102 floors,
New York City, 1931
Aon Center (Amoco Building)
346 m, 83 floors
Chicago, 1973
John Hancock Center 344 m, 100 floors
Chicago, 1969
Chrysler Building 319 m, 77 floors
New York City, 1930
Bank of America Plaza 312 m, 55 floors,
Atlanta, 1992
US Bank Tower 310 m, 73 floors,
Los Angeles, 1990
AT&T Corporate Center 307 m, 60 floors,
Chicago, 1989

Africa
Carlton Centre 202 m, 36 floors,
Johannesburg, 1973
Hassan II Mosque 198 m,
Casablanca, 1993

Australia
120 Collins Street 264 m, 52 floors,
Melbourne, 1991
Rialto Towers 251 m, 63 floors,
Melbourne, 1986
Central Park 249 m, 52 floors,
Perth, 1992
Citigroup Centre 243 m, 50 floors
Syndey, 2000
Chifley Tower 243 m, 50 floors,
Sydney, 1992
MLC Center 228 m, 60 m,
Sydney, 1977
Governor Phillip Tower
227 m, 54 floors
Sydney 1993

Europe
Commerzbank Tower 259 m, 63 floors,
Frankfurt, 1997
Triumph Palace 264 m, 54 floors
Moscow 2004
Messeturm 257 m, 64 floors,
Frankfurt, 1991,
Moscow University 240 m, 32 floors,
Moscow 1953
One Canada Square 235 m, 56 floors,
London 1991

Towers and Antennas
Reaching for the Sky

Towers have been used for thousands of years and for many different purposes, including defensive, navigational, and observation use. Most modern towers were built to transmit broadcast waves over great distances.

Huge radio and television antennas can be found all over the planet. These thin steel structures often rise several hundred meters into the air and play an important part in global communications.

The Tallest Towers

CN Tower 553 m, 1976
Toronto, Canada
Ostakino Tower 540 m, 1967,
Moscow, Russia
Oriental Pearl Tower 468 m, 1995,
Shanghai, China
KL Tower 421 m, 1996,
Kuala Lumpur, Malaysia
Tianjin Tower 415 m, 1991,
Tianjin, China
Central Radio & TV Tower 405 m, 1992
Beijing, China
Tashkent Tower 375 m, 1985,
Tashkent, Uzbekistan
Television Tower 375 m, 1969,
Berlin, Germany
Stratosphere Tower 350 m, 1996,
Las Vegas, Nevada
Tokyo Tower 333 m, 1958,
Tokyo, Japan
Sydney Tower 305 m, 1958,
Sydney, Australia
Eiffel Tower 301 m, 1889,
Paris, France
Barcelona Tower 288 m, 1992,
Barcelona, Spain

Antennas/Transmitting Towers

KHTI tower 555 m,
Fargo, United States
WBIR television tower 533 m,
Knoxville, United States
WTVM/WBRL tower 533 m,
Columbus, United States
KFVS TV tower 510 m,
Cape Girardeau, United States

Bridges and Tunnels
Vital Connections

Great bridges span powerful bodies of water, withstand the forces of nature, connect islands to the rest of the world, and could one day even connect entire continents.

Tunnels are in many ways subterranean bridges – they run through mountains or beneath bodies of water.

Satellite technology and future advancements in engineering could one day make it possible to construct gigantic bridges over the deep bodies of water that separate the continents including the Bering Strait and Strait of Gibraltar.
Tunnels are vital transportation links in many of the world's mountainous regions. These underground roadways stretch through mountains, reduce distances, and connect many mountainous areas to the world. Underwater tunnels are especially impressive engineering achievements. The 50-kilometer-long Channel Tunnel was completed in 1994 despite the technical difficulty of its construction. Travelers can now travel by train between northern France and southern England in less than 35 minutes.

Visionary Bridges
(futuristic proposals)

Gibraltar Bridge 10 kilometers,
Spain/Morocco
Strait of Messina Bridge 3.3 kilometers,
Sicily, Italy

The Longest Cable-Stayed Bridges
length of the main span

Tatara Bridge 890 m, 1999,
Japan
Pont de Normandie 856 m, 1994,
France
Second Nanjing Bridge 628 m, 2001,
China
Wuhan Bridge 618 m, 2000
China
Quinzhou-Minjiang Bridge 605 m, 1996
China
Yangpu Bridge 602 m, 1993
China

Xupu Bridge 590 m, 1997
China
Meiko Central Bridge 590 m, 1998,
Japan
Skarsundet 530 m, 1991,
Norway
Jueshi 518 m, 1998,
China 518 m,
Tsuruma Tsubasa 510 m, 1994,
Japan
Jingzhou 500 m, 2002,
China

The Longest Suspension Bridges

Akashi Kaikyo 1,991 m, 1998
Japan
Store Belt 1,624 m, 1998
Denmark
Humber Bridge 1,410 m, 1981,
United Kingdom
Jiangyin Bridge 1,385 m, 1998
China
Ts'ing-Ma-Bridge 1,377 m, 1997
China

The Longest Bridges by Continent
(length in meters)
S= suspension bridge, CS= cable-stayed bridge, A= arch bridge, C= cantilever bridge

Europe
Store Belt (S) 1,624 m, 1997,
Denmark
Humber (S) 1,410 m, 1981,
United Kingdom
Hoega Kusten (S) 1,210 m, 1997,
Sweden
F.S. Mehmet (S) 1,090 m, 1998,
Turkey
Kemal Atatürk (S) 1,074 m, 2004
Turkey

Asia
Akashi-Kaikyo (S) 1,991 m, 1998,
Japan
Jiangyin Bridge (S) 1,385 m, 1998,
China
Tsing Ma Bridge (S) 1,377 m, 1997,
China

Australia/Oceania
Sydney Harbour Bridge (A) 509 m, 1932,
Australia
West Gate Melbourne (CS) 336 m, 1974
Australia
Gladesville Bridge (A) 305 m, 1964
Australia

North America
Verrazano Narrows (S) 1,298 m, 1964;
United States
Golden Gate Bridge (S) 1,280 m, 1937,
United States
Mackinac Straits (S) 1,158 m, 1957,
United States
George Washington (S) 1,067 m, 1931,
United States
Pierre LaPorte (S) 908 m,1970,
Canada

South America
Urdaneta Bridge (S) 712 m, 1967
Venezuela
Rio Parana (CS) 330 m, 1978,
Argentina
Costa e Silva (C) 300 m, 1974,
Brazil

Africa
Bircbenough (A) 329 m, 1935,
Zimbabwe
Wadi Kuf (CS) 282 m,
Libya

The Longest Tunnel
Rail and road tunnels

Seikan Tunnel 53.90 kilometers
Japan
Channel Tunnel 49.94 kilometers,
United Kingdom/France
Iwate-Ichinoe 25.81 kilometers,
Japan
Laerdal 24.51 kilometers,
Norway
Dai-Shimizu 22.17 kilometers,
Japan
Simplon II 19.82 kilometers,
Italy/Switzerland
Simplon I 19.80 kilometers,
Italy/Switzerland
Shin-Kanmon 18.68 kilometers
Japan
Apennin 18.49 kilometers
Italy
Qinling 18.45 kilometers,
China
St. Gotthard Tunnel 16.91 kilometers,
Switzerland/Italy
Rokkou 16.25 kilometers,
Japan
Furka Pass 15.44 kilometers,
Switzerland
Haruna 15.35 kilometers,
Japan
Severomuyskiy 15,35 kilometers,
Russia

Index of Names

The Index of Names gives each name only once. Descriptions are shown in symbol form.
References show the largest scale maps in which the object appears.
Names are listed alphabetically. Umlauts are treated as vowels, diacritical characters as standard Latin characters.
Multiple names are treated as a single word, e.g. Garmisch-Partenkirchen is listed under G, not P. However, in proper name/common name combinations the proper name is placed first, e.g. Canaveral, Cape.

Legend

■ Country	① Capital	▣ Administrative unit	② Administrative HQ
● City	▬ Landscape	▲ Mountains	▲ Mountain
▨ Valley	▨ Volcano	▨ Basin	▨ Island
▨ Ocean, sea	▨ Lake	◹ River, canal	▨ Glacier
▨ Hydraulic structure	▨ Cape	✦ Park, reserve	★ Tourist site
▨ Ruins	▨ Submarine relief	⊞ Airport	

217

Juža ◼ **41** J 3
Južna Morava ⬃ **37** E-F 4
Južno-Sahalinsk ◼ **53** K 4
Jylland ▬ **21** C 5-6
Jyväskylä ② **19** H 5

K

K2 ▲ **54** A 3
8616 m. World's second highest mountain, in Pakistan.

Kaalualu Bay ⬔ **83** D 4
Kaaresuvanto ◼ **18** G 2
Kaatoan ▲ **69** D 3
Kabale ◼ **97** D 2
Kabalo ◼ **97** C 2
Kabardino-Balkaria ② **60** D 3
Kåbdalis ◼ **18** E-F 3
Kabinda ◼ **96** C 2
Kabir ▲ **65** D 2
Kabo ◼ **94** A 3
Kabompo ◼ **98** C 2
Kabongo ◼ **96** C 2
Kabul ① **48** C 4
Kabwe ◼ **98** C 2
Kachchh, Gulf of- ⬃ **66** A 2
Kachchh, Rann of- ▬ **66** A-B 2
Kachin ▬ **67** D 2
Kachovka ◼ **43** F 4
Kachovs'ke vodoschovyšče ⬔ **43** F-G 4
Kaçkar Dağı ▲ **59** H 2
Kacug ◼ **52** F 3
Kadınhanı ◼ **58** D 3
Kadirli ◼ **59** F 4
Kadnikov ◼ **41** H 2
Kadom ◼ **41** J 4
Kadoma ◼ **98** C 2
Kaduj ◼ **40** F 2
Kaduna ◼ **93** D 1
Kaduqli ◼ **94** B 2
Kadyj ◼ **41** J 3
Kadyjivka ◼ **43** J 3
Kadžaran ◼ **61** F 5
Kaédi ◼ **88** B 4
Kaesong ◼ **56** D 3
Kafan ◼ **61** F 5
Kaffa ▬ **95** C 3
Kafia Kingi ◼ **94** B 3
Kafirēvs, Ákra- ⬃ **38** D 3
Kåfjord ◼ **18** H-J 1
Kafrayya ◼ **62A** B 1
Kafue ◼ **98** C 2
Kafue ⬃ **98** C 2
Kafue National Park ⬔ **98** C 2
Kaga Bandoro ◼ **94** A 3
Kagalnik ◼ **43** K 4
Kagen ◼ **18** F 1-2
Kagera ⬃ **97** D 2
Kağızman ◼ **60** D 4
Kagoshima ◼ **57** D-E 4
Kahakuloa ⬔ **83** C 3
Kaharlyk ◼ **42** E 3
Kahiu Point ⬔ **83** C 1
Kahoolawe ⬔ **82** C 3

Kahramanmaraş ◼ **59** F 4
Kâhta ◼ **59** G 4
Kahuku ◼ **83** B 1
Kahuku Point ⬔ **83** B 1
Kahului ◼ **83** C 2
Kahului Bay ⬔ **83** C 2
Kai, Kepulauan- ⬔ **69** E 4
Kaifeng ◼ **55** E 3
Kaikoura ◼ **79** C 4
Kailu ◼ **56** C 2
Kailua (Hawaii-USA)
◼ **83** C-D 3
Kailua (Oahu-Hawaii-USA)
◼ **83** B 1
Kaimana ◼ **69** E 4
Kainji Reservoir ⬔ **93** D 1
Kainuunselkä
▬ **18-19** J-K 4
Kairouan ⬛ **89** D-E 2
Kaiserslautern ◼ **30** E-F 4
Kaitaia ◼ **79** C 3
Kaivy ⬃ **43** F 4
Kaiwi Channel ⬔ **83** B 1
Kaiyuan (Laoning-China)
◼ **55** F 2
Kaiyuan (Yunnan-China)
◼ **54** D 4
Kajaani ◼ **19** J 4
Kakabeka Falls
⬔ **112** A-B 1
Kakamega ◼ **97** D 1
Kakinada ◼ **66** C 3
Kaktovik ◼ **104** E 1
Kalabahi ◼ **69** D 4
Kalač ◼ **43** K 2
Ka Lae ⬔ **83** D 4
Kalahari Desert ▬ **98** C 3
Kalakan ◼ **52** G 3
Kalamata ◼ **38** C 4
Kalamazoo ◼ **112** B 2
Kalamits'ka zatoka
⬔ **43** F 5
Kalan ◼ **59** G 3
Kalapana ◼ **83** E 3
Kälarne ◼ **20** F-G 2
Kalat ▲ **65** F 2
Kalaus ⬃ **60** D 2
Kalávrita ◼ **38** B-C 4
Kale (Turkey) ◼ **58** B 4
Kale (Turkey) ◼ **58** B-C 4
Kalecik ◼ **58** D 2
Kalemie ◼ **97** C 2
Kálfafell ▲ **44** E 4
Kalgoorlie ◼ **80** B 3
Kaliakra, nos- ⬔ **37** J 4
Kalima ◼ **97** C 2
Kalimantan → Borneo
⬔ **68** C 3-4
Kálimnos ⬔ **38** C 4
Kaliningrad (Russia)
◼ **40** F 4
Kaliningrad (Russia)
② **22** F 4
Kalinino (Armenia)
◼ **61** E 4
Kalinino (Russia) ◼ **60** B 2
Kalinkavičy ◼ **35** J 2
Kalispell ◼ **110** D 2
Kalisz ◼ **34** D 3
Kalitva ⬃ **43** K 3

Kalix ◼ **18** G 4
Kalixälv ⬃ **18** G 3
Kaljazin ◼ **40** F-G 3
Kalkan ◼ **58** B 4
Kalkfontein ◼ **98** C 3
Kallas ▲ **54** B 3
Kallaste ◼ **23** J 2
Kallavesi ⬃ **19** J-K 5
Kallsedet ◼ **20** E 2
Kallsjön ⬃ **20** E 2
Kalmar ② **21** G 5
Kalmar ② **21** G 5
Kalmarsund ⬔ **21** G 5
Kalmius ⬃ **43** H-J 4
Kalmykia ② **61** E-F 2
Kalocsa ◼ **36** D 2
Kalofer ◼ **37** G 4
Kalohi Channel ⬔ **83** B 2
Kaloli Point ⬔ **83** E 3
Kalomo ◼ **98** C 2
Kalpákion ◼ **38** B 3
Kaluga ◼ **50** D 3
Kalumburu Mission
◼ **80** B 1
Kalundborg ◼ **21** D 6
Kaluš ◼ **42** B 3
Kalynivka ◼ **42** D 3
Kama ◼ **97** C 2
Kama ⬃ **50** F 2
Kamaishi ◼ **57** G 3
Kamalo ◼ **83** C 1
Kaman ◼ **58** D 3
Kamaran ⬔ **63** D 5
Kambove ◼ **97** C 3
Kamchatka Peninsula
▬ **53** L-M 3
Kamen ▲ **52** E 2
Kamenjak, Rt- ⬔ **36** A 3
Kamenka (Russia)
◼ **41** J-K 5
Kamenka (Russia) ◼ **43** J 2
Kamen-na-Obi ◼ **51** J 3
Kamennik ▲ **40** D 3
Kamennoe ⬔ **19** L 4
Kamennomostski ◼ **60** C 2
Kamenskoje ◼ **53** M 2
Kamensk-Šahtinski ◼ **43** K 3
Kamensk-Uralski ◼ **51** G 3
Kamień Pomorski ◼ **34** B 1-2
Kamina ◼ **96** C 2
Kamin'-Kašyrs'kyj ◼ **42** B 2
Kamjanec-Podilskyj
◼ **42** C 3
Kamjanka ◼ **43** F 3
Kamjanka-Buzka ◼ **42** B 2
Kamjanka-Dnjprovs'ka
◼ **43** G 4
Kamloops ◼ **106** D 3
Kampala ① **97** D 1
Kampar ⬔ **68** B 3-4
Kampene ◼ **97** C 2
Kampot ◼ **67** E 3
Kamsar ◼ **92** B 1
Kamskoe vodochranilišče
⬔ **50** F 3
Kamyšin ◼ **50** E 3-4
Kanab ◼ **111** D 4
Kananga ◼ **96** C 2
Kanaš ◼ **41** L 4
Kanazawa ◼ **57** F 3
Kanchipuram ◼ **66** B-C 3

Kandalakša ◼ **50** D 2
Kandangan ◼ **68** C 4
Kandavu ⬔ **78** C 1
Kandi ◼ **93** D 1
Kandıra ◼ **58** C 2
Kandy ◼ **66** C 4
Kaneohe ◼ **83** B 1
Kanevskaja ◼ **60** B 1
Kangal ◼ **59** F 3
Kangan ◼ **63** F 3
Kangaroo ⬔ **81** C 3
Kangasniemi ◼ **19** J 6
Kangean ◼ **68** C 4
Kanggye ◼ **56** D 2
Kangnung ◼ **57** D 3
Kanin, poluostrov-
▬ **50** E 2
Kanin Nos, mys- ⬔ **50** E 1
Kaniv ◼ **42** E 3
Kanjiža ◼ **36** E 2
Kankaanpää ◼ **19** G 6
Kankakee ◼ **112** B 2
Kankan ◼ **92** C 1
Kanmon Strait ⬔ **57** E 4
Kano ◼ **93** D 1
Kanoya ◼ **57** E 4
Kanpur ◼ **66** B-C 2

Kansas ② **108** D 2
Pop. 2.5 m. US state, capital: Topeka.

Kansas City ◼ **108** D 2
Kansk ◼ **52** E 3
Kantchari ◼ **92** D 1
Kantemirovka ◼ **43** J 3
Kantishna ◼ **104** D 2
Kanye ◼ **98** C 3
Kaohsiung ◼ **55** F 4
Kaolack ◼ **92** B 1
Kaouar ▬ **89** E 3-4
Kapanga ◼ **96** C 2
Kapellskär ◼ **21** H 4
Kapingamarangi ⬔ **75** C 2
Kaposvár ◼ **36** C 2
Kapsan ◼ **57** D 2
Kapuas ⬃ **68** C 3
Kapuas Hulu Range
▲ **68** C 3
Kapuskasing ◼ **107** H 4
Kaputjug ▲ **61** E-F 5
Kapyrevščina ◼ **40** D 4
Karabogaz-Gol ⬃ **50** F 4
Karabük ◼ **58** D 2
Karaburun ◼ **58** A 3
Karacabey ◼ **58** B 2
Karaca Dağ ▲ **59** G 4
Karačajevsk ◼ **60** C-D 3
Karacaköy ◼ **58** B 2
Karacasu ◼ **58** B 4
Karačev ◼ **40** D 5
Karachay-Cherkessia
② **60** C-D 3
Karachi ◼ **66** A 2
Kara Dağ ▲ **58** D 4
Karadah ◼ **61** F 3
Karaghandy ◼ **51** H 4
Karaginskij, ostrov-
⬔ **53** M 3
Karaj ◼ **63** E-F 1
Karak, Al- ◼ **64** B 2

Karakoçan ◼ **59** G-H 3
Karakol ◼ **51** H 4
Karakoram Shankou
▲ **54** A 3
Karakorum ⬛ **54** D 2

Karakorum Range ▲ **66** B 1
Central Asian mountains between Himalayas, Pamir and Kunlun.

Karaköse ◼ **60** D 5
Karaköy ◼ **60** C 5
Karakum ▬ **50-51** F-G 4
Karaman ◼ **58** D 4
Karamay ◼ **54** B 2
Karamiran Shankou
▲ **54** B 3
Karapınar ◼ **58** D 4
Karasberge ▲ **98** B 3
Karasburg ◼ **98** B 3
Kara Sea ⬃ **51** G-H 1
Karasjok ◼ **18** H 2
Karasu ◼ **58** C 2
Karasu Dağları ▲ **59** H 3
Karasuk ◼ **51** H 3
Karataş ◼ **59** E 4
Karatau ▲ **51** G 4
Karbala ◼ **64** C 2
Karcag ◼ **37** E 2
Kardeljevo ◼ **36** C 4
Kardhítsa ◼ **38** B-C 3
Kärdla ◼ **23** G 2
Kärdžali ◼ **37** G 5
Karelia ② **19** L 4
Karelia ▬ **50** D 2
Karen ◼ **67** D 3
Karesuando ◼ **18** F 2
Kargapazarı Dağı ▲ **59** H 2
Kargı ◼ **59** E 2
Kariai ◼ **38** D 2
Kariba ◼ **98** C 2
Kariba, Lake- ⬃ **98** C 2
Karibib ◼ **98** B 3
Karigasniemi ◼ **18** H 2
Karima ◼ **94** C 2
Karimata Strait ⬔ **68** B 4
Karin ◼ **95** D 2
Karis ◼ **19** G 6
Karisimbi ▲ **97** C 2
Káristos ◼ **38** D 3
Karkar ⬔ **74** B 3
Karkaralinsk ◼ **51** H 4
Karkas ▲ **65** E 2
Karkheh ⬃ **65** D 2
Karkinits'ka zatoka
⬔ **43** F 5
Karkkila ◼ **19** H 6
Karlino ◼ **34** B 1
Karliova ◼ **59** H 3
Karlivka ◼ **43** G 3
Karlobag ◼ **36** B 3
Karlovac ◼ **36** B 3
Karlovo ◼ **37** G 4
Karlovy Vary ◼ **31** H 3
Karlsborg ◼ **21** F 4
Karlshamn ◼ **21** F 5
Karlskoga ◼ **21** F 4
Karlskrona ◼ **21** F 5
Karlsruhe ◼ **30** F 4
Karlstad ◼ **21** E 4

225

227

229

Mosquitos, Golf de los-
[img] 115 D 3-4
Moss [•] 21 D 4
Mossaka [•] 96 B 2
Mosselbaai [•] 98 C 4
Mossendjo [•] 96 B 2
Mossoró [•] 123 E 2
Most [•] 31 H 3
Mostar [•] 36 C 4
Mosterøy [img] 21 A 4
Møsting, Kap-
[img] 105 G-H 3
Mostovskoj [•] 60 C 2
Mosty's'ka [•] 42 A 3
Motala [•] 21 F 4
Motilla del Palancar
[•] 29 E 4
Motril [•] 28 D 5
Motu One [img] 76 C 3
Mouchoir Bank [img] 117 C 3
Mouchoir Passage
[img] 117 C-D 2
Moudjéria [•] 88 B 4
Moúdros [•] 38 D 2-3
Mouila [•] 96 B 2
Moulins [•] 27 E 4
Moulmein [•] 67 D 3
Moulouya [img] 89 C 2
Moultrie [•] 113 C 4
Moundou [•] 94 A 3
Mountain Home [•] 110 C 3
Mount Gambier [•] 81 D 3
Mount Hagen [•] 74 B 3
Mount Isa [•] 81 C 2
Mount Magnet [•] 80 A 2
Mount Morgan [•] 81 D-E 2
Mount Vernon [•] 112 B 3
Moura (Brazil) [•] 122 E 2
Moura (Portugal) [•] 28 B 4
Mourne Mountains
[img] 25 C-D 4
Moussoro [•] 94 A 2
Moûtiers [•] 27 G 5
Moyale [•] 95 C 3
Moyamba [•] 92 B 2
Moyen Atlas [img] 88-89 C 2
Moyobamba [•] 120 C 3
Možajsk [•] 40 F 4
Mozambique [flag] 99 D 2-3
Mozambique Basin
[img] 99 D-E 4
Mozambique Channel
[img] 99 D-E 2-3
Mozambique Ridge
[img] 99 D 3-4
Mozdok [•] 61 E 3
Mpanda [•] 99 D 2
Mpika [•] 99 D 2
Mrayyah, Al- [img] 88 C 4
Mscislav [•] 35 K 1-2
Msta [•] 40 C 2
Mtubatuba [•] 99 D 3
Mtwara [•] 97 F 2
Muang Pakxan [•] 67 E 3
Muarasiberut [•] 68 A 4
Muaratewe [•] 68 C 4
Mubarraz, Al- [•] 63 E 3
Mubi [•] 93 E 1
Muchinga Mauntains
[img] 99 D 2
Mucur [•] 59 E 3

Mudanjiang [•] 55 F-G 2
Mudanya [•] 58 B 2
Muddus nasjonalpark
[img] 18 F 3
Mudurnu [•] 58 C 2
Mueo [•] 78 B 2
Mufulira [•] 98 C 2
Muğla [•] 58 B 4
Mugodzhar Hills [img] 50 F 4
Muhammad, Ras-
[img] 64 A 3
Muhammad Qawl
[•] 95 C 1
Muharraq, Al- [•] 65 E 3
Mühlhausen [•] 31 G 3
Muhos [•] 19 H 4
Muhu [img] 23 G 2
Mujezerski [•] 19 L-M 5
Mujnak [•] 50 F 4
Mukačeve [•] 42 A 3
Mukah [•] 68 C 3
Mukalla, Al- [•] 63 E-F 6
Mula [•] 29 E 4
Mulanje, Mount- [img] 99 D 2
Mules, Mont des- [img] 45 B
Mulhacén [img] 28 D 5
Mulhouse [•] 26 G 4
Mull [img] 24 C-D 3
Mullewa [•] 80 A 2
Mullingar [•] 25 C 5
Mulobezi [•] 98 C 2
Multan [•] 66 B 1

Mumbai = Bombay [2] 66 B 3
Pop. 11.9 m. Capital of Indian
state Maharashtra.

Mumbwa [•] 98 C 2
Muna [img] 52 G 2
Muna [img] 69 D 4
Munamägi [img] 23 J 3
Muncie [•] 112 B-C 2
Munda [•] 75 C 3
Munera [•] 29 D 4
Mungbere [•] 97 C 1
Munhango [•] 98 B 2
Munich [2] 31 G 4
Munkedal [•] 21 D 4
Munku-Sardyk [img] 52 E-F 3
Munsfjället [img] 20 F 1
Münster [img] 30 E 2-3
Munster [2] 25 B 5
Muntok [•] 68 B 4
Munzur Dağları [img] 59 G 3
Muodoslompolo
[•] 18 G 2-3
Muojärvi [img] 18 K 4
Muonio [•] 18 G 3
Muonioälv [img] 18 G 2
Muqayshit [img] 65 E 4
Mur [img] 36 B-C 2
Murallón [•] 125 B 4
Muraši [•] 41 M 2
Murat [img] 59 H 3
Murat Dağı [img] 58 B 3
Muratli [•] 59 H 2
Muravera [•] 33 B 6
Murchison [img] 80 A 2
Murcia [2] 29 E 4
Murcia [2] 29 E 5
Murfreesboro [•] 113 B 3

Murilo [img] 74 C 2
Müritz [img] 31 H 2
Müritz, Nationalpark-
[img] 31 H 2
Murmansk [•] 50 D 2
Murom [•] 50 E 3
Muroran [•] 57 G 2
Muros [•] 28 A 2
Muroto [•] 57 E 4
Murray [img] 81 C-D 3
Murray Bridge [•] 81 C 3
Murrumbidgee [img] 81 D 3
Mururoa [img] 77 E 4
Murwara [•] 66 C 2
Muş [•] 60 C 5
Musala [img] 37 F 4
Musan [•] 57 D 2
Musayjid, Al- [•] 64 B 4
Mus Chaja [img] 53 K 2
Musgrave Range
[img] 81 C 2
Musi [img] 68 B 4
Muskegon [•] 112 B 2
Musoma [•] 97 D 2
Mustafakemalpaşa
[•] 58 B 2
Mustvee [•] 23 J 2
Musu Dan [img] 57 D-E 2
Mut (Egypt) [•] 90 C 3
Mut (Turkey) [•] 58 D 4
Mutarara [•] 99 D 2
Mutare [•] 99 D 2
Mutoko [•] 99 D 2
Mutsu [•] 57 G 2
Muurola [•] 18 H 3
Muzaffarpur [•] 66 C 2
Muztag [img] 54 B 3
Mvuma [•] 99 D 2
Mwali [img] 99 E 2
Mwanza [•] 97 D 2
Mweka [•] 96 C 2
Mwene Ditu [•] 96 C 2
Mwenezi [•] 99 D 3
Mwenga [•] 97 C 2
Mweru, Lake-
[img] 98-99 C-D 1
Mwinilunga [•] 98 C 2
Myanmar [flag] 67 D 2
Myingyan [•] 67 D 2
Myitkyina [•] 67 D 2
Mýkenai [img] 38 C 4
Mykolaijw [•] 42-43 E-F 4
Mykolajiv [•] 42 B 3
Mykonos [img] 39-40 D 4
Mymensingh [•] 66 C-D 2
Myolo [•] 94 B-C 3
Myre [•] 18 C 2
Mýri [•] 44 E 2
Myrkárjökull [img] 44 D 2
Myronivka [•] 42 E 3
Myrtle Beach
[•] 113 D 4
Mysen [•] 21 D 4
Myškino [•] 40 G 3
Myślenice [•] 34 D-E 4
Mysore [•] 66 B 3
Mysovoje [•] 43 G 5
Mys Šmidta [img] 53 O 2
My Tho [•] 67 E 3
Mytilini [2] 39 E 3

Mytišči [•] 40 F-G 4
Mývatn [img] 44 E 2
Mzuzu [•] 99 D 2

 N

Naab [img] 31 G-H 4
Naalehu [•] 83 D 3
Naantali [•] 19 F 6
Naas [•] 25 C 5
Nabash [img] 112 B 3
Nabatia [•] 62A B 1
Naberežnye Celny [•] 50 F 3
Nabire [•] 69 E 4
Nabk, An- [•] 64 D 2
Nabk Abu Qsar, An-
[•] 64 B 2
Nabulus [•] 62A B 2
Nacala [•] 99 E 2
Náchod [•] 31 K 3
Nachuge [•] 67 D 3
Nacozari de Garcia
[•] 114 B 1
Nadi [img] 78 C 1
Nador [•] 89 C 2
Nadym [•] 51 H 2
Náfplio [•] 38 C 4
Nafud, An- [img] 63 C-D 3
Nafusah, Jabal- [img] 90 B 2
Naga [•] 69 D 2
Nagaland [2] 67 D 2
Nagano [•] 57 F 3
Nagaoka [•] 57 F 3
Nagasaki [•] 57 D-E 4
Nagaur [•] 66 B 2
Nagercoil [•] 66 B 4
Nago [img] 19 F 6

Nagorno-Karabakh [2] 61 F 5
Pop. 190,000. Armenian enclave
in Azerbaijan.

Nagornyi [•] 52 H 3
Nagoya [•] 57 F 3
Nagpur [•] 66 B 2
Nagqu [•] 54 C 3
Nagua [•] 117 D 3
Nagyatád [•] 36 C 2
Nagykanizsa [•] 36 C 2
Nahariyya [•] 62A B 1
Nahavand [•] 65 D 2
Nahodka [•] 55 G 2
Nahr Ouassel [img] 29 F-G 6
Nahsholim [•] 62A B 2
Nahud, En- [•] 94 B 2
Nahuel Huapi, Lago-
[img] 124-125 B 4
Naikliu [•] 69 D 4
Naiman Qi [•] 56 C 2
Nain (Canada) [•] 107 K 3
Nain (Iran) [•] 63 F 2

Nairobi [1] 97 D 2
Pop. 1.5 m. Capital of Kenya.

Najaf, An- [•] 63 D 2
Najafabad [•] 65 E 2
Najd [img] 63 D-E 4
Najin [•] 57 E 2
Najran [•] 63 D-E 5

Nakhon Phanom [•] 67 E 3
Nakhon Ratchasima
[•] 67 E 3
Nakhon Sawan [•] 67 D 3
Nakhon Si Thammarat
[•] 67 D-E 4
Naknek [•] 104 D 3
Nakuru [•] 97 D 2
Nalčik [2] 60 D 3
Nallihan [•] 58 C 2
Nalut [•] 90 B 2
Nam [•] 67 E 3
Namacurra [•] 99 D 2
Namak, Daryachen-ye-
[img] 63 F 2
Namangan [•] 51 H 4
Namapa [•] 99 D 2
Namaqualand [img] 98 B 3-4
Nam Co [img] 54 B-C 3
Namdal [img] 20 E 1
Nam Dinh [•] 67 E 2
Namib Desert [img] 98 B 2-3
Namibe [•] 98 B 2
Namibia [flag] 98 B 3
Namjagbarwa [img] 54 C 4
Namlea [•] 69 D 4
Namoluk [img] 74 C 2
Namonuito [img] 74 C 2
Namorik [img] 75 D 2
Nampa [•] 108 B 1
Nampo [•] 56 C-D 3
Nampula [•] 99 D 2
Namsos [•] 20 D 1
Namu [img] 75 D 2
Namúli, Serra- [img] 99 D 2
Namur [•] 26 F 2
Namur [2] 26 F 2
Namuzu [•] 57 F 3
Nan [img] 67 E 3
Nanaimo [•] 106 D 4
Nanakuli [•] 83 A 1
Nanam [•] 57 D-E 2
Nanao [•] 57 F 3
Nancha [•] 55 F 2
Nanchang [2] 55 E 4
Nanchong [•] 54 D 3
Nancy [•] 26 G 3
Nanda Devi [img] 66 B-C 1
Nanded [•] 66 B 3
Nangnim Sanmaek
[img] 56-57 D 2-3
Nanjing [2] 55 E 4
Nan Ling [img] 55 E 4
Nanning [2] 54 D 4
Nanpan Jiang [img] 54 D 4
Nanping [•] 55 E 4
Nanpo-shoto [img] 57 G 4
Nan Shan [img] 54 C-D 3
Nansio [•] 97 D 2
Nantes [2] 26 C 4
Nantong [•] 55 F 3
Nanumanga [img] 75 E 3
Nanumea [img] 75 E 3
Nanuque [•] 123 E 3
Nanyang [•] 55 E 3
Nanyuki [•] 97 D 1
Napamute [•] 104 C-D 2
Napier [•] 79 C 3
Naples [•] 113 C 5
Naples → Napoli [2] 33 E 5
Napo [img] 120 C 2

O

Oak Ridge INDEX | LEXICON

245

CREDITS/CONTRIBUTORS

© 2004/2005 Verlag Wolfgang Kunth GmbH & Co. KG, Munich

Coordination: GeoGraphic Media GmbH, Munich
Cartography: Legenda, Novara (Italy)
Text translation: Demetri Lowe
Editors: Christopher Kunth; Büro Norbert Pautner, Munich;
Design: Um|bruch; Christopher Kunth, Munich
Cover design: Derrick Lim
Cover photograph © NASA

The information and facts presented in the atlas have been extensively researched and edited for accuracy. The publishers, authors, and editors, cannot, however, guarantee that all of the information in the atlas is entirely accurate or up to date at the time of publication. The publishers are grateful for any suggestions or corrections that would improve the content of the atlas.